WHAT'S WRONG
WITH MY KID?

WHAT'S WRONG WITH MY KID?

Wh n

DATE DUE

Hazelden
Center City, Minnesota 55012
hazelden.org

ISBN: 978-1-61649-119-2

Library of Congress Cataloging-in-Publication Data

Leary, George E., 1943-
  What's wrong with my kid? : when drugs or alcohol might be a problem and what to do about it / George E. Leary, Jr.
     p. cm.
  Includes bibliographical references.
  ISBN 978-1-61649-119-2 (softcover)
  1. Youth—Substance use. 2. Youth—Drug use. 3. Youth—Alcohol use. 4. Substance abuse—Treatment. 5. Drug abuse—Treatment. I. Title.
  HV4999.Y68L43 2012
  649'.48—dc23
                              2012004295

Editor's note
The names, details, and circumstances may have been changed to protect the privacy of those mentioned in this publication.

This publication is not intended as a substitute for the advice of health care professionals.

Alcoholics Anonymous and AA are registered trademarks of Alcoholics Anonymous World Services, Inc.

Hazelden offers a variety of information on chemical dependency and related areas. The views and interpretations expressed herein are those of the author and are neither endorsed nor approved by AA or any Twelve Step organization.

This book is for educational and informational purposes only and should not be considered, or used as a substitute for, professional medical/psychological advice, diagnosis, and treatment. Hazelden makes no warranty, guarantee, or promise, express or implied, regarding the effectiveness of this book in the prevention of suicide in specific situations. Hazelden does not take responsibility for any loss, injury, or damage caused by using the book information and in no event shall Hazelden, its employees, or its contractors or agents be liable for any special indirect or consequential damages or any loss or damages whatsoever resulting from injury, loss of income or profits, whether in an action of contract, negligence, or other tortious action, arising in connection with the use or performance of any information contained in the book or associated materials.

In chapter 11, the information on family roles draws from Sharon Wegscheider-Cruse's *Another Chance: Hope and Health for the Alcoholic Family* (Palo Alto: Science and Behavioral Books, 1981).

14 13 12   1 2 3 4 5 6

Cover design by Theresa Jaeger Gedig
Interior design and typesetting by Madeline Berglund

To Ondria, my wife of more than four decades,
my sons, and grandchildren, Kobi, Elizabeth, Jaiden;
the joys of my life.

CONTENTS

ACKNOWLEDGMENTS

This book is the result of the help and support of many people, with special mention to my wonderful and gracious wife, who not only gave me the time and space to write, but was my main support throughout. Special thanks to Dr. Rhonda L. Allen, who not only mentored me as I learned the ins and outs of working in the addiction field under her tutelage, but provided personal support to me and my family when drugs assailed us. I would not be who I am without you in my life. To Michael Johnson, M.D., and Deborah Rawlings, I extend my deepest appreciation for not only reading the manuscript but also motivating me to finish the work. I also thank Janice Stevenson, Ph.D., who became my cheerleader, encouraging me and validating my work. I am appreciative to James McCollum Jr. for his advice and support, as well as Peter Schletty, who guided me and this work from initial submission to final product. Finally, I acknowledge my accomplished and supportive sons, George and Mark. You two are the greatest sons a father could ever want.

INTRODUCTION

"What's wrong with my kid?" "How can I find out what's happening?" "What can I do as a parent?" These questions are all too often asked by mothers and fathers as they watch a son or daughter plummet out of control. Searching for answers, Mom and Dad often look at their young person's peers and possible school issues, but a valid explanation remains evasive. Despite a trail of therapists, doctors, and counselors, the troubling self-destructive behaviors continue and intensify. Parents are caught between introspection and self-deception as they ignore or refuse to consider the possibility that their young person is using brain-altering substances. All too often, substance abuse is the reason for these disturbing behaviors, but parents fail to acknowledge it because they lack awareness of the criteria to determine its existence, or are terrified of what it might mean for them and their family. Unaware or unwilling to acknowledge the signs and symptoms of substance abuse, Mom and Dad continue in their quandary.

The extent of substance abuse among teens is exemplified by the 2010 Monitoring the Future survey, which was sponsored by the National Institute on Drug Abuse (NIDA) and covers illicit substance abuse during the year 2010:

- **Daily marijuana** use increased among 8th, 10th, and 12th graders from 2009 to 2010. Among 12th graders it was at its highest point since the early 1980s at 6.1%. . . . [In 2010,] perceived risk of regular marijuana use also declined among 10th and 12th graders, suggesting future trends in use may continue upward.

- In addition, most measures of marijuana use increased among 8th graders between 2009 and 2010 (past year, past month, and daily), paralleling softening attitudes for the last 2 years about the risk of using marijuana.

- **After marijuana, prescription and over-the-counter medications** account for most of the top drugs abused by 12th graders in the past year. Among 12th graders, past-year nonmedical use of Vicodin decreased from 9.7% to 8%. However, past-year non-medical use of OxyContin remains unchanged across the three grades and has increased in 10th graders over the past 5 years [2005 to 2010]. Moreover, past-year nonmedical use of Adderall and over-the-counter cough and cold medicines among 12th graders remains high at 6.5% and 6.6%, respectively.

- After several years of decline, current and past-year use of Ecstasy [or MDMA] has risen among 8th and 10th graders. From 2009 to 2010, lifetime use of Ecstasy among 8th graders increased from 2.2% to 3.3%, past-year use from 1.3% to 2.4%, and current use [from] 0.6% to 1.1%. This follows declines in perceived risk associated with MDMA use seen over the past several years.

- Alcohol use has continued to decline among high school seniors with past-month use falling from 43.5% to 41.2% and alcohol binge drinking (defined as five or more drinks in a row in the past two weeks) declining from 25.2% to 23.2%.[1]

The survey also found that in 2010, 71 percent of high school seniors were illegally drinking alcohol and nearly half of all seniors were using illicit substances. This is undeniably a national problem that affects the majority of U.S. households. The illicit use of these substances is fostered by a widespread plague of parental ignorance about addiction as well as a troubling poor awareness of the telltale signs of substance abuse. This parental unawareness allows drug and alcohol abuse to evolve into dependency upon brain-altering substances.

The U.S. Department of Health and Human Services recently published the results of a 2009 National Survey on Drug Use and Health, which found that adult lack of awareness fostered an increase in the abuse of prescription medication, a major concern for those working in addictions. The survey found, for instance, that 55.3 percent of those twelve and older who obtained illicit pain medicine from a friend or relative didn't pay for the pills.[2] Could this be intentional adult involvement, or might it be a sign of a general ignorance about drugs among Americans?

On the other hand, the survey did show that parents can play a positive role in controlling the use of illicit drugs. It found, for instance, that for youth whose parents strongly disapproved of the use of marijuana and hashish, only 4.8 percent used these drugs, while 31.3 percent of those youth without strong parental disapproval used these drugs.[3] This book is for you, Mom and Dad—the true motivators in keeping youth from illicit drug use.

Given these troubling statistics, it is obvious that parents must become educated about the use of illicit substances by our youth—the purpose of this book—which begins by showing parents how to recognize substance abuse. Throughout the early parts of this book, parental denial and guilt are met head-on so that parents can undertake the difficult task of parenting an addicted son or daughter, unencumbered by the crippling effects of those dual demons. The second section is dedicated to educating parents about the truth of addiction to brain-altering substances. Parents can't combat substance abuse without understanding the nature of addiction. The third section builds upon the foundation developed in the preceding sections by exposing the reader to weapons that are effective in combating addiction. The fourth section illustrates the concepts of the first three sections as we attend an Al-Anon meeting.

This is your handbook. As you begin reading, you are asked to be open-minded and receptive. Since most parents have no idea how to effectively address a young person who has a drug and/or alcohol problem, this book will serve as your guide. You can read it cover to cover, and I encourage you to do so. You can also reference the information specific to your situation using the table of contents. Please take your time to absorb the information so that you can again be a knowledgeable and effective parent.

Section 1

Determining If Your Young Person Is Addicted

CHAPTER 1

Solitary Agony: Bill and Susan's Story

This is the story of Susan, a woman who suspects her son is using drugs, and Bill, her friend and neighbor, who uses his own experience with addiction to help her with her son. We will return to their story several times to illustrate the concepts in this book.

An ominous, shrill voice suddenly pierced the peace and tranquility of an unusually mild Sunday afternoon in early March. "Good afternoon, neighbor!"

Bill glanced in the direction of the voice, which came from his rapidly approaching neighbor, Gladys.

Approaching his driveway, she announced, "Car looks nice."

Bill replied, "Thank you. Everything looks better when we remove winter's remains."

"How is your family?" She was beside his car.

Bill and his wife, Gloria, had been divorced for two years, and neither she nor their daughter, Barbara, had visited the neighborhood for at least three years. "They are doing well. Thank you for asking. And how are you doing this fine day?"

"Oh, I'm good. It's too nice a day to feel otherwise."

"What can I do for you this afternoon, Gladys?"

"Well, actually, I came to see if there was anything I could do to help."

"Help? I didn't know anything was wrong."

"I saw the police at Susan's twice this weekend and I was concerned. Since you two are so close, I figured you would know if there was anything I could do to help."

Bill was flooded with concern for his good friend and neighbor. *What happened?* he wondered.

He stared at his neighbor, unsure of what to say next. Memories of his daughter, Barbara, and the drug issues his family dealt with that had brought him to his knees. Powerless over her drug addiction, Bill endured years of turmoil and feelings of helplessness before he discovered his only true source of strength: God, his higher power. He had managed to ignore God throughout most of his life, but that was before his God accomplished what he couldn't do—brought his daughter out of her addiction without any permanent damage. Bill committed his life and began making significant behavioral changes.

He controlled himself, courteously saying, "I'll talk to Susan as soon as I can. If there is anything you can do, I'll be sure to let you know."

Bill bent over to gather his cleaning materials. From his stooped position, he heard, "Be sure to call me, Bill. I'll be waiting to know how I can be of assistance."

Bill and Susan were indeed close friends. Over the years, Susan's family had formed a healthy friendship with Bill and his wife, Gloria. They created a bond that solidified when her husband tragically died, and her two sons became fatherless. Without hesitation, Bill assumed the role of surrogate father for her boys, coaching their Little League teams, taking them to the city to watch professional sporting events, routinely putting a male slant to their problems and concerns. He attended father-son affairs that the school and community offered and looked forward to warm weather when he and the boys worked the shared family garden. Blessed with only one child, a daughter, Bill had to admit that he enjoyed the male-bonding process.

While he spent time with the boys, Gloria and Susan became best friends, spending countless hours talking. Gloria was a strong support for Susan after her husband's sudden death, and later, when Barbara's drug use hastened the end of Bill and Gloria's troubled marriage, Susan returned the support by upholding Gloria. Yet, to her credit, she remained neutral and was one of the few people who didn't treat him with disparagement during those dark hours of his life. His family splitting up may have been the latest neighborhood scandal, but Susan remained considerate and supportive. Now she was in trouble. He would return the support, something he should have done months ago.

He knew he should have reached out to Susan long before now, but he had been held back by the fear of reliving those wretched days, which he knew would be his fate if he honestly addressed the evil he believed had assailed Susan's family. Over the past few months, he had become increasingly concerned about the behavioral changes that he noticed in her oldest son, Sean. His behaviors replicated those Barbara exhibited when she was using drugs, but Bill had remained silent. *If only I had done something earlier. If only I had said something. If only I had shared my concerns.* Bill resolved that he would be silent no longer.

Rolling up the garden hose, he began indicting himself. He had failed his good friend and Sean, whom he loved as if he were his own son. He had failed himself by not adhering to his personal program of recovery. *How quickly I can slip back into those old behaviors,* he thought.

Bill took exception to his quick judgment. Maybe Sean wasn't the cause of the police visit. Just as quickly, he accused himself of again retreating into denial. He would face his fear and take action. *Susan needs support and today she will get that, no matter how uncomfortable it might be.*

Bill struggled to recall when his concerns about Sean first began. He concluded that it was late last summer, when he first noticed Sean acting moody and rebellious, which was so unlike him. Over time, Sean's formerly neat hair had become unkempt, while baggy pants and offensive shirts with sleazy slogans advertised his new life. The clean and happy appearance that had characterized him for so many years had vanished, and by the time winter had set in, Bill recognized Sean's behavioral changes as signs of substance use—just like his daughter had exhibited. Unsure if he could endure that agony again, Bill chose to do nothing, hoping against hope that he was wrong.

Crossing into Susan's yard, Bill thought of the last time he saw Sean. He was running late for the airport and was tossing his luggage into the car when he heard Sean defiantly telling his mother, "I ain't no kid you can boss around."

This polite, pleasant, cheerful young person, who was the envy of every parent in the neighborhood, had vanished, just as Bill's daughter's pleasant personality was annihilated when brain-altering substances took control. Yet he had done nothing, using the excuse that he was late for his flight as a reason to continue his avoidant behavior.

"Gladys tells me that the police have been visiting you," Bill announced as Susan opened the front door.

"Come on in," a somber voice responded. "She doesn't miss a thing, does she?"

Standing in the vestibule while Susan shut the door to the rest of the world, Bill asked, "What has been going on?"

"Sean ran away," Susan replied, her voice cracking in pain.

Bill's heart went out to Susan. Knowing firsthand the anguish a child can bring by running away, he embraced his friend. Without hesitation, Susan accepted his support, "Oh Bill, I don't know what to do. It hurts so much."

She burst into tears. Softly, he reminded her, "I know the pain. Barbara ran away three times. It never gets any easier."

Susan sobbed in pain and grief. Bill held her until she was calm enough to speak. In a quavering voice, she said, "I never knew anyone could break my heart the way he has. This is worse than when my husband got killed."

Pulling away from Bill, she attempted to gain control by serving as hostess. "Can I get you anything? Soda? Coffee?"

"No thanks. I just want to be here for you."

"Thanks. I could use an ear. It's been a rough weekend."

Bill watched Susan plop down on the couch, and his concern escalated. He had never seen her this unkempt. Her hair was in disarray and her clothes hung on her slumping body. Struggling to control her emotions, Susan began. "First Sean would talk back and defy me. I tried to work with him, but things only got worse. We kept arguing and fighting. I just couldn't reach him anymore. Friday was the clincher. I told him that he couldn't go out because he violated curfew."

Fearful of the response, Bill asked, "And what happened?"

"He told me, 'Don't tell me what to do. I'll be home when I'll be home.' And then he burst out the door."

Bill's wife once equated their broken dreams and lost hope for Barbara to an invaluable keepsake that crashes onto the floor, shattering irreparably. Many were the times when his daughter became belligerent or ran away, and Bill would fear that her precious life was lost forever. Yes, he knew the pain that follows annihilated hope and dreams, yet he couldn't find the comforting words he knew she needed. Just as he had anticipated, troubling memories were clogging his thinking and leaving him too impotent to help. All he could do was fight off his ghosts.

Susan's head dropped as tears resumed flowing down her cheeks. Moving closer, he grasped her hand. She raised her head, exposing pained brown eyes sitting listlessly in a backdrop of grief.

Those desperately sad eyes tore down the protective walls he had constructed to contain the memories of Barbara's drug-crazed days. Helpless, he barely heard Susan's question, "What did I do wrong? How did I fail?"

It was a familiar, agonizing cry that Bill knew all too well and had repeated far too often, and which stirred up his own past feelings of guilt, self-pity, remorse, resentment, and anger. He struggled to stop the emotional turmoil overwhelming him. *Get it together. This is about Susan, not your stuff. You need to decide what you are going to do and say. Think only of Susan. Focus only on her.*

Bill then found himself saying, "You are not a failure. You've been an excellent parent. As your friend and neighbor, I can attest to the conscientious way that you've raised your sons. What has happened is not because of you. It happened because of circumstances beyond your control."

Grief blocked any possibility that Susan would absorb Bill's words. "I failed my child. He is supposed to be with me—safe at home—not out, God only knows where."

Bill wrapped his arm around her shoulder and held her tightly. "It's not your fault, Susan. Sean made a choice independent of you."

Bill wanted to tell Susan that she wasn't alone, that her situation wasn't unique, that the heartache she was experiencing was shared by hundreds of thousands of parents. He wanted to explain to her that in time she would realize that her son's behaviors were most likely drug induced and not reflective of her parenting, but he cautioned himself that this was not the appropriate time to bring up the subject of drugs. For a moment he wondered if this was again his own escapism and avoidance, but with Susan's fear for Sean so deep and painful, Bill concluded introducing the possibility of drug use would be too much for Susan to bear. Opting to provide her with what she needed most, companionship and solace, Bill simply held her. Today, Susan would receive the sponsorship her broken spirit desperately needed. Everything else could wait.

As Susan's tears soaked his shirt, Bill sympathized with her. She had endured nearly forty-eight hours of unmitigated terror and dread, with no word of her son's safety or well-being. Alone, confused, and frightened, Susan had spent the past two days uselessly wracking her brain for elusive answers to the heart-wrenching questions "What did I do wrong? How did I fail?"

Bill had seen it before with other parents. He knew personally what it felt like to have a drug-induced crisis beset his family and cause him to question his parenting. Until his daughter plunged the family into the foreign, wretched world of addiction, Bill too had considered himself to be a good parent. *Welcome to the world of addiction,* he thought.

Bill's daughter had introduced him to that world, one populated by parents watching powerlessly while drugs negated everything that they had nurtured in their offspring. Sean is introducing Susan to that world, and in the upcoming months, she will become intimately acquainted with the ability of drugs to override a person's value system, thought processes, and behaviors. As she acknowledges her loss of control over her son, she will come to appreciate addiction's power and eventually learn that she can't hold herself culpable. This, however, will be a long, torturous, and onerous process, just as it is for any other parent of an addicted offspring.

When this awareness finally occurs, Susan will discover that she has become part of a group of families whose membership comes from every socioeconomic group. She will come to understand that her family has become another casualty in a growing roster of families victimized by the power of drugs. For now, however, with Bill's brief, supportive visit being a notable exception, Susan is fated to remain isolated, devastated, and heartbroken, lingering in silent agony while addiction dismantles her family and rips her heart apart.

Many parents fail to identify unusual, impulsive, extreme, and excessive behaviors that they have been witnessing in their children as signs of substance abuse, preferring to attribute these behaviors to anything but drug use and the stigma that comes with addiction. Having lived through his daughter's addiction, Bill recognized Sean's behaviors as signposts pointing toward the presence of drugs, but he didn't want to believe Sean had succumbed to drugs, choosing to engage in avoidance instead. Like most parents, this surrogate father surrendered to denial, which for Bill was manifested by his avoidance—even though he knew intimately the signs of drug use. Now that a crisis has occurred, he is finally willing to acknowledge that the behavioral indicators of drug use are present in Sean's life.

When parents finally make that aching admission that drugs have overtaken a loved one, they are forced to confess that they no longer can control that addicted son or daughter. With that acknowledgment, parents must accept the reality that normal parenting techniques are ineffective for a son or daughter who is operating under the influence of brain-altering substances. Parenting an addicted offspring is different than parenting a normal young person. This book will introduce you to some of the tools that can effectively deal with substance abuse in a young person, just as Bill will eventually guide and educate Susan.

Drugs also impact the entire family, not just the addicted individual, and the resultant dysfunctional, maladaptive, and unhealthy behaviors the family adopts in the wake of substance abuse must be exposed, examined, and acknowledged. Parental approaches in dealing with the entire family must also be adjusted if addiction's power over the family unit is to be countered. As Bill held Susan closely, he promised that in the upcoming weeks he would help her understand the impact drugs had upon her non-addicted son as well as herself. In section 2 of this book, the reader will experience that same enlightenment.

An African proverb reminds us, "It takes a village to raise a child." Parenting an addicted offspring shouldn't be a solo effort. Outside assistance and support from a community of knowledgeable and caring people is necessary for parents. They need to be supported, encouraged, and guided by those who are personally acquainted with substance abuse within their families and have learned from personal experience how to practically counter drugs within the family setting. Bill will introduce Susan to the support groups that sustained him; likewise, the reader will learn how to access this support. Parents of addicts and alcoholics must be sustained and buttressed by informed supports. Solitary agony must be replaced by access to experienced and knowledgeable help.

We will temporarily leave Susan and Bill so we can begin an exploration of the behaviors associated with drug and alcohol abuse. But before we do this, a few clarifying words are in order. First, the reader should realize that the intent of this book is to provide parents with a fundamental understanding and appreciation of what it means to be addicted to brain-altering substances. It is neither designed nor intended to provide a detailed, exhaustive discourse on the many complex topics that make up the field of addiction. Our library shelves and the Internet are filled with such information. What is missing is a down-to-earth, functional book that offers practical insight and guidance for parents with sons or daughters addicted to drugs and alcohol. Once parents understand the basic truths about addiction (the goal of the early chapters of this book), they will have a foundation to understand the practical weaponry that can effectively challenge the disease of addiction. The latter portion of this book is dedicated to introducing the reader to these invaluable parenting tools.

Second, it should be noted that the term *drugs* will be used as a general label, and the routine absence of the term *alcohol* should not be seen as discounting or ignoring this brain-altering substance's gravity. For our purposes, we are considering a *drug* to be a nonfood, chemical substance that alters the normal condition of the brain and body when consumed. Alcohol contains the drug ethanol, a colorless, volatile, flammable liquid that serves as the intoxicating ingredient in fermented and distilled liquors. Ethanol is a depressant that alters the normal functioning of the mind and body, and thereby meets the definition of a drug.

Another characteristic that distinguishes alcohol from other drugs is that it happens to be legal, culturally sanctioned, and socially accepted and supported, which tends to mask its devastating impact. For many youth, being "wasted" is a permissible, desirable, and often applauded behavior that, while illegal for those who are under twenty-one years of age, is socially tolerated for and by our youth. This mind-set has led to a widespread, dangerous abuse of alcohol by our youth, and parents who intentionally or unintentionally sanction this mind-set place their sons and daughters in serious danger.

Alcohol abuse is widespread and affects all age groups, but it severely impacts our youth. Read what the Centers for Disease Control and Prevention (CDC) says about alcohol use:

Alcohol is one of the most widely used drug substances in the world. Alcohol use and binge drinking among our nation's youth is a major public health problem:[1]

➡ Alcohol is used by more young people in the United States than tobacco or illicit drugs.[2]

➡ Excessive alcohol consumption is associated with approximately 75,000 deaths per year.[3]

➡ Alcohol is a factor in approximately 41% of all deaths from motor vehicle crashes.[4]

➡ Among youth, the use of alcohol and other drugs has also been linked to unintentional injuries, physical fights, academic and occupational problems, and illegal behavior.[5]

➡ Long-term alcohol misuse is associated with liver disease, cancer, cardiovascular disease, and neuro-logical damage as well as psychiatric problems such as depression, anxiety, and antisocial personality disorder.[6]

➡ Drug use contributes directly and indirectly to the HIV epidemic, and alcohol and drug use contribute markedly to infant morbidity and mortality.[7]

As mentioned above, the reader will notice that there is an intentional absence of the term *alcohol* in this book. The routine use of the term *drugs* includes alcohol unless a specific drug is being discussed. Using the term *drugs* to include alcohol is for literary clarity and ease of understanding the concepts involved. Don't let the absence of the term *alcohol* be interpreted as minimizing the seriousness of the widespread, dangerous, and all-too-often-fatal drug, alcohol.

Literary clarity also affects the frequently used terms *parents* and *mom and dad*. If you are a single parent, step-parent, or another significant presence in the life of a young person, consider yourself included when these phrases are used. What is said in this book to "parents" is applicable to siblings, grandparents, aunts, uncles, extended family members, close friends, pastors, and others who have a significant role in the life of the young person.

CHAPTER 2

Halting Addiction's Progression by Confronting Denial

Ask the average person to describe an addict or alcoholic, and you will hear such phrases as "a stumbling drunk," "a disheveled, homeless person," or "someone who robs to get money for drugs." While these responses may be accurate for those substance abusers in the late stages of addiction, they don't represent the vast number of addicts who have yet to reach this point. When the image of addiction is limited to late-stage substance abusers, those who have yet to reach this point in addiction's progressive march are overlooked. The legions of people advancing steadfastly toward that day when drugs completely dismantle their lives, but are currently able to hold down jobs, attend school, maintain basic social interactions, and generally function tolerably within our society, are disregarded.

How a parent views addiction is critical. When parents limit their view of addiction, they miss invaluable opportunities to help their young person while time is still on their side. Blinded by stereotypical images, they miss the signs of substance abuse, fail to procure early help and intervention, and subject their son or daughter to an unnecessary journey on addiction's dangerous and progressive pathway. To avoid this potentially fatal behavior, it's important to know how addiction spawns, grows, and, in time, totally controls the individual.

Substance use begins with experimentation (stage one) and occurs on a hit-or-miss basis. It is propelled primarily by curiosity and peer group influence. Over time, this irregular, unplanned, experimental use of drugs evolves into a pattern of planned weekend recreational use (stage two). The recreational user quickly discovers that drugs have a social lubrication effect that relaxes and eases them in social settings. The awkward, uncomfortable emerging adult who suffers from low self-esteem and often feels inadequate in social settings (common for many teens) discovers that through the use of drugs and alcohol, he or she can feel more comfortable and relaxed. Social interactions are easier, which becomes an enticing reason to use brain-altering substances.

Thanks to substance-induced social ease, a mind-set develops that equates "having fun" and "partying" with substance use. This is in stark contrast to drug-free peers, who view "having fun" and "partying" as an opportunity to enjoy life by visiting with friends, dancing, talking, and "hanging out." For the emerging addict, these activities pale in comparison to the drug-induced blissfulness, euphoria, and pleasure that they define as "partying" and "having fun"—getting high.

Over time, this pattern of recreational use progresses to excessive consumption, heavy drinking, and bingeing. While some of the consequences of alcohol consumption have already been mentioned, the following information on alcohol poisoning from the National Institute on Alcohol Abuse and Alcoholism (NIAAA) is well worth considering. Not only does the NIAAA article discuss the ways in which excessive alcohol consumption affects the brain and its potentially fatal consequences on the body and brain, but it also serves as an excellent guide for that all-important talk about alcohol poisoning that every parent of an emerging adult should have.

Alcohol depresses nerves that control involuntary actions such as breathing and the gag reflex (which prevents choking). A fatal dose of alcohol will eventually stop these functions.

It is common for someone who drank excessive alcohol to vomit, since alcohol is an irritant to the stomach. There is then the danger of choking on vomit, which could cause death by asphyxiation in a person who is not conscious because of intoxication.

You should also know that a person's blood alcohol concentration (BAC) can continue to rise even while he or she is passed out. Even after a person stops drinking, alcohol in the stomach and intestine continues to enter the bloodstream and circulate throughout the body. It is dangerous to assume the person will be fine by sleeping it off.

Critical Signs and Symptoms
of Alcohol Poisoning

➡ Mental confusion, stupor, coma, or person cannot be roused.

➡ Vomiting.

➡ Seizures.

➡ Slow breathing (fewer than eight breaths per minute).

➡ Irregular breathing (10 seconds or more between breaths).

➡ Hypothermia (low body temperature), bluish skin color, paleness.

(continued)

What Should I Do If I Suspect Someone Has Alcohol Poisoning?

➥ Know the danger signals.

➥ Do not wait for all symptoms to be present.

➥ Be aware that a person who has passed out may die.

➥ If there is any suspicion of an alcohol overdose, call 911 for help. Don't try to guess the level of drunkenness.

What Can Happen to Someone with Alcohol Poisoning That Goes Untreated?

➥ Victim chokes on his or her own vomit.

➥ Breathing slows, become irregular, or stops.

➥ Heart beats irregularly or stops.

➥ Hypothermia (low body temperature).

➥ Hypoglycemia (too little blood sugar) leads to seizures.

➥ Untreated severe dehydration from vomiting can cause seizures, permanent brain damage, or death.[1]

The article also points out this significant fact: "Even if the victim lives, an alcohol overdose can lead to irreversible brain damage. Rapid binge drinking (which often happens on a bet or dare) is especially dangerous because the victim can ingest a fatal dose before becoming unconscious."[2]

Youth do respond positively when parents knowingly talk with them about alcohol and drugs, so please educate yourself so you can share this information with your emerging adult. As you engage in this imperative discussion, make sure you share what the article so strongly emphasizes: "Don't be afraid to seek medical help for a friend who has had too much to drink. Don't worry that your friend may become angry or embarrassed—remember, you cared enough to help. Always be safe, not sorry."[3]

Every parent needs to be familiar with the dangers of alcohol poisoning so they can share this critical information with their sons and daughters. Binge drinking is a peer-instigated activity and often occurs without any restrictions—except the guidelines and counseling you impart.

As recreational use continues, the emerging addict's attention becomes more and more centered upon the upcoming weekend's drug and alcohol activities. This increased mental fixation evolves into an ongoing mental preoccupation that advances into a pattern of daily drug use. At this stage, the young person is truly addicted, and illicit drug use occurs daily and eventually several times a day. Addiction's progressive march has now reached preoccupation (stage three). The addict's life is now centered almost exclusively upon obtaining and using drugs. There is an increase in the frequency of use as well as the amount and the types of drugs used. At this stage, obtaining and using drugs is more and more an all-consuming activity that the addict cannot control. Over time, the addict's life becomes totally consumed by seeking and using drugs, which leads to a state of total powerlessness over drugs (stage four). At this point, nothing matters but finding and consuming drugs. The stereotypes depicted at the start of this chapter are now a likelihood. There is only one more stage left in addiction's progressive march: death, which will occur unless treatment is initiated and the strategies to sustain a drug-free lifestyle are maintained.

All users of brain-altering substances can be found somewhere along addiction's progressive pathway. Individuals at the experimental or recreational stages are still able to maintain themselves, except when they are engaged in heavy drinking and bingeing. Since drugs haven't yet taken control, the developing addict is more often than not capable of masking her drug use, thereby preventing any early parental discovery. Eventually, undetected drug use progresses to the preoccupation stage, where social, ethical, and moral standards take a backseat to the obsession to seek out and consume drugs on a daily basis. It is at this progressive stage of addiction that the brain becomes so altered that behaviors associated with drug use become blatantly evident to anyone close to the young person.

Fortunately, most youth do not progress this far down addiction's pathway because experimenting with drugs was only a phase they went through. Another reason they don't is because their parents talk about drugs. Studies have shown that kids react positively to parental concerns and expressed disapproval regarding drugs. For many parents, however, denial rules, and instead of positively interacting, they react to bizarre acting-out by mimicking their addicted offspring's behaviors: making excuses, blaming others, covering up, ignoring, rationalizing, and minimizing. Parents who are normally rational, insightful, and intelligent adults will resort to seemingly protective and safeguarding acts, which in reality are harmful, unprincipled behaviors that would not occur under normal circumstances. In short, they do anything but admit that a beloved son or daughter has a substance abuse problem.

Denial by parents is understandable. What parent is going to unreservedly admit that a son or daughter, whom they've loved, nurtured, and ethically and morally trained since birth, has a problem with drugs or alcohol? Such an admission would be a condemnation of their parenting and open them up to negative societal and cultural innuendos. While denial is understandable, it must be confronted because, if it is allowed to continue, a parent's ability to treat the addicted young person in a rational and effective manner is almost impossible.

Denial also rules the addicts, who tenaciously maintain that they don't have a problem. A distinctive characteristic of addicts is their adamant insistence that drugs are not a problem, as exemplified by their ignoring, rationalizing, or minimizing the impact of drugs. To validate this mindset, they blame others: "It's my parents' fault because they don't like/understand/care for me," "It's the teachers and their attitudes," "It's my boss, who is crazy and doesn't know how to talk to people." Substance abuse is never acknowledged to be the problem, even when it is blatantly obvious that a problem with drugs or alcohol exists. Listen to addicts as they continually blame others, and you will come to appreciate the authenticity of the saying "Addiction is a blaming disease."

Denial, especially parental denial, must be overcome and illicit substance use must be verified. Since there is little chance that a parent will stumble upon a son or daughter using brain-altering substances, it is imperative that an easy-to-use method to detect and validate drug use be established. One such method is evaluating behaviors, looking for specific behaviors that are associated with substance use. Behavioral evaluation is a valid methodology to detect the use of brain-altering substances because the brain controls behavior, and when drugs are introduced, the brain changes. Its normal regulatory authority is destabilized and undermined, which leads to bizarre and extreme behaviors. As these foreign behaviors emerge, substance abuse becomes more and more obvious, but, unfortunately, far too many parents remain in denial and excuse away the behaviors.

In the next chapter, a behavioral test is presented. Following this test is an explanation of why the behaviors in question are indicative of substance use. While these behaviors are valid indicators of drug use, they are only as usable as the objectivity that the parent brings. You, therefore, are encouraged to approach the thirteen main behavioral indicators and their multiple sub-behaviors in a straightforward, honest manner. If you find that some of the listed behaviors are present, admit it without rationalizing by telling yourself, *Many drug-free teens act this way. This behavior is part of the changes all teens go through. This behavior can be pointing toward something other than drug use. The transition from childhood to adulthood is marked by turmoil, and this is likely part of growing up.*

It's true that the years from twelve to twenty-five are marked by turmoil and chaos, as well as impulsive and compulsive negative actions. The behaviors listed on the upcoming test can be reflective of these youthful indiscretions and confusion, but they are also behaviors that are found with those who engage in the use of brain-altering substances. Since the behaviors in question can arise from multiple causes, no parent should infer from a specific behavior that drug use is occurring. What you are observing may be reflective of school problems, undesirable peers, or the turmoil that all young people experience as they transition from childhood to adulthood. Concentrate instead on the totality of the multiple behavioral indicators and avoid getting hung up on any specific behaviors.

⚜

CHAPTER 3

The Unlucky Thirteen Behavioral Test

Below are thirteen behavior categories. Under each category are listed several sub-behaviors that are reflective and characteristic of the main behavior category. If your child demonstrates any of these sub-behaviors on a consistent basis, check the box in front of the described behavior. If the behavior isn't part of your child's behavioral repertoire, leave the box empty.

1. Mood Swings That Are Unusually Excessive and/or Dramatic (___/09)

☐ Does your son or daughter have periods of excessive aggressiveness?

☐ Does your son or daughter become argumentative much too quickly?

☐ Is your son or daughter excessively sensitive?

☐ Is your son or daughter more and more unpredictable?

☐ Does your son or daughter have periods of explosiveness, which are often accompanied by violence?

☐ Are your parent-child interactions marked by senseless arguments and clashes?

☐ Do your parent-child interactions leave you fearful at times?

☐ Has your son or daughter punched holes in doors, walls, and so on?

☐ Are you considering placing a lock on your bedroom door for your personal safety?

2. Extreme Isolation (___/04)

☐ Are you concerned about the amount of time your young person spends isolated from the family?

☐ Do you consider the amount of time your young person spends alone when at home to be excessive?

☐ Is your young person spending excessive amounts of time in a locked bathroom or bedroom?

☐ Does your son or daughter engage in whispered conversations?

3. Extreme Remoteness (___/09)

☐ When asked about his or her whereabouts, does your young person offer you excessive amounts of useless information that provides you with virtually no information or idea about what he or she has been up to?

☐ Does your son or daughter offer sketchy and minimal information about his or her activities?

☐ When questioned, does your son or daughter lie or avoid giving a straight answer?

☐ During family gatherings, does your young person disappear?

☐ Does your son or daughter avoid or refuse to interact with relatives?

☐ Is your young person remote and moody with family members?

☐ Has your young person ruined a family gathering or holiday?

☐ Is your young person neglecting household chores and duties to excess?

☐ Have such qualities as basic respect disappeared or begun to disappear from your son's or daughter's life?

4. Excessive Time Spent Away from the Home (___05)

☐ Do you consider the amount of time your son or daughter spends away from home to be excessive?

☐ Has the amount of time your son or daughter spends away from home increased dramatically in recent months?

☐ Are you uncomfortable with the amount of time your son or daughter spends away from home?

☐ Are you unaware of where your son or daughter spends time when he or she is away from home?

☐ Are you unfamiliar with those whom your son or daughter associates with when he or she is away from home?

5. Old Friends Replaced by New, Phantom Friends (___/07)

☐ Have your son's or daughter's old friends disappeared?

☐ Are the reason(s) given for their disappearance unclear and ambiguous?

☐ Are you receiving vague responses to your inquiries about new friends?

☐ Are you in the dark regarding the type of people your young person associates with?

☐ Are you without such basic information as names, addresses, and phone numbers of his or her friends?

☐ Has your son or daughter managed to keep his or her new friends away from you?

☐ Are you uncomfortable with your lack of knowledge regarding your son's or daughter's friends?

6. Deterioration in Physical Health and Appearance (___/09)

☐ Have you noticed your son or daughter with bloodshot eyes?

☐ Have you noticed your son or daughter with dilated (wider/larger than usual) or constricted pupils?

☐ Does your son or daughter use products that are designed to remove red from the eyes?

☐ Has there been a dramatic and significant change in your son's or daughter's appearance?

☐ Is your son's or daughter's skin tone pallid or sickly in appearance?

☐ Has there been an increase in the number of infections your son or daughter has acquired?

☐ Has there been a decrease in your son's or daughter's appetite?

☐ Has there been a noticeable and significant decrease in your son's or daughter's weight?

☐ Has your son or daughter increased his or her consumption of sweets?

7. Preoccupation with Drugs (___/05)

☐ Have drug/alcohol jokes and references become more and more commonplace in your son's or daughter's conversation?

☐ Is your son or daughter fascinated with drug-centered songs and musical groups?

☐ Is your son's or daughter's room decorated with drug-related posters, pictures, and slogans?

☐ Are your son's or daughter's T-shirts littered with drug references?

☐ Do your son's or daughter's attire, possessions, and living environment endorse using drugs/alcohol?

8. Disciplinary and Academic Deterioration in School (___09)

☐ Has there been an increase in the number of falling or failing grades?

☐ Has there been an increase in disciplinary problems in school?

☐ Has your son or daughter lost interest in school?

☐ Has your son or daughter been tardy in arriving to class?

☐ Has your son or daughter been skipping class?

☐ Have you been told that your son or daughter is being truant?

☐ Have the teachers complained about your son or daughter being sleepy or sluggish in class?

☐ Have the teachers complained about your son or daughter spending a lot of time gazing into space?

☐ Have you been avoiding meeting with your young person's teachers?

9. Dramatic Changes in the Way the Phone Is Used (___07)

☐ If your son or daughter uses the home phone, are rules over phone usage not followed?

☐ Are many of your son's or daughter's phone conversations unusually brief?

☐ Does the monthly record of your son's or daughter's cell phone use indicate abuse of the phone, such as making calls that violate the hours he or she is supposed to be using the phone?

☐ Are your young person's phone conversations conducted in a whispered tone?

☐ When you happen to overhear phone conversations, does your son or daughter use "code words" (phrases or words that make little or no contextual sense)?

☐ If your son or daughter has a cell phone, does the monthly report of phone usage indicate many calls of brief duration to the same number?

☐ Are you unaware of whom those numbers on the cell phone bill belong to?

10. Irregularities Regarding Money (___/07)

☐ Does your son or daughter have excessive and abnormal amounts of money on him or her?

☐ Does your son or daughter experience unexplainable shortages of money?

☐ Is there a discrepancy between the amount of money your son or daughter has and his or her income (wages and/or allowance)?

☐ Is there a discrepancy between the amounts of money your son or daughter should have and what he or she has been purchasing?

☐ Have you found money or other valuables such as jewelry missing?

☐ Have there been unexplained ATM withdrawals from your bank account?

☐ Have you found purchases on your charge accounts that you didn't make?

11. Inability to Maintain a Job (___/05)

☐ Is your son or daughter frequently late reporting for work?

☐ Is your son or daughter prone to unexcused absences at work?

☐ Does your son or daughter go from job to job, unable to hold any job for very long?

☐ Does your son or daughter do a poor job at work?

☐ Are your son's or daughter's work habits so poor that you wouldn't hire him or her if you had the option?

12. Change in Things That Were Once of Interest (___/04)

☐ Has your son or daughter suddenly lost interest in cherished hobbies and activities?

☐ Have long-held dreams and ambitions suddenly vanished from your son's or daughter's life?

☐ Are you unable to explain these sudden changes in interests?

☐ Are you uncomfortable with the lack of interests in your son's or daughter's life?

13. Memory, Speech, Energy, Sleep Changes (___/08)

☐ Has your son or daughter been displaying either long- or short-term memory loss?

☐ Has your son or daughter shown signs of poor concentration?

☐ Have you observed your son or daughter with slurred and/or incoherent speech?

☐ Has your son or daughter shown signs of listlessness?

☐ Is your son or daughter too easily fatigued?

☐ Does your son or daughter sleep more than you think is healthy?

☐ Have you observed a significant increase in your son's or daughter's agitation?

☐ Have you observed a significant change in your son's or daughter's sleep patterns?

Scoring the "Unlucky Thirteen"

1. Count the number of checked boxes under each of the thirteen main behavioral headings.

2. Place that number on the blank space within the parentheses.

3. If the written number is half or more of the typed number, write a plus sign in the margin alongside the numbered behavior. If the written number is less than half but exceeds zero, make a check mark in the margin alongside the numbered behavior. If the written number is zero, write a zero in the margin alongside the numbered behavior.

4. Now add up the number of plus scores, the number of check marks, and the number of zeros.

5. Place the totals in the appropriate places below:

    + scores = _____   √ scores = _____   0 scores = _____

Interpreting the Results

Consider any plus score as an indicator that your young person is exhibiting behaviors that are characteristic of addicted young people. No single plus score should be treated as a definitive sign that your child is involved in drug use. That plus score may be reflective of other issues and problems. For instance, if your young person earned a plus rating for the Disciplinary and Academic Deterioration in School category, he may have a learning disability or other academically centered problems that need your attention. Likewise, a plus score for the Deterioration in Physical Health and Appearance category may be a warning of an underlying medical problem that should be brought to the family doctor's attention. If, however, your son's or daughter's behaviors earned more than two plus scores, the results should be considered a competent measurement that drug use is most likely a part of your young person's life. One or two plus scores may be underscoring problems other than substance abuse, but when the scores reach three or more, you are most likely looking at a young person with a substance abuse problem. With so many behaviors that are indicative of the use of illicit substances, the possibility of drug use cannot and must not be ignored.

A zero rating suggests the absence of behaviors that are indicative of the presence of brain-altering substances. If your young person's behavior comes up with multiple zero scores, take a moment to let your teen know how grateful you are that he or she is not involved with drugs.

Each behavioral category that merits a check should be treated as an indicator that your young person might be leaning toward involvement in the drug culture. The presence of these behaviors must be treated with cautious, rational concern, and you would be wise to closely observe your son or daughter to see if any additional behaviors develop. Those checked boxes can be reflective of other issues and problems in an emerging adult's life, but often they function as a forewarning of developing involvement in the drug culture. If your son or daughter earned several checks among the thirteen categories, do not overreact, but do remain on the alert for the presence of additional sub behaviors. Multiple checks should be addressed through parent-child communications regarding the danger of drugs. Many youth who remain drug free or stop drug use early attribute their sobriety to parental concern and communication. If your knowledge of addiction and drugs is limited, the upcoming chapters will present you with sufficient knowledge to carry on an intelligent discussion. In addition to the information you will find in this book, an assortment of websites and resources is offered through notes and within the text. Utilize these references to further enhance your knowledge of various drugs and the disease of addiction.

If there are multiple check ratings along with more than two plus scores, consider this combination to be a strong validation of drug use that should be immediately addressed before the substance abuse advances further.

If both parents are involved in the child's life, it is strongly recommended that both independently take this test and then compare the results. Often, one parent views a young person's behavior differently than the other, and these discrepancies should be openly discussed if you intend to effectively address drug use. Conflicting viewpoints, attitudes, and beliefs will have to be understood and appreciated so that they can be married into a workable, unified consensus. An integrated, united approach is essential to effectively combat drug use, and this can occur only when both parents understand and appreciate each other's mind-set. What better way to initiate the meaningful unification dialogue than by comparing and discussing the differing test results? Understanding the mind-set of each other and then working toward striking a balance from divergent viewpoints is a fundamental early step in effectively combating addiction within the family.

CHAPTER 4

The Impact of Drugs on the Brain

Having just endured the uncomfortable task of determining whether a son or daughter is exhibiting behaviors that might be indicative of the use of brain-altering substances, you might now be able to appreciate the connection between drugs and behavior. To help you, I've provided here a basic presentation about the brain. As we begin exploring this relationship, shun the tendency to allow denial to blind you. Remain open-minded. This book intentionally avoids comprehensive presentations of complex and technical topics, such as the working of the brain. A more detailed discussion would bog down the average reader and unnecessarily expand the scope of this book. If you need further information, do not limit yourself to what is presented here. There are many books that can provide you more detailed information, and so can your family physician. If you need additional information, by all means seek it out.

The brain is a complex and effective system that ordinarily works quite well to provide an individual with normal, controlled mood swings and adequate thinking and behaviors. It consists of 100 billion neurons, which are nerve cells that conduct electrochemical impulses. Neurons can also be found within the central nervous system, which receives sensory impulses from internal and external sources and then converts these impulses to a signal that travels to the spinal cord. The spinal cord is the main pathway for information transmission between the brain and the nervous system. Neurons communicate with each other through impulses that pass through a synapse, a minute space separating the neurons. The synapse contains nerve terminals and chemicals that are called neurotransmitters, which determine mood and behavior. Neurotransmitters pass through the synapse to specialized receiving locations called receptor sites. If the receptor site accepts the neurotransmitter, it begins to function as an operations manager by controlling the neurotransmitter's energized waves. Proper management by the receptor site is essential to keep brain functions such as feeling, thinking, judgment, behavior, and emotional control intact.

To see how substances impact this system, let us look at the neurotransmitter dopamine, which provides motivation, pleasure, and enjoyment, and affects cognition. This neurotransmitter is released when a person is engaged in actions that bring pleasure, such as eating. Dopamine neurotransmitters bind to specific receptor sites. This action releases the chemical in a controlled way, which ensures that the dopamine is discharged for an adequate duration and at acceptable levels. Receptor sites are also tasked with maintaining a sufficient amount of dopamine in reserve so that when the pleasurable action ceases, the individual will not experience an extreme negative mood swing, but rather will be able to return to an acceptable mood level.

When brain-altering substances, such as the stimulant drug methamphetamine, are introduced into the body, an excessive amount of dopamine is suddenly released, overwhelming the receptor site and causing it to fail in its regulatory function. This failure results in a sudden, intense surge of the "feel-good" dopamine, causing a highly invigorated state that is characterized by remarkable pleasure, something that the users of methamphetamine find very enticing. Various body organs respond to this rapid, unregulated inundation through heightened excitement and activity that leaves the individual energized, vigorous, fully awake, and believing that she is able to do anything. The user feels competent, capable, and optimistic. The world becomes a beautiful, wonderful, enthralling place!

Since methamphetamine causes an excessive rush of the feel-good chemical dopamine, there is an insufficient reserve of this neurotransmitter to uphold normal and acceptable mood levels when the drug wears off. Without an adequate supply, the individual crashes into a state of depression. This mood collapse is severe enough that the user must ingest more methamphetamine in order to stop the mood crash. A cycle of use, euphoria, and impending crash continues until the user's supply of methamphetamine runs out, at which point she plunges into a state of severe depression. Parents see this pattern exemplified by wide, extreme mood swings as the drug user is thrust from a state of restlessness, euphoria, and high energy to one of lethargy, excessive irritability, and depression.

Many other sections of the brain are impacted by drugs. These areas include the motor cortex, which is responsible for controlling body movements; the sensory cortex, which controls sensation; the visual cortex, which controls vision; the cerebellum, which is responsible for motor coordination; and the hippocampus, which controls memory.

Drugs affect all these crucial areas of the brain. When heroin is ingested, its naturally occurring analgesic properties impact these parts of the brain. The hippocampus is unable to recall what happened during the heroin-induced high, save a vague recollection of a blissful, altered state. The motor cortex, sensory cortex, and cerebellum are altered to such an extent that the user descends into a state of being that is void of normal sensations. The observer sees the heroin user leaning slightly forward as he enters a blissful state of being. Street slang for this is a "heroin nod."

Alcohol, which contains the sedating drug ethanol, offers another example of the effect brain-altering substances have on the brain. When excessive consumption of alcohol occurs, the individual experiences blurred and distorted vision (impaired visual cortex functioning), is unable to walk normally (impaired motor cortex and cerebellum functioning), and cannot recall what he did while under the influence of alcohol (impaired hippocampus functioning). While many readers may never have seen someone under the influence of methamphetamine or heroin, they most likely have seen the effects of alcohol as just described. Some readers may have personally experienced the effects for themselves.

The brain is composed of three parts. The brain stem makes up 10 percent of the brain and provides vital body functioning automatically. The largest part of the brain, called the cortex, makes up 70 percent of the brain. The remaining 20 percent of the brain, the limbic system, is the unconscious, emotional part of the brain—its pleasure system. This pleasure system motivates the individual to do things that feel good and/or are species preserving, such as eating, the fight-or-flight instinct, fear, and sexual attraction and reproduction.

The frontal lobe is the brain's conscious effort to control the highly emotional, unconscious limbic system. The frontal lobe offers concentration, impulse control, ethics and moral code, problem solving, reasoning, decision making, and appropriate social functioning, among other things. The limbic system responds to pleasure cues more quickly than the conscious response of the frontal lobe, which means values and reasoning arrive more slowly than the emotions and feelings arising from the environmental cue.

The frontal lobe in essence confronts the limbic system. An example of this would be an individual who has been using heroin and whose reward system has adapted to an immediate desire to use the drug whenever an environmental cue is presented. The emotional reward system charges ahead before the frontal lobe can question if using heroin is worth the risk or effort. If the frontal lobe is unsuccessful in stopping the limbic system, the impulse travels down the spinal cord and a reaction to use heroin occurs—the person consumes heroin.

Parents should also know that the frontal lobe doesn't fully mature until the young person is about twenty-five years old. This fact should help parents understand why teens tend to react more emotionally to situations, and not as rationally as adults typically do. The frontal lobe simply isn't mature enough to counter the emotional pull of the limbic system. Since teen drug use delays frontal lobe development, a substance-using young adult will continue to react emotionally beyond age twenty-five unless certain actions are taken. Parents can help speed up the maturation of the frontal lobe by encouraging their young person to exercise, seek out fun activities and new experiences, stay in the present, engage in meditation, and volunteer, all of which lead to positive emotions.

Another characteristic of the brain is plasticity, which means the brain is constantly changing itself based on individual experiences. This is why parents should promote positive activities, so that maturation of the frontal lobe can be accelerated. The brain also has competitive plasticity, which means if you don't use it, you lose it. So help your son or daughter lose those old pleasures by replacing them with new, positive pleasures.

Having been exposed to this brief, fundamental overview of the workings of the brain and the impact brain-altering substances have, you can understand why the behaviors listed in the Unlucky Thirteen test, a result of actions in the brain, can be symptomatic of drug use.

CHAPTER 5

The Unlucky Thirteen Explained

Now that you are aware of how drugs impact normal operations of the brain, you are ready to consider how specific behaviors are markers for illicit substance abuse. As you read the explanations for each of the behavioral categories, please remain open-minded and unencumbered by preconceptions, fear, and the various forms of mental gymnastics designed to keep denial alive.

Mood Swings That Are
Unusually Excessive and/or Dramatic

Knowing how drugs alter the brain's ability to control emotions and mood, it shouldn't come as a surprise that when substance abusers' emotions burst forth, they are unchecked, highly charged, extremely intense, and often explosive eruptions. When judging the severity of emotions and mood swings, parents should look at the behavioral excesses that are displayed. If the behaviors/emotions are significantly different from the expected ups and downs youth normally undergo during their teen years, consider that as indicative of an altered brain at work. Mood changes, which occur when drugs are introduced, have a greater severity and impetuousness than what you would expect of those in a normal adolescent. To differentiate between expected "normal" adolescent mood swings and drug-centered mood swings, parents should consider the degree of excessiveness displayed. The emotions and mood swings that come from drug-free youth may be disturbing and uncomfortable for parents, but they tend to remain within acceptable boundaries, unlike those of their substance-abusing peers, who display extreme mood swings that lack fixed parameters.

When brain-altering substances are ingested, the altered brain's receptor sites are unable to control the flow of neurotransmitters. One can, therefore, expect that excessive, potentially volatile, unpredictable, and extreme emotions will follow. This explains why interacting with a son or daughter impacted by drugs can be so fundamentally frightful that parents come to fear for their own safety. Attempts to communicate with someone whose brain has been altered by drugs or alcohol all too often result in senseless, irrational clashes. Many homes contain holes in walls and doors, scars that serve as visible testimony to the explosive, excessive, and impulsive behaviors that brain-altering substances render. Parents who live with an addicted young person know intimately what it means to fear for their safety. These moms and dads are experiencing firsthand the wide, excessive, unpredictable, and dramatic mood swings and resultant behaviors that drugs cause, visible proof of brain alterations that leave many feeling like they are being held hostage in their home.

Extreme Isolation

Occasionally, everyone needs to retreat from the "madding crowd" and seek out solitary refuge from life. Seeking out and enjoying private moments can be a healthy, often invigorating action that leaves one with clarity and peace of mind. The need for solitary "time-outs" spans all ages, but it is a particularly significant activity for maturing young people who need privacy and space to reflectively sort through the various messages they receive about themselves. While an important part of the healthy maturation process, isolation carried to an extreme should be an alarm for all parents.

While extreme isolation can serve as an indicator of depression and/or suicidal ideation (chapter 24 offers a discussion about the warning signs that indicate when suicide is being considered), it also is a signpost that a young person may be using brain-altering substances. Privacy is essential when using illicit substances, and while the preferred environment, especially for those engaged in early drug use, is to be surrounded by their supportive drug-using peer group, solitary use does occur. When the youthful substance abuser engages in solitary drug use, there is a need for steadfast security from any unwanted company, especially intrusive parents. Unfailing isolation is imperative, so around the home the young drug user becomes reclusive, existing behind locked doors in order to maintain undetected solitary drug use.

As with mood swings, the differentiating factor between drug-centered and normal, healthy adolescent isolation is the degree of excessiveness. One sign of abnormal isolation is an inordinate amount of time cloistered behind locked doors, usually the bedroom and the bathroom. The bedroom provides ample space to hide drugs and their associated paraphernalia while permitting use in a relatively comfortable environment. It is also a fairly secure area since most parents, aware of the emerging adult's need for privacy, seldom burst into the bedroom unauthorized. The bathroom, with its locked door, not only offers a secure environment to use drugs, but it has the additional advantage of camouflaging the various smells and sounds that are indicative of drug-related activities.

Whispered conversations are also a concern. If there is nothing to hide or cover up, why talk in a hushed tone? For many teens involved in drugs, especially those dealing drugs or living in rural areas where access to drugs can demand tricky planning, the phone serves as a lifeline. To avoid detection, drug acquisition or the selling of drugs necessitates secrecy.

Extreme Remoteness

Your developing young person is independently evaluating, exploring, and reflecting upon the world; discovering self; and acquiring her own unique set of values—normal developmental activities that parents accept reluctantly and often with considerable discomfort. However, should your young person's remoteness reach the point of excessiveness (there is that word again), you have valid justification for concern.

To determine if your son's or daughter's remoteness has become excessive, examine the specifics of your parent-child interactions. When you communicate with your adolescent, does she offer circumstantial and confusing details that leave you with worthless bits of information and absolutely no idea about what she is doing? Are legitimate questions routinely answered with evasive responses or an outright refusal to give a straight answer? Does your young person lie, engage in dishonesty, or hedge? If you responded yes to these questions, you have a person who is hiding something—and drug use may be it.

Family gatherings are not events most young people look forward to attending. Spending a day with all those ancient aunts and uncles instead of friends is not on the average adolescent's top ten list of things they like doing. For the substance abuser, family gatherings and holidays are especially unwelcome events. Not only do they force the substance abuser away from his drug-using friends, but those visitors pose a real threat to his ability to get high in secrecy. There are too many people roaming the house who might accidentally catch him using drugs, or he's in an unfamiliar place. At least parents have fairly predictable patterns of coming and going, around which the substance abuser can maneuver. It is much more advantageous to become obnoxious, secluded, or abandon home and family altogether than to civilly interact with an unwelcome assortment of inquiring relatives who have the potential to jeopardize or expose the substance use.

Parents of addicts have ample horror tales of holiday celebrations and family gatherings marred by the addict. It is not unusual for an addicted young person to either disappear or destroy the festivities with moodiness, remoteness, rudeness, and other behaviors. If your son or daughter's behavior during family events exceeds the typical adolescent disinclination, it may be illicit substance use that's the reason.

Excessive remoteness and detachment from the family can also be seen in defying normal household responsibilities. While battling over household chores is an ongoing struggle for all parents, extreme disregard of household responsibilities and duties can serve as a signal that substance abuse exists. Operating with a mind that is obsessed with seeking out and using drugs, the addict becomes oblivious to her surroundings and responsibilities. Hauling the trash to the curb, doing the dishes, and complying with other ordinary responsibilities do not register as important, their significance having been lost on the drug-altered brain that is centered solely on getting and using substances. Neglect of responsibilities is a hallmark of substance abusers, both young and old.

Typically, adolescents and young adults find themselves in a fluctuating relationship with their family. They seek independence and freedom from their parents, yet they want to remain connected, desiring the nurturing and protection the family offers (although they will rarely admit it). This duality sustains the typical adolescent's affiliation with the family unit while endorsing the independence the emerging adult needs for healthy maturation. With the addict, this is not the situation. Having only one purpose in life—to satisfy that urge to use drugs—family attributes such as nurturance, respect, and interaction, as well as values and morals that their parents taught, become irrelevant. Those positive, socially beneficial attributes that were so diligently instilled have no place in a life centered upon using drugs. Excessive remoteness becomes imperative for drug use to continue without conflict.

Excessive Time Spent Away from the Home

Away from the watchful eyes of parents, any young person's social skills are developed and solidified through peer relations, an essential and wholesome part of any emerging adult's striving toward healthy maturation and autonomy. This process is misshapen for the substance abuser. Influenced by the authority of the drug-centered peer group, who offer the easy solution of drug use, there is no need to learn socially acceptable coping skills. Failing to develop positive social skills, the young adult is unable to deal with life's problems—except by escaping into drug use. This is why addiction workers believe that the social maturation age of an addict is the age at which the person started using drugs and stopped coping with and handling life's problems. In addition, this social immaturity further highlights what was discussed in the preceding chapter when we considered drug-induced delay of the frontal lobe's development. Your young person may be seventeen, but if he started using drugs at age fourteen, that is the social maturation age at which he operates, and his coping skills are those of the typical fourteen-year-old.

The commanding influence that the peer group holds is indispensable in the initiation and development of substance abuse. Ask older addicts what influences were present when they began using brain-altering substances, and you will most likely hear it was the dual combination of curiosity and peer influence. Rarely did they begin using brain-altering substances alone. Most addicts need encouragement to begin drug use, so they spend an inordinate amount of time with drug-using peers, who value and endorse drug use. Alliance with fellow substance abusers is essential for the development of drug use.

Operate on your instincts. Parents are often gifted with a "sixth sense," feeling discomfort and concern whenever something isn't right with a son or daughter. If your sixth sense is activated by your young person's excessive absences from the home, don't disregard it.

Old Friends Replaced by New, Phantom Friends

Old childhood pals and loyal school friends disappear once a youngster becomes involved in drugs. Drug-free youth will not endanger their sobriety and reputation by associating with drug-using peers. The drug-using young person does not want to be associated with drug-free youth either, since they don't offer the encouragement and support that is essential for hassle-free, unchallenged drug use. Given this, the young person engaged in drug use will leave those old friends (unless they also have succumbed to drug use) since they no longer have anything in common. As addiction takes hold, associations are exclusively with the peer drug group, who offer crucial encouragement, acceptance, and approval, qualities that are so essential for any teenager.

If old friends have disappeared, investigate the reason. While it may be difficult, try to find out who replaced those longtime friends. Drugs do affect cognition, but not to the point that the drug-using son or daughter ignores the perils of bringing home drug-using friends. Aware of what would befall her if her parents learned with whom she is associating, the young person offers nameless "phantom" friends whom she can't seem to bring home.

Honestly ask yourself, "How much do I know about my son's or daughter's friends? Who are they? What are their names? Where do they live? What are their phone numbers? Who are their parents?" If you cannot answer these questions to your satisfaction, your son or daughter may be concealing friends who are caught up in drugs. Remember, you knew those old friends, their parents, and where they lived. The same expectations should hold for these new, phantom-like friends.

Deterioration in Physical Health and Appearance

Drugs affect the physical body in numerous, often-visible ways. Even parents without medical training can detect such telltale signs of drug use as bloodshot eyes and dilated (wider or larger than normal) pupils. The addict knows he must mask these, so eye care products become an everyday companion. What other explanation can there be for that "remove the red" product that you saw in your son's jacket pocket?

Skin tone is another easily observable clue pointing to drug use. If your child's skin tone has changed from healthy and robust to pallid and sickly, you should regard this as a possible sign of substance abuse. If your young person is of a dark complexion, look for increased darkness and/or dark blotches on the skin. Drugs also affect the digestive and respiratory systems, so an increase in the number of digestive or respiratory infections and complaints can serve as a sign of drug use. Naturally, there very well may be medical reasons for these physical alterations and concerns, but drugs must not be discounted. A complete physical examination, during which you ask the doctor to rule out drug use, would be in order.

Abusing illicit substances is a very effective way to lose weight. Many addicts are underweight, alcoholics who flood their bodies with empty calories being a major exception. While weight loss and a change in appetite may be attributed to many causes, drug use is one possibility that you should ask your doctor to rule out. It should also be noted that with marijuana, there is often an increase in cravings for sweets and other snacks. Watch your young person's intake of junk food, since this can serve as a sign of marijuana use.

Preoccupation with Drugs

Substance-abusing young people will not openly admit that they use or abuse drugs, but some will openly advertise their allegiance to the drug culture by surrounding themselves with drug-related merchandise and accessories. A fascination with songs laced with drug lyrics and groups associated with the drug scene, conversations mixed with phrases and slogans associated with drugs, wearing T-shirts and hats emblazoned with drug-centered images and slogans (including alcohol), are common examples of how young adults advertise their allegiance to the drug culture. If your young person's room has become a shrine to the drug culture, or his clothing a walking advertisement for drugs and/or alcohol, you have good reason for concern. No one litters their possessions or personal space with slogans, posters, and pictures unless that individual has an allegiance to that which is being promulgated. It does not take a rocket scientist to figure out that there is a connection.

Disciplinary and Academic Deterioration in School

Because a young substance abuser often attends school in an altered mental state, it is virtually impossible for him or her to maintain good grades or remain free from disciplinary problems within the school setting. Granted, from time to time drug-free students will lose interest in school and their grades and conduct will mirror, but these changes are not as dramatic and extreme as they are for the substance-abusing student. When drugs begin altering the brain, a significant, often-rapid deterioration in grades occurs because drugs affect the brain's ability to think, concentrate, and behave appropriately. Needing to satisfy drug cravings by getting a "smoke," "drink," or "blast," substance abusers are frequently late for class or miss class altogether. Incidents of truancy rise as the need to use drugs surpasses the need to be in school. When the substance abuser is in the classroom, drugs overpower any possibility of focusing and comprehending what is being taught.

School is an excellent place to investigate any suspicions you may have regarding drug use. Your youngster's teachers spend more time with her than any other adult, including you, and can serve as an invaluable resource—so why not talk with them? Ask if they have observed the behaviors just mentioned, as well as any issues with memory, speech, energy, or sleeping during class. Be aware, however, that for a variety of valid reasons, it is not advisable for teachers to affirm or deny drug use. That determination should be reserved for you, the parent, so do not try to foist your parental responsibilities onto them.

Do, however, consider your son's or daughter's teachers as excellent resources to confirm or negate the presence of addiction's signposts. Teachers can also function as powerful allies when you begin to tackle the problem, if one exists—more on that later. By the way, are you seeing your young person's teachers on a regular basis? If not, why? Are you fearful of what you might learn, or has your teenager conned you with that "I'm not a kid now" line?

Dramatic Changes in the Way the Phone Is Used

Young adults often go through adolescence as if they had developed an added appendage: the phone. Domination of the house phone is always a problem in homes with adolescents, which may partly explain the prolif- eration of cellular phones among our youth. Most families have rules regarding phone use: The cell and house phone cannot be used at specific times, take messages, and click over when a second call comes in. How well is your young person following phone rules? If you live in a suburban or rural area, remember that the phone often serves as a lifeline for acquiring drugs. Even when parental regulations prohibit phone use, the drug user will find a way to contact his dealer and phone rules will not stand in the way.

When the abuser of illicit substances picks up the phone, his need for drugs overrides rule impositions. Seeking out (or selling) drugs requires calls of extremely short duration. They will be made and received at odd hours, possibly against rules regulating use of the phone, and conducted in whispered tones. If you happen to be nearby, you may hear code words, which are words and phrases that make no contextual sense to the casual observer but make complete sense to those cognizant of the meaning of these clandestine terms. The use of code words permits your son or daughter to make a drug transaction right under your watchfulness. This is in stark contrast to the typical teen who is long-winded, will talk for hours if allowed, often loudly, but will also adhere to family guidelines regarding phone use.

Because there are few controls over the use of cell phones, short of confiscating the phone, you may be wondering, "How can I expect to monitor calls made away from home?" Actually, you have a very good means to do this—the monthly bill. Examine that bill. If there is a pattern of multiple calls being made to a certain number(s) that last for a very brief period, find out who owns the number(s). Ask your son or daughter, "Who owns this number? I see you made several calls to this number but the calls never last more than a minute." If your young person becomes an obstructionist, substance abuse is a possibility.

Irregularities Regarding Money

Drugs and money are inherently related. Money drives drug traffic and is one of the most tangible indicators of involvement in the drug scene. Sudden, unexplainable extra money can serve as an indicator that your young person is dealing drugs to finance her addiction and/or earn extra money. An unexplainable shortage of money can also serve as an equally strong warning. Drugs cost money and will inevitably drain the user's finances, something that is especially true for those who have chosen not to sell drugs.

Many young people, propelled by their drug cravings, will often turn to parents to fund their habit. Bumming money from parents initially works, but as drug use increases, this is no longer a sufficient revenue source. At this point, some youth turn to outright stealing. Taking money and other valuables, pawning jewelry stolen from Mom, making unauthorized purchases on credit cards and then selling or pawning the ill-gotten goods, removing money from Dad's wallet, pilfering a parent's bank account through unauthorized use of an ATM card, slipping money out of the family "cookie jar" or off Mom's dresser—these are everyday ways that youthful substance abusers finance their addiction. If you are missing money or other valuables, or if there have been irregularities in your credit card and ATM accounts, you may be underwriting your young person's addiction. Secure your valuables and closely monitor your young person's money flow as well as yours.

Inability to Maintain a Job

Individuals addicted to brain-altering substances have difficulty holding on to a job. While many adult substance abusers can function adequately in the workplace, reporting for work on time and giving the employer a full day's work by delaying drinking or drug use, others have drug-induced problems on the job. For these addicts, behavior on the job is characterized by disappearing for extended periods of time, tardiness, absenteeism, poor work quality, and inadequate work output.

Youthful addicts exhibit job difficulties more quickly than their addicted adult counterparts because they have yet to acquire a proficiency in work skills and habits that can temporarily mask substance abuse. For the young drug user, drugs quickly become the substance abuser's "boss." Getting high becomes more important than reporting for work on time or even showing up. Urges to use drive the abuser to unscheduled and extended breaks, and the powerful influence of drug-using peers causes him to give away food or merchandise in order to ensure membership in the peer group and as barter for "free" drugs.

If your young person goes from job to job, unable to remain employed for very long, be alert for the presence of drugs. Don't settle for such common excuses as "I can't stand my boss," "That place is a sweatshop," "I can't get decent hours," or "My boss plays favorites." Minimum-wage jobs frequently warrant such comments, but are the problems truly related to the job, or might they be drug centered? Not sure? Why don't you talk with your young person's current and former employers? Ask if these behavioral traits were characteristic of your young person on the job. Your emerging adult will resent you for interfering in her life, and you will probably be uncomfortable talking with her employers, but if job performance and retention have become a problem, you have an obligation as a concerned parent to investigate. It would be rare for an employer to indicate suspected drug use, but if the supervisor indicates irresponsible behaviors and poor attendance on the job, you might want to consider that possibility, especially if there were other "plus" scores on the Unlucky Thirteen Behavioral Test.

Still unsure whether drugs have impacted your young person's ability to perform adequately in the workplace? A good litmus test would be to ask yourself, "If I had the opportunity, would I hire my son or daughter?" Except for those in deep denial, parents of substance abusers would have a difficult time answering in the affirmative.

Change in Things That Were Once of Interest

As substance abuse takes hold of your young person, cherished hobbies and activities lose their importance and eventually vanish from his life. Drugs alter thinking and values, which results in a loss of interest in hobbies and other activities that were once cherished. Drugs also demand more and more of the user's time and energy, leaving little left for constructive pastimes. With thinking impaired and drug cravings making time demands, the athletic adolescent ends up quitting sports, and the teen who historically has been active in various school activities suddenly drops out of her extracurricular activities, announcing, "I'm tired of all that junk."

Adolescence is a period when sudden, unexpected, and impulsive changes occur. This is common, but how often do these fluctuations take such an extreme turn? If cherished activities, dreams, and goals have disappeared from your young person's life, drugs may now be in control. Use your parental intuition. If you are uncomfortable with the changes you are seeing, find out the real reason for these radical shifts, refusing to accept superficial excuses.

Memory, Speech, Energy, Sleep Changes

Drugs produce toxic effects within the brain. While scientists can prove this microscopically, the untrained person is able to see this manifested through memory lapses, limited attention spans, poor concentration, and incoherent or slurred speech. Since teachers are usually the first to notice these signs, regular communication with your son's or daughter's teachers is crucial. Just remember: You are looking for confirmation or negation of signposts pointing toward illicit substance use, not for the teacher to verify or deny substance use on the part of your young person.

Ambition flows from the brain, and since drugs alter the brain, the longer a person abuses drugs, the more his ambition decreases. Listlessness becomes more and more the norm while the addict becomes a shell of his former hopeful and motivated self. Considering the detrimental impact that drugs have upon the brain, it is common for the typical addict to be lethargic, feel hopeless and helpless, and sleep too much. It should be noted, however, that while under the immediate influence of stimulant drugs such as amphetamine, Ecstasy, and cocaine, there would be an obvious increase in agitation, activity, and sleeplessness, with abusers going for extended periods of time without any sleep.

In Summary

Remember, no single behavior can substantiate the presence of drugs in your young person's life. Taken alone, any given behavior may be expected in the tumultuous developmental process all teens experience, or it may function as a marker of other mental or physical problems that need to be addressed. If your responses to three or more of the thirteen behavioral categories rated a "plus" score, substance abuse is very likely the problem. The volume of behaviors is more than what one would expect from normal adolescent developmental chaos and turmoil, so don't dismiss or ignore these multiple signs. Do something about them by immediately contacting a physician to rule out medical problems and ensure that there have been no medical complications due to the abuse of brain-altering substances. Since substance abusers are at high risk for acquiring HIV, hepatitis C, and STDs (sexually transmitted diseases), request that your doctor test for these illnesses.

Then educate and prepare yourself. Use those scores to stimulate yourself into action. Learn all you can about addiction. Be knowledgeable and skilled in executing the antidrug weaponry effective in countering addiction and explained in section 3 of this book. Make those "plus" scores a big plus for your young person's future by taking action—this can happen only if you accept their authenticity and avoid the urge to engage in denial.

If you have been blessed by a teen who doesn't display these behaviors, don't put this book down. Drugs may not have touched your immediate family as of yet, but the same cannot be said of your "village" of extended family, friends, neighbors, co-workers, and church members. Drugs are too widespread to not have touched someone you know and care about, and just because your family has been spared by addiction so far, there is nothing to guarantee that it won't happen later. Don't let drug abuse go undetected by being uninformed. And don't forget relatives or your "village" who may one day need your informed help. Continue reading so you can be prepared to assist those who were not as fortunate as you.

CHAPTER 6

Environmental Clues

Behavioral clues aren't the only indicators that point toward substance abuse. Drug use can also be detected through the presence of paraphernalia that are specific to the various ways drugs are packaged and used. The presence of these items serves as specific, tangible, and irrefutable verification of drug involvement that confronts not only any parental denial that may remain, but also any lingering doubts that parents may be harboring regarding the legitimacy of those scores from the behavioral test.

To determine if drug paraphernalia is in your child's life, you will have to search areas that your young person frequents—an action that many parents, including myself, are uncomfortable doing. Violating a young person's trust or privacy is not something parents should take lightly, since emerging adults should be accorded as much trust and space as possible. But we must also recognize that occasionally trust and privacy must be violated for the health and welfare of the emerging adult. If you have solid grounds to fear substance use but remain uneasy about violating your young person's privacy, please ask yourself, *What would be worse, violating my young person's privacy and temporarily damaging trust or not acting, and through my inaction damaging his future with the misery and the dangers that drugs extend?*

As you prepare to search, realize that you will have to thoroughly inspect book bags, clothing, the bedroom and bathrooms, the car, and any other places that your son or daughter frequents. Put on some old clothes before you begin pulling up those loose corners of carpeting and looking under furniture and dresser drawers, searching for objects that might be taped or stuck with gum to the undersides. Grab a flashlight so you can inspect the lower portions of bathroom cabinets, making sure that you thoroughly check those small crevices, hidden ledges, and deep recesses. In addition, you will have to proceed cautiously as you examine clothing, paying particular attention to pockets and hems since torn linings function nicely as entrées to secreted hiding places. Take time to examine your son's or daughter's book bag by inspecting those many compartments while checking for holes or torn linings. If your young person uses the car, don't forget to look for small burn holes, matches, ashes, and drug paraphernalia that may have been left behind. Pay particular attention to ashtrays, areas under the seats, side door compartments, and the glove compartment. Some of the things you are looking for are normal, everyday household items, but notice whether they're out of place, hidden away, or used in excess. Tweezers, cotton balls, and rubbing alcohol are common in the bathroom. But when they're squirreled away in hiding places, or in large amounts, be suspicious.

Words of warning before you actually start your search: Be very cautious, especially when you go through pockets, examine torn linings, or reach your hand into areas with poor visibility. The last thing you want is a finger or hand cut by a needle, razor, or other sharp object containing an unwanted virus. It is highly recommended that you use some form of protection, such as thick gloves, and proceed with extreme caution.

Environmental Indicators

The items listed below are specific to the drug culture. How they are associated with drugs will soon be explained, but before that occurs, carefully and cautiously search your young person's environs for the following:

- ☐ cigarette papers (thin sheets of white paper designed to roll tobacco into cigarettes)
- ☐ clips and tweezers

☐ small screens and pipes, including water pipes

☐ burn holes in clothing, furniture, or car upholstery

☐ plastic bags, aluminum foil, and vials

☐ a small scale

☐ razor blades

☐ strange odors

☐ missing or watered-down liquor

☐ baby pacifiers and/or glow sticks

☐ syringes

☐ lighters, matches, steel wool

☐ spoons or bottle caps

☐ blood-stained cotton balls

☐ rubbing alcohol

As you read the ways these items relate to drug use, remember that the possession of these items is very specific to the drug culture. Do not minimize the significance of any of your findings by attempting to justify or rationalize their presence. Denial must not rule.

Cigarette Papers

Most convenience stores sell small packs of white paper designed to roll tobacco into cigarettes. Drug users roll their marijuana into thin, cigarette-like objects that are referred to as "joints." Given the ease that our youth have in acquiring commercially prepared cigarettes, despite the laws against it, there is no rational explanation for the presence of this paper, save smoking pot.

Many advanced addicts began their journey along addiction's pathway with marijuana. Should you not consider marijuana to be an unsafe drug, please realize that today's marijuana is not the same as what was available during your younger years. Twenty-first-century marijuana is much more potent (thanks to improved breeding and growing processes) and contains many more ingredients than the marijuana that was available a couple of decades ago. Today's pot smokers also mix other brain-altering chemicals into their marijuana. One such mixture is called love boat, the highly potent and dangerous combination of marijuana laced with PCP. If marijuana use does not concern you, these additional drugs certainly should.

Clips and Tweezers

Unlike regular cigarettes, which have filters to protect fingers and are seldom smoked to the very end, marijuana smokers prefer to maximize their drug consumption by smoking the entire joint, including the butt end, which is called a "roach." In order to prevent burned fingers, clips or tweezers are used to hold that last small portion of the marijuana cigarette. Clips or tweezers make sense in the bathroom or a makeup kit, but may otherwise indicate drug use.

Small Screens and Pipes, Including Water Pipes

Water pipes, often referred to as bongs, are used to smoke various drugs. These pipes range in size from a few inches to over a foot and consist of three sections: the pipe, a water chamber, and a bowl. Many substance abusers do not get this elaborate, preferring to create their own crude version of a pipe. If you stumble upon a homemade contraption that has a bowl and stem to it, you most likely have found something other than a creative school project.

Marijuana seeds tend to pop out of the pipe's bowl when heated, so marijuana smokers find it necessary to place a screen over the pipe bowl so that the exploding seeds do not burn their clothing, hands, or arms. Creative youth often discover that the small, screenlike filter at the mouth of the faucet makes for a useful screen. If you have been wondering why the water is not flowing from the faucet the way it once did, check to see if the filter screen has been removed. Some youth get their screens from window screens in the home. You might want to check to see if any of your window screens have small holes cut out.

Burn Holes in Clothing, Furniture, or Car Upholstery

Since marijuana seeds tend to pop when they are hot, it is common to find small burn holes on the clothing of marijuana smokers and on car upholstery. Should you find tiny holes, please curtail the impulse to burst forth with a lecture about the damaged items. Instead focus upon drug use, a far more significant concern than any damaged clothing, furniture, or upholstery.

Plastic Bags, Aluminum Foil, and Vials

Drugs are packaged and prepared for distribution in small plastic bags, bottles, and vials. Should you find any of these items within your young person's environment, carefully inspect them for drug residue. A powdery residue in a container is an indicator that your young person most likely has used the item to store drugs. Dried, crushed brown particles most likely are indicative of marijuana remains. If you discover a small vial containing a liquid, powdery substances, or crystalline objects, you may have stumbled upon a container containing a drug, possibly a psychedelic or a stimulant like crack/cocaine. If you do not find any residue or other indicators that drugs were once in the container, you should at least make it a point to find out why the packaging item is in your young person's possession.

A Small Scale

Drugs must be packaged and weighed before they can be sold. Small scales, such as the one in your kitchen, are a handy, easily available item to weigh drugs prior to packaging and distribution. If a small scale is in your son's or daughter's environment, you may have a young person who is making money by selling or packaging drugs. By the way, do you know what happened to your small kitchen scale?

Razor Blades

If your youngster is involved in selling drugs, she must have some way to divide the merchandise into easily marketable quantities. The old-fashioned single-edge razor is an excellent tool for separating drugs into retail portions. For those involved in the drug culture, this increasingly obsolete item also serves as an excellent tool to create "lines" of heroin, cocaine, and other drugs. The term *lines* refers to the practice of placing the powered form of a drug into a thin row to facilitate snorting, or nasal consumption. If you happen to find razor blades in your young person's environment, find out the reason they are there. With the evolution of disposable razor cartridges, it's unlikely they're used for shaving. Unless your young person is actively engaged in woodworking or model making, he will have a difficult time explaining the presence of razor blades.

Strange Odors

If you have detected strange odors in your home, especially in the bathroom or bedroom, consider the possibility of drug usage. Drugs give off various odors, and you should be alert for their presence. Some of the odors you should be vigilant for are

1. Sweet aromas, which are produced by marijuana
2. Acid odors, which occur when cooking implements are burned
3. Sulfur, which is given off whenever a match has been struck
4. Incense, room deodorizers, or mouthwash, all of which are regularly used to mask the odors of smoked drugs as well as alcohol

Missing or Watered-Down Liquor

Youth abusing brain-altering substances often consider the family liquor cabinet as a way to get high for free, especially when other drugs are difficult to obtain or alcohol is their drug of choice. Many youth prefer alcohol and often will help themselves to the family's liquor supply in order to satisfy their alcohol craving. To prevent detection, small amounts will be removed from several bottles. Sometimes tap water is added to replenish the missing liquid. Since few parents conscientiously monitor the amount of liquor in each bottle, raiding Dad's liquor cabinet can continue undetected for a while. When it's finally discerned, either through missing liquid or a difference in taste, parents realize something is amiss, but all too often conclude that they are imagining things or they have consumed more liquor than they thought.

Inventory your liquor cabinet, mark the bottles, and watch for dilution. Removing alcohol from the home would be ideal, but if you are not ready to make this sacrifice for your substance-abusing young person's well-being, at least tightly secure that liquor cabinet and closely monitor your liquor supply.

Baby Pacifiers and/or Glow Sticks

Baby pacifiers and glow sticks are found among users of the drug Ecstasy. This drug delivers a heightened state of sensory arousal, which glow sticks further magnify. A baby pacifier helps to prevent grinding of teeth, and it also increases the pleasurable sensation that Ecstasy produces. Since there is little reason for a teen to possess baby pacifiers or glow sticks, the presence of either of these items should serve as an indicator that your son or daughter is using Ecstasy. Often, water bottles are found at parties where Ecstasy is used because there is nonstop dancing, and the availability of water prevents dehydration.

Syringes

For many addicts, injecting is the preferred method for consuming drugs because it provides a more rapid and intense euphoric surge than other ways of consuming drugs. Some of the drugs that can be consumed through injection are amphetamine, cocaine, heroin, and methamphetamine. Sharing syringes is the most common reason that drug users acquire hepatitis C and HIV/AIDS.

If you happen to find a syringe in your child's environment, take strong decisive action. Unless your young person suffers from a medical problem that requires intravenous medication, such as diabetes, there is absolutely no reason for syringes to be in your young person's environment. If there are signs of intravenous use, quickly get your son or daughter tested for HIV/AIDS, hepatitis C, and STDs. Also have the doctor test your young person for illicit drugs, and if the test is positive, have your physician assist you in enrolling your young person in a drug treatment program.

Lighters, Matches, Steel Wool

Some drugs are smoked, and others are "cooked" so that they can be consumed intravenously. Addicts tend to carelessly discard spent matches, so look carefully around window frames and the corners of the bathroom and your young person's bedroom. If used matches are found, don't succumb to the typical parental reaction of focusing on cigarette smoking or the dangers of starting a fire. While these are very legitimate concerns, they ignore the possibility of drug usage and feed into denial. Spent matches must be treated as more than a fire hazard or a sign of cigarette use. When matches are unavailable, steel wool can be placed onto an electrical outlet to create a spark sufficient to light a joint. Bits of steel wool can also be used as a makeshift pipe filter. Did you find any steel wool?

Be particularly on the lookout for butane lighters. These instruments provide an excellent source of flame for your young person to "cook" his narcotics. If you discover a burned spoon or bottle cap along with a butane lighter (the preferred flame source), it's a fairly safe bet that you have found the tools of an addict who prefers intravenous consumption of his drugs.

Butane can also function as an inhalant, which produces hallucinations and can kill. Middle school youth and even late elementary school students are generally the abusers of butane. When this highly compressed liquid enters the throat, it quickly expands and can get cold enough to freeze the larynx. When this happens, the lungs rapidly fill up with fluid and death quickly occurs. Butane also serves as a propellant in deodorant aerosol sprays. If you discovered a container of butane or butane lighter, please take immediate action. Butane can be lethal!

Spoons or Bottle Caps

Your typical kitchen spoon serves as an excellent utensil for sniffing drugs that come in powder form, such as cocaine, heroin, methamphetamine, and amphetamine. Should you find spoons in your young person's room, don't dismiss this as another act of irresponsibility or conclude that she has again been sneaking food into her room. Inspect the spoon, looking for any powdery residue. Turn the spoon over and look for burn marks. That innocent kitchen item serves as an excellent utensil to "cook" drugs so that they can be consumed intravenously. If you find scorch marks, accept the fact that you are holding an item that has been used to prepare drugs for injection.

Bottle caps also serve the same purpose as spoons, but they have the advantage of being less likely to spark a parent's interest. Typically, parents noticing bottle caps lying around will presume that their youngster failed to throw them away and dismiss it as another example of carelessness or irresponsibility. Pick up that bottle cap and examine it. Does the outside of the cap show signs of contact with a flame, or does the inside have any residue related to drug usage, such as a white powder? If it does, you have definitive proof that your young person is involved in drug use.

You might want to inventory your everyday kitchen spoons as well as fine-dining spoons secured in a dining-room cabinet. Are any spoons missing? If your inventory is inexplicably low, consider the likelihood of drug use.

Blood-Stained Cotton Balls

Cotton balls are common in the bathroom, and your child might be using them to remove makeup or apply acne medication, but there are other uses too. For example, after an injection, a nurse will use a cotton ball to stop the bleeding and cover up the area where the needle entered the vein. Many intravenous drug users follow the same procedure. If the inspection of your young person's environment uncovers cotton balls, you should be alarmed, especially if there is evidence of dried blood on any of the cotton balls. Regardless of whether or not the cotton balls are blood stained, investigate why they are among your son's or daughter's possessions.

Rubbing Alcohol

Rubbing alcohol is used to sterilize needles and clean up skin abscesses that develop due to intravenous drug use. Should you find a bottle of rubbing alcohol in a strange place or large amounts of rubbing alcohol, it may be an indicator that your young person is engaged in intravenous drug usage. There may be legitimate reasons your teen is using rubbing alcohol, such as treating a cut or a pimple. But if your parental instincts tell you something is not right, make a note of it.

In Summary

If you happened upon any of the listed paraphernalia while searching your child's environment, you may be in possession of direct evidence of drug usage. Act quickly and decisively. This is not the time to engage in excuse making, entertaining lies, debating, or weighing the pros and cons about what you have discovered. If you found syringes, scorched bottle caps or spoons, blood-stained cotton balls, and/or rubbing alcohol, you have distinct signs of intravenous drug use, which places your young person at high risk for the acquisition of HIV/AIDS or hepatitis C. Immediately take your young person to the doctor and have him tested for hepatitis C, HIV/AIDS, and other STDs. In addition, have a complete physical done and ask the doctor to assist you in initiating the process for entering substance abuse treatment. With some insurance plans, especially HMOs, access to drug treatment often goes through the family physician.

Addressing intravenous drug use is not something you can postpone nor waste time denying. Your beloved will resist going into treatment—of this you can be assured—but you have to take control regardless. You have no choice but to act swiftly and decisively in order to save your young person from a drug overdose, drug-related violence, death from hepatitis C, or an AIDS-compromised immune system.

The Centers for Disease Control and Prevention (CDC) reports the following statistics for 2004 regarding HIV/AIDS:

- An estimated 4,883 young people [ages 13–24] received a diagnosis of HIV infection or AIDS, representing about 13% of the persons given a diagnosis during that year.
- An estimated 2,174 young people received a diagnosis of AIDS (5.1% of the estimated total of 42,514 AIDS diagnoses) and 232 young people with AIDS died.
- An estimated 7,761 young people were living with AIDS, a 42% increase since 2000, when 5,457 young people were living with AIDS.
- Since the beginning of the epidemic, an estimated 40,059 young people in the United States had received a diagnosis of AIDS and

an estimated 10,129 young people with AIDS had died. They accounted for about 4% of the estimated total of 944,306 AIDS diagnoses and 2% of the 529,113 deaths of people with AIDS.[1]

These are scary statistics for parents. While they may be a few years old, there hasn't been any significant change in youth acquisition of HIV. As a matter of fact, with better medication to control HIV, youth have become less concerned about acquiring it. Their attitude increasingly is "They've got medication for it, so it won't kill me." Talk with your kids before you wish you had.

HIV (human immunodeficiency virus) is a virus that attacks the immune system. The immune system is designed to fight off infections and keeps a person from getting sick. HIV weakens the immune system. AIDS (acquired immunodeficiency syndrome) develops when the HIV virus has compromised the immune system to the point the individual's CD4 count (cells designed to fight off infections) drops to a threshold of 200 or below. This is determined by blood testing. When people with AIDS die, they die from an opportunistic infection or illness which their weakened immune system cannot counter.

HIV/AIDS is a part of our modern life and impacts our youth. With intravenous drug use being a leading cause for the acquisition of HIV, you have no option but to act immediately if you find paraphernalia directly related to intravenous use. Many parents react to evidence of intravenous use with shock and paralyzing fear, but this must be immediately overcome. Hepatitis C and HIV are spread by sharing "dirty" needles—so act responsibly. Seek out immediate medical attention, including testing for HIV, and get that young person into drug treatment. How you can effectively access drug treatment will be discussed in section 3 of this book, but in the meantime, begin by talking with your family doctor and ask how to facilitate getting your son or daughter into substance abuse treatment.

For now, I will close this discussion about HIV/AIDS by quoting the CDC report about HIV/AIDS and substance abuse among our youth:[2]

> Young people in the United States use alcohol, tobacco, and other drugs at high rates.[3] Both casual and chronic substance users are more likely to engage in high-risk behaviors, such as

unprotected sex, when they are under the influence of drugs or alcohol.[4] Runaways and other homeless young people are at high risk for HIV infection if they are exchanging sex for drugs or money.

As if HIV/AIDS were not sufficient to strike fear into the heart of every parent whose young person is engaged in intravenous drug use, there is an even greater concern that parents must be aware of—hepatitis C (HCV). Please take note what the CDC says about HCV:

> Hepatitis C virus (HCV) infection is the most common chronic blood-borne infection in the United States: approximately 3.2 million persons are chronically infected. Although HCV is not efficiently transmitted sexually, persons at risk for infection through injection drug use might seek care in STD treatment facilities, HIV counseling and testing facilities, correctional facilities, drug treatment facilities, and other public health settings where STD and HIV prevention and control services are available.[5]

Since hepatitis C is a blood-borne disease, intravenous drug addicts are vulnerable to acquiring it. If you find any environmental sign of intravenous drug use, your young person is at risk of acquiring HCV. Since hepatitis C affects the liver, there eventually may be scarring of the liver (cirrhosis of the liver). This is another reason for parents to immediately address signs of intravenous drug use. Do not let your denial or passivity enhance the possibility that your beloved son or daughter will acquire HCV and join the already 3.2 million people with hepatitis C.

✽

CHAPTER 7

Drugs of Abuse Our Youth Prefer

This chapter is dedicated to the principal drugs our youth abuse, but for this to be done properly, it is important to introduce a few basic concepts and terms directly related to the use of drugs. The first term we will examine is *triggers,* which refers to cues that suddenly and powerfully spark the urge to use drugs. These cues can be directly related to drugs, such as entering an area where drugs are sold, or they can be seemingly innocent events most people—except for the substance abuser—would not consider to be drug related. One such seemingly innocent trigger is spilled salt. For the person not addicted to cocaine, spilled salt is a minor nuisance that needs to be cleaned up, but for the person with a history of cocaine abuse, it is anything but innocuous. Due to a history of prior cocaine abuse, the addict's conditioned brain perceives the salt as cocaine (both are white granular substances), and this reactive image gives rise to strong urges to again experience cocaine's delights.

Many people use incense to cover up home odors, and unless someone is allergic to incense, they will not be affected by the smell. This, however, is not true for the person who burned incense to mask the smell of marijuana. For this individual, walking into a home with incense burning can trigger sudden cravings to again experience the blissfulness that marijuana produces.

Another example is hearing songs from the past on the radio. This is an enjoyable experience for all of us, but when a former drug user hears a song that is intimately connected with her past drug use, remembrances of old euphoric sensations arise, sparking urges to repeat the drug-induced pleasures.

Addicts in recovery know that they must conscientiously avoid triggers by removing themselves from people, places, things, and other cues that have the potential to trigger the urge to use drugs again. Appreciating the power of conditioned, programmed cues and the need to avoid these cues is imperative for any recovering addict who wishes to maintain a drug-free life. Parents must also develop an appreciation of the power of cues. They must accept the truth that their son's or daughter's mind has been so conditioned (programmed) by drugs that it responds quickly and powerfully to drug-related cues. Parents must also accept the need to minimize triggers by making necessary adjustments to their lifestyle. For instance, if Dad maintains a liquor cabinet or must have his daily after-work cocktail, he must make some changes. He may not be responsible for his offspring's substance abuse, but he should feel an obligation to remove triggers from her life by not drinking in front of her and removing or tightly securing his alcohol supply. Regardless of whether your young person is in active addiction or in recovery, if that person is living in a home with a cabinet full of alcohol or if you drink in front of her, you are unnecessarily allowing your addicted offspring to experience sudden urges to drink. Parents, please become aware of cues, remove them, and change your behavior, no matter what the inconvenience.

Another term parents should be familiar with is *tolerance,* which refers to the fact that regular and repeated consumption of drugs leads to a progressive increase in the amount of brain-altering substances consumed. This occurs because, over time, current use patterns are no longer able to achieve the desired effect, so the addict resorts to additional dosages, more frequent use, more powerful drugs, and the combining of drugs. As you read on, you will come to appreciate the importance of tolerance.

Another addiction term is *withdrawal,* which refers to the uncomfortable and distressing physical and mental effects that occur when the concentration of drugs in the blood and body tissues declines. Not willing to endure the anguish that occurs when drug concentration drops, the addict seeks out substances to stop the pain, a pattern that promotes tolerance. Fear of withdrawal is a major factor in keeping addicts from stopping their use of drugs and seeking treatment.

Addicts and alcoholics live with a condition called psychological and physical dependence. This refers to a state of being in which an individual relies upon the ingestion of substances in order to maintain a sense of normalcy and avoid the pain and discomfort of withdrawal. Mentally, the addict depends on brain-altering substances to feel good and suppress distress, anxiety, restlessness, depression, and other forms of psychological uneasiness. Physically, the absence of drugs can result in aches and pains, body sweats, nausea, delirium tremens (physical tremors, hallucinations, and other symptoms), sleeplessness, headaches, seizures, and more. Fearful about the dreadful mental and physical effects that occur when a person doesn't have the brain-altering substances upon which he is dependent, the addict keeps ingesting drugs and alcohol.

It should also be noted that drugs affect an individual's mood in a manner that is similar to the way a pendulum operates. To the extent that a pendulum swings in one direction, to the same extent it will then swing in the opposite direction. Likewise, to the extent that a drug-induced mood swings in one direction, so it will swing in the opposite direction. This is called the *rebound effect,* and it is seen in the tireless, overly alert, exhilarated, hyperactive person who has consumed cocaine swinging into a "down" state that is marked by sluggishness, a depressed mood, and lethargy. With cocaine, especially in its crack form, providing only a brief period of euphoria, the rebound effect pushes the addict to consume additional crack in order to stop the inevitable, a coke crash. The rebound effect explains in part why addicts will expend so much money and consume so much cocaine during a run, which is an extended period of drug use.

Armed with this additional information, we will now look at some of the drugs that our youth prefer. Space limitation doesn't permit a discussion of all the drugs our youth consume, so we will focus upon the more commonly used drugs. It should be noted that new drugs regularly appear while other drugs fall out of favor, so this list will change. Educate yourself on the current trends.

Alcohol

In the opening chapter of this book, the term *drug* was defined as "a non-food, chemical substance that alters the normal condition of the brain and body when consumed." Alcohol meets this definition. Alcohol is the most popular of the brain-altering substances that our youth abuse because it's legal (for people of drinking age) and widely available, either through older friends or through stealing it from parents or retail stores.

While there has been a noticeable reduction in the pattern of youth alcohol consumption compared to past data, levels are still high. With 63.5 percent of high school seniors illegally drinking annually, 40 percent monthly, and 25 percent getting drunk at least once a month, there is cause for concern.[1] Parents, talk to your sons and daughters now. They are under a lot of social pressure to drink, and for many teens it is cool to get drunk. This behavior can be a preamble to what all too frequently occurs in college, namely drinking in excess. This can lead to a number of short- and long-term consequences, such as problems with school, trouble holding a job, physical or sexual assault, legal and financial issues, an increased risk of alcohol-related car crashes and other potential accidents, and a higher risk of alcoholism. Elsewhere in this book, we talked about alcohol poisoning. This occurs when one drinks too much too fast and the nerves that control involuntary actions, such as breathing and the gag reflex, are affected. Since alcohol can be an irritant, often someone who has drunk too much will vomit. With involuntary actions compromised, the person may end up suffocating on his or her own vomit and die.

Alcohol abuse is not a rite of passage. Alcohol abuse is not something to be expected as part of the journey to adulthood. Instead, it is a setup for future alcohol dependency. We all know people with alcohol problems. Talk to your sons and daughters now.

Marijuana

Marijuana is the most commonly used illicit drug by our youth. It is often referred to on the streets as *pot, weed,* or *grass.* Marijuana presents as a dry green or brown mixture of buds, stems, seeds, and leaves. This mixture is from the hemp plant *cannabis sativa,* and its main active chemical is THC (delta-9-tetrahydrocannabinol). Users may roll the marijuana into cigarette paper (called a *joint*), put it into a cigar wrapper (called a *blunt*), or smoke it through a pipe. When smoked, the THC rapidly enters the bloodstream and quickly goes to the brain and other organs, producing a relaxed, blissful experience. Marijuana has a very distinctive odor and is rising in popularity with youth.

Part of this increase in use can be attributed to a softening of negative attitudes toward marijuana. Today, our youth witness many of their peers as well as adults smoking marijuana without any negative consequences. This, combined with increased advocacy toward legalizing marijuana, especially for medical purposes, negates prohibitions toward use. Given this state of affairs, talking to your young person about not smoking marijuana can seem as if you are swimming against the current.

To assist parents in their efforts to intelligently discuss marijuana with their teenager, here are some points to consider and discuss with your child. The main areas of the brain affected by the THC in marijuana are called *cannabinoid receptors,* which are responsible for the feeling users get. The largest areas of receptors are in parts of the brain dealing with memory, concentration, sensory perception, movement, and pleasure. Because of this, marijuana use can cause problems with coordination, awareness, problem-solving skills, memory, ability to feel pleasure when not using, and learning ability. The effects of marijuana can last for days or weeks after the initial "high" wears off, so someone who uses it daily is likely functioning well below his or her abilities nearly all the time. Finally, high levels of marijuana use have been linked to schizophrenia and related mental illnesses. Users may find that it calms disturbing thoughts or quiets voices in their head. It may also trigger the onset or recurrence of a mental illness in someone who is already at risk, either due to genetics, stress, or exposure to violence or trauma.

For all of these reasons and more, it's important for you and your teen to understand the risks and consequences marijuana use poses to his or her well-being.

Synthetic Drugs

Before we close our discussion about marijuana, it should be noted that many youth are turning to synthetic drugs, including synthetic marijuana, which has many names including *K2* and *Spice.* It is a mixture of herbs and spices that are sprayed with chemicals similar to THC, the active chemical in marijuana. In 2011, the first year this drug was tracked, 11.4 percent of high school seniors used this drug.[2] It's marketed as incense and can be found in paraphernalia and tobacco shops as well as various other retail and Internet outlets. It is sold in small, silver plastic bags. The Drug Enforcement Agency (DEA) banned five of the chemicals used to make K2 and Spice on March 1, 2011, but manufacturers and retailers continue to find ways to skirt the law and keep this popular illicit drug available under a variety of names.

In addition, new synthetic drugs hit the market all the time, using a variety of names and chemicals, and delivering a number of effects. One especially troubling new drug is methylenedioxypyrovalerone (MDPV), better known as *bath salts.* These are not the same compounds found in commercially available bath salts sold in a pharmacy. This drug gets its name because of its similar appearance (white or colored powder) and because packaging it that way allows it to go undetected. The drug can be smoked, snorted, or injected, and it is meant to provide feelings of euphoria, increased energy, and other effects. However, the side effects can be deadly and include psychotic hallucination, suicidal thoughts, violence, seizure, respiratory failure, liver failure, and death.

Synthetic drugs change all the time, so it's impossible to cover all possibilities in one book. They change names, use different chemicals, and become available through different channels. They are often sold online or through legitimate storefronts, and this gives them an air of safety among teenagers. They are easy to locate, cheap to buy, and you don't have to go through drug dealers to get them. Educate yourself about the synthetic drugs currently trending among youth, especially in your area, and talk to your kids about them before they become addicted to these brain-altering substances.

Opiates

Prescription Drug Abuse

Opiates contain drugs derived from the opium poppy. These drugs are commonly referred to as narcotics and function as legitimate prescription medications. They include morphine, codeine, OxyContin, Dilaudid, Percocet, Vicodin, Demerol, and Darvon, all of which are pain relievers, but, unfortunately, often end up diverted to illicit uses. Properly used, these medications are effective, but they have the potential for abuse, which can lead to addiction.

Abuse of prescription medication is a rapidly growing problem. If your doctor has prescribed any of the above-listed medications, secure them. Do not allow your young person the opportunity to experiment with these substances or be tempted by their easy availability. Opiates that are prescribed by doctors can lead to addiction, particularly if they are abused or misused. Given the increasing abuse of prescription medications among our youth, parents cannot afford to ignore the potential hazards of these medications.

To understand the rapidly growing concern over illicit prescription use, let us examine the active ingredient in many narcotics, oxycodone, which is an opiate analgesic (a pain suppressant). Oxycodone is a Schedule II controlled substance, which means it is a drug that has a high potential for abuse but also has acceptable medical uses and is in such narcotics as OxyContin and Percocet, two commonly prescribed pain relievers and two drugs that are most often used illicitly.

Those who seek to acquire OxyContin for illegal purposes use fake prescriptions, doctor and emergency room "shopping," stealing from a parent's medication, and buying it from the elderly. OxyContin abuse has created some interesting terms to describe the ways the drug is obtained: *doctor shopping* (the practice of going from doctor to doctor in order to obtain OxyContin prescriptions) and *pill ladies* (female senior citizens who sell the OxyContin they get from their doctors).

The prescription drug OxyContin comes in pill form with its milligrams stamped on one side of the pill and "OC" on the other side of the pill. Since it is a control-released drug, the abuser crushes the tablet to negate the time-release factor, which then allows the user to snort it or mix it with water so that it can be injected. Once the time release has been compromised, this drug produces a rapid and extremely intense euphoric surge. Because this surge is so powerful, the user will rapidly consume additional

OxyContin, a practice that can lead to an overdose because the active ingredient, oxycodone, is released into the blood system too rapidly.

The number of abusers of oxycodone-based medications greatly exceeds the number of individuals who use the opiate heroin because the high is similar to a heroin high, but its use lacks the stigma associated with heroin. It is also favored by abusers since, unlike heroin, with its relatively brief period of blissfulness, oxycodone-based medications will produce a high that lasts considerably longer. Tolerance to oxycodone occurs rapidly, which leads to the need for higher and higher dosages and explains, in part, the widespread abuse of prescription medications.

Oxycodone-based medications directly affect the respiratory system by slowing down breathing, and serious complications can arise when mixed with other drugs that act upon the respiratory system. One such drug is antihistamine, which is designed to treat allergy symptoms such as runny nose, sneezing, and itchy eyes. Another drug type is barbiturates, which are legitimately used to improve sleep and decrease anxiety and tension. Excellent in treating what they were designed for, these two drugs pose serious health consequences when mixed with oxycodone-based medications.

When oxycodone-based drugs are withdrawn abruptly, physical withdrawals are similar to heroin: body aches and pain, sleep disturbance, diarrhea, vomiting, sweats, and hot and cold flashes. Withdrawal discomfort can be severe enough to cause addicts to turn to heroin to prevent further withdrawals.

In the United States, the abuse of prescribed medications is increasing rapidly and is a growing concern for medical personnel and addiction workers. The following research report from the National Institute on Drug Abuse (NIDA) on prescription drug abuse is offered to awaken parents to the extent of illicit prescription abuse.

Prescription drug abuse remains a significant problem in the United States.

➡ In 2009, approximately 7.0 million persons were current users of psychotherapeutic drugs taken nonmedically (2.8 percent of the U.S. population). This class of drugs is broadly described as those targeting the central nervous system, including drugs used to treat psychiatric disorders (NSDUH 2009). The medications most commonly abused are

- Pain relievers—5.3 million
- Tranquilizers—2.0 million
- Stimulants—1.3 million
- Sedatives—0.4 million

➡ Among adolescents, prescription and over-the-counter medications account for most of the frequently abused drugs by high school seniors (excluding tobacco and alcohol).

- Nearly 1 in 12 high school seniors reported nonmedical use of Vicodin; 1 in 20 reported abuse of OxyContin.
- When asked how prescription narcotics were obtained for nonmedical use, 59% of 12th graders said they were given to them by a friend or relative. The number obtaining them over the Internet was negligible.

➡ Among those who abuse prescription drugs, high rates of other risky behaviors, including abuse of other drugs and alcohol, have also been reported.

(continued)

What is driving this high prevalence?

Multiple factors are likely at work:

➥ *Misperceptions about their safety.* Because these medications are prescribed by doctors, many assume that they are safe to take under any circumstances. This is not the case: prescription drugs act directly or indirectly on the same brain systems affected by illicit drugs; thus their abuse carries substantial addiction liability and can lead to a variety of other adverse health effects.

➥ *Increasing environmental availability.* Between 1991 and 2010, prescriptions for stimulants increased from 5 million to nearly 45 million, a 9-fold increase, and opioid analgesics increased from about 30 million to approximately 180 million, a 6-fold increase.

➥ *Varied motivations for their abuse.* Underlying reasons include to get high; to counter anxiety, pain, or sleep problems; or to enhance cognition (although they may, in fact, impair certain types of cognitive performance). Whatever the motivation, prescription drug abuse comes with serious risks.

Risks of commonly abused prescription drugs

➥ Opioids (used to treat pain):

- *Addiction.* Prescription opioids act on the same receptors as heroin and therefore can be highly addictive. People who abuse them sometimes alter the route of administration (e.g., snorting or injecting vs. taking orally) to intensify the effect; some even report moving from prescription opioids to heroin.

(continued)

- *Overdose.* Abuse of opioids, alone or in combination with alcohol or other drugs, can depress respiration and lead to death. Overdose is a major concern: the number of fatal poisonings involving prescription pain relievers has more than tripled since 1999.
- *Heightened HIV risk.* Injecting opioids increases the risk of HIV and other infectious diseases through use of unsterile or shared equipment.

➥ CNS [central nervous system] depressants (used to treat anxiety and sleep problems):

- *Addiction and dangerous withdrawal symptoms.* These drugs are addictive and, in chronic users or abusers, discontinuing them absent a physician's guidance can bring about severe withdrawal symptoms, including seizures that can be life-threatening.
- *Overdose.* High doses can cause severe respiratory depression. This risk increases when CNS depressants are combined with other medications or alcohol.

➥ Stimulants (used to treat ADHD [attention deficit/hyperactivity disorder] and narcolepsy):

- *Addiction and other health consequences.* These include psychosis, seizures, and cardiovascular complications.[3]

If your home is typical, it contains medications that the family doctor legitimately prescribed. These medications are approved by the Food and Drug Administration (FDA), and when properly used they are effective in addressing your medical problem. Unfortunately, all too many teens liberate pills to satisfy their curiosity, to get high, or for social functions such as "Skittle parties." At these parties, tweens and teens bring pills that have been liberated from Mom and Dad's medicine bottles. Upon arrival, they place the pills in a candy dish, and the partygoers help themselves to the multicolored, multishaped pills as if they were candy—oblivious of the serious medical consequences that could occur.

At home, curiosity takes over, and some youth will experiment with your medications to see how the pills affect them. It doesn't take long for these youth to want the feeling that your medications offer, and since they think they are medically safe (after all, the doctor did prescribe them), they begin to use and abuse them.

Talk to your kids about the dangers of abusing prescription drugs. Our youth see them as safe, and this mind-set contributes in part to prescription drug abuse's growing invasion of our communities. Explain to your young person that misusing prescription pills is not safe. Give your children the guidance, support, and education they need before they fall prey to these medications. If your doctor has prescribed medication for anyone in your home, secure those medications, count the number of pills in each container, and monitor those pills daily. If you are no longer taking a medication, or it's expired, remove it from the home but do not flush it down the toilet, since the chemicals in the medication will end up in various water systems. Your local pharmacy will instruct you on how to dispose of them.

The abuse of prescription medication is a major concern. Do not minimize its abuse. Talk with your sons and daughters. Monitor and secure those medications. Don't allow your offspring to fall victim to the illicit use and abuse of prescription medications. It is the third-most-abused drug category, exceeded only by alcohol and marijuana. Remember, as was pointed out earlier, most prescription pills abused by our young people are obtained from family and friends.

Morphine

Another opiate drug that has a high potential for abuse is morphine, a powerful analgesic (painkiller). This drug is used to stop or significantly reduce pain from such body traumas as major injury, cancer treatment, body pain, and tooth extractions. Morphine was initially used to not only relieve pain but also as a "cure" for opium addiction. Since it is highly addictive, this drug should be carefully monitored, and when it is time to discontinue use, a medically supervised protocol should be conscientiously followed in order to prevent withdrawals. If your son or daughter has a history of opiate abuse, be sure to let the doctor know so that this drug isn't prescribed. Many opiate addicts have relapsed after being prescribed morphine by a doctor or dentist.

Codeine

Codeine, an analgesic that is often found in cough syrup, is also available in capsule and tablet. Codeine can be obtained by prescription as a time-released tablet, and it is also found in such commonly used products as Tylenol with Codeine #3. The 3 represents 30 milligrams of codeine contained in the pill. Codeine is also available in liquid form for intravenous use in hospitals.

This drug is used to treat pain as well as coughs. In the United States, products with codeine must be prescribed, but in other countries, they can be purchased over the counter. Youth will consume bottle after bottle of cough syrup so they can experience an opiate-induced state of blissfulness, often at the urging of their friends, who tell them they can get high by drinking a lot of cough syrup.

Heroin

Heroin is the best-known member of the opiate family of drugs. Initially, it was synthesized from morphine and marketed as a cough syrup. Heroin appears as either a white to brown powder or a tarlike substance and has multiple street names, such as *junk, smack, dope, brown sugar, big H,* and *horse.* It can be injected into the vein, which is called *mainlining,* or by *skin popping,* the practice of inserting a needle just under the surface of the skin. Additionally, heroin is consumed by *snorting,* a term referring to the practice of breathing in the powered form of the drug or inhaling it through a straw. Until recently, intravenous use was the favored method of administration, since this practice provides a more powerful, immediate, and blissful effect. Today, more and more heroin users are choosing to snort heroin, a switch that was motivated by fear of acquiring HIV through shared needles. Interestingly, there exists within the addict population the belief that nasal consumption is less grave an act than intravenous use. I have repeatedly heard heroin addicts, who had been nasally consuming heroin for years, confess, "Only when I began using needles did I realize that I had a problem."

This history of heroin in this country is interesting. When first marketed, the addictive properties of heroin were unknown, so the drug was not included on the list of drugs prohibited by the Harrison Act of 1914, a law that began to regulate narcotics. Those who had been addicted to opiates such as morphine, a drug on the list of prohibited substances, switched to heroin, and "dope" realized an instant popularity. In 1924, heroin was added to the list of prohibited drugs, and those addicted to heroin were pursued by governmental law enforcement, much like today. Heroin use is decreasing, but not fast enough. In some parts of the United States it remains high.

When heroin enters the body, the user experiences a sense of peace because the drug functions as a depressant upon the central nervous system. Internally, this alteration is manifested in slower breathing and pulse rates, as well as a drop in blood pressure. Parents can detect external signs of heroin use through slowed speech and gait as well as constricted pupils and droopy eyelids. Heroin users often experience a "heroin nod," in which the nodding individual appears as if she is going to fall. (But in my years of street work, I have not seen an addict experiencing a heroin nod actually fall.)

For many, initial use can cause nausea, but the euphoria "hooks" the user, and repetitive consumption begins, despite the side effects. Thanks to the development of tolerance, long-term heroin addicts can consume the drug in amounts large enough to kill a novice.

As a very rapid-acting opiate, heroin attacks endorphins, which are groups of proteins within the brain that possess naturally occurring analgesic properties. When consumed, heroin interrupts the pain stimulus in the brain and changes how pain is perceived. Heroin affects the functioning of the brain stem, which controls automatic body functions. Breathing is slowed and other alterations in normal body functions occur. As a result of these drug-induced alterations, the individual experiences a peaceful, tranquil, trancelike state marked by an absence of pain.

Heroin causes multiple health problems and risks. Deaths occur from overdoses and by injecting harmful substances that were used to "cut" the purity of the heroin prior to it being sold on the streets. In addition, there is the risk of blood poisoning or acquiring HIV and hepatitis C through the sharing of contaminated needles, as well as deterioration in the individual's health due to the muting of pain signals that forewarn an individual of problems within the body. With pain signals blocked, physical problems go undetected, which allows ailments to advance without treatment. Of course, by obsessively "chasing" after heroin, even if the person is aware of health problems, he most likely would have no time or motivation to seek out medical intervention.

Opiate Detoxification Medication

Opiate addiction requires supervised detoxification due to severe withdrawals. Until buprenorphine and Suboxone, synthetic opiate medications, were approved for doctor-monitored detoxification, the process of removing opiates from the body was very unpleasant. The individual was extremely sick for three to five days, and it was very difficult to convince addicts enduring severe opiate withdrawal to remain in treatment. With the new drugs that are available, the withdrawals are much milder and can be done without inpatient treatment. If you learn that your son or daughter is addicted to an opiate, immediately seek out a medically monitored detoxification program. Do not try to do it on your own. It is virtually impossible to detoxify on one's own, since the severe sickness and extreme discomfort will be so intense that fleeing back to heroin is likely.

Methadone is a synthetic opiate that is used to detoxify those addicted to opiates and greatly reduce the withdrawal symptoms. This drug has been used for more than forty years and is effective, but it must be carefully monitored since addicts tend to "boost" the effects of the drug with cocaine, alcohol, and prescription drugs such as Xanax. For those with a history of multiple relapses, methadone maintenance is worth considering. Relapse, a return to the use of brain-altering substances after a period of sobriety, is a very common occurrence, and placing a relapse-prone individual on methadone maintenance allows her to avoid opiates and regain her life. When it is determined that methadone maintenance should end, there must be a gradual tapering of the amount taken daily. To suddenly cease taking methadone will result in withdrawal symptoms that are severe enough that they probably will propel the individual into another relapse. The same need for a gradual tapering applies to buprenorphine and Suboxone, even though the withdrawal symptoms with these new drugs are significantly less severe.

Inhalants

This group of drugs is included early in this chapter because its abuse is vastly underreported, and many parents are unaware of its impact upon our younger youth. Review these statistics from NIDA:

> According to the Monitoring the Future survey, a significant increase in past-month inhalant use was measured among 10th-graders from 2008 to 2009; prevalence of use rose from 2.1 percent to 2.2 percent among that population. Other prevalence measures remained stable. Lifetime [at least once during a respondent's lifetime] use of inhalants was reported by 14.9 percent of 8th-graders, 12.3 percent of 10th-graders, and 9.5 percent of 12th-graders in 2009; 8.1 percent of 8th-graders, 6.1 percent of 10th-graders, and 3.4 percent of 12th-graders reported use in the past year. However, investigators are concerned that perceived risk associated with inhalant use has been in decline for several years, which may leave young people open to renewed interest.[4]

The obvious must be emphasized: Inhalant use not only begins in middle school, but perceived risk of the dangers of inhalant use has been in decline, leaving our youngsters more susceptible than ever to inhalant use. The above citation also shatters the myth that drug use begins in high school. Middle school youth are drawn to inhalants because they are easily accessible and are found everywhere, especially within the home. Inhalants consist of ordinary, everyday products that have the capability of being inhaled or sniffed. The list of inhalants is extensive and includes such common household items as dry-cleaning fluids, correction fluids, felt-tip marker fluid, glue, hair and deodorant sprays, fabric protector sprays, vegetable oil sprays, whipped cream aerosols, room deodorizer, leather cleaners, video head cleaners, compressed-air computer cleaners, and paint thinners. If you want a more comprehensive listing of inhalants, go to NIDA's website: http://www.nida.nih.gov/Infofacts/inhalants.html.

Inhalants are consumed by bagging, which is the practice of putting the substance in a bag and then holding the bag around the nose; by huffing, or soaking a rag with an inhalant and then putting the rag in the mouth; or by inhaling the chemicals directly from the container. NIDA discusses how inhalants affect the brain:

> The effects of inhalants are similar to those of alcohol, including slurred speech, lack of coordination, euphoria, and dizziness. Inhalant abusers may also experience lightheadedness, halluci-nations, and delusions. With repeated inhalations, many users feel less inhibited and less in control. Some may feel drowsy for several hours and experience a lingering headache. Chemicals found in different types of inhaled products may produce a vari-ety of additional effects, such as confusion, nausea, or vomiting.
>
> By displacing air in the lungs, inhalants deprive the body of oxygen, a condition known as hypoxia. Hypoxia can damage cells throughout the body, but the cells of the brain are especially sensitive to it. The symptoms of brain hypoxia vary according to which regions of the brain are affected: for example, the hip-pocampus helps control memory, so someone who repeatedly uses inhalants may lose the ability to learn new things or may have a hard time carrying on simple conversations.
>
> Long-term inhalant abuse can also break down myelin, a fatty tissue that surrounds and protects some nerve fibers. Myelin helps nerve fibers carry their messages quickly and efficiently, and when damaged, can lead to muscle spasms and tremors or even permanent difficulty with basic actions such as walking, bending, and talking.[5]

Parents, note what inhalants can do to your son's or daughter's memory and their ability to converse with you. Talk to your young person about the dangers of inhalants before these drugs affect her mind and an intelligent talk is impossible.

As an example of inhalant use, let us look at a recent "in" activity—inhaling computer cleaner. On the *Today* show, correspondent Peter Alexander exposed this increasingly popular practice to the public.[6] The report showed that young people are using cans of compressed aerosol computer cleaners, the type that blow dust from the small crevices of a keyboard, as a cheap and easy high. Called "dusting," in part from the most popular brand of cleaner, Dust-Off, the means to this high is available in any office supply store and as close as the living-room computer desk.

For the sake of your young person's mental and physical health, become alert, be vigilant, and above all talk with your children now. Your middle school youngsters are fully aware that inhalants exist and are being used around them, so it is imperative that you immediately talk with them about the dangers of inhalant use while they are still alert and able to comprehend what you have to say.

Over the many years I have been working in addictions, I have seen far too many young adults permanently damage their brain after engaging in inhalant use. When I would conduct assessments of addicts who had used inhalants, a pattern emerged: The young person did adequately in elementary school, but in middle school the grades began to fall, and during high school the inhalant user usually dropped out, his or her brain no longer able to adequately function. Conducting these assessments was difficult, as the individual exhibited poor concentration and an inability to complete sentences. My heart went out to these young people who had destroyed their brains, their lives, and their future by using inhalants.

If you are uncomfortable with the prospect of talking with your offspring due to your limited knowledge about inhalants, don't let this stop you from conducting that all-important conversation. There are plenty of opportunities to learn all you need to know to carry on an intelligent and informed conversation with your son or daughter. Go to the NIDA website, www.nida.nih.gov, and search for "inhalants." Educate yourself and hold that needed conversation before it is too late. Inhalants are one of the illicit substances that produce severe, irreparable brain damage.

Stimulants

This category of drugs refers to substances that arouse activity within the central nervous system, which consists of the spinal cord and brain. When stimulants impact the central nervous system, various muscle systems receive stimulant-induced impulses that energize the individual, leaving him feeling alert, attentive, and energetic.

While doctors legally prescribe stimulants, some are illegal and abused. We will focus upon three illegally used stimulant drugs—amphetamine, methamphetamine, and cocaine—but first we will briefly touch upon one stimulant drug that is legal and used by most Americans on a regular basis.

Caffeine

Americans routinely consume items containing the stimulant drug caffeine, such as chocolate, tea, coffee, sodas, and energy drinks. This stimulant provides a burst of energy, and many of us need our morning cup(s) of coffee and our afternoon caffeine boost to function well. Some Americans want an additional energy lift, so they turn to energy drinks, which are loaded with caffeine. In recent years, we have seen a proliferation of coffee-houses throughout the country. As we begin discussing stimulants, you might want to keep yourself from being too judgmental by asking, *How dependent am I upon the legal stimulant caffeine?*

Recently we have seen canned drinks introduced into the marketplace containing the equivalent of several beers and a significant amount of caffeine—an unhealthy combination since alcohol is a depressant and caffeine a stimulant. Mixing a depressant with a stimulant can cause, and has caused, deaths. If you haven't yet talked to your young person about these products, please do so.

Cocaine

Cocaine is extracted from the leaves of the coca plant and appears as a white powder or as a white crystalline form. Cocaine has various street names, such as *coke, big C,* and *snow.* The drug is consumed by snorting, by smoking, or by intravenous injection. Crack, cocaine in its crystal form, appears as white to tan pellets or crystalline rocks and is consumed through smoking.

Cocaine was initially considered to be a good local anesthetic. It was an ingredient in various ointments, cigarettes, liquor, and, from 1886 to 1903, it was found in Coca-Cola. Freud considered it to be a magical drug and personally used it. During a six-day cocaine binge, Robert Louis Stevenson wrote his novel *The Strange Case of Dr. Jekyll and Mr. Hyde*.[7]

In the 1930s, amphetamine replaced cocaine in popularity because it served as an alternative, similarly acting drug. In the 1970s, cocaine's popularity was revived in the United States when it became linked with glamour, sophistication, and wealth. Seen as a recreational drug that was not physically addictive, cocaine was embraced by those with elevated social status. Then, in the early 1980s, cocaine's image was shattered by the media's fascination with a new phenomenon, the crack baby—a newborn who must spend his first weeks of life undergoing wretched detoxification due to the crack his mother smoked during her pregnancy. With the intro- duction of the inexpensive drug crack, the glamorous image of powder cocaine was destroyed. Since then, crack has devastated the social structure of many of our poorer communities, hooking numerous victims into a cycle of dependence and corrupting the values of cities and communities unable to control it.

Crack is made by combining baking soda with cocaine hydrochloride and then heating the mixture until the water is vaporized. This process removes impurities from the mixture, leaving a final product that offers an unbelievably sensuous experience. This drug, "ready rock" (street slang for *crack),* transports the user to a state of being far beyond comprehension and experience. Some crack users have described the experience as the greatest they have ever felt. The term *crack* comes from the crackling sound that is produced when it's smoked.

NIDA summarizes the harmful effects of cocaine as follows:

> Cocaine usually makes the user feel euphoric and energetic, but also increases body temperature, blood pressure, and heart rate. Users risk heart attacks, respiratory failure, strokes, seizures, abdominal pain, and nausea. In rare cases, sudden death can occur on the first use of cocaine or unexpectedly afterwards.[8]

In addition to the above, cocaine users also risk increased exposure through intravenous use to hepatitis C and HIV. Cocaine boosts the intensity of the sexual experience and stimulates users so powerfully that they will not slow down long enough to prepare for safe sex, so the spread of STDs rises. How cocaine is ingested determines the length and intensity of the high as well as its effects. NIDA offers the following information so parents can appreciate the importance of the various ways that cocaine is introduced to the body:

> The intensity and duration of cocaine's effects—which include increased energy, reduced fatigue, and mental alertness—depend on the route of drug administration. The faster cocaine is absorbed into the bloodstream and delivered to the brain, the more intense the high. Injecting or smoking cocaine produces a quicker, stronger high than snorting. On the other hand, faster absorption usually means shorter duration of action: the high from snorting cocaine may last 15 to 30 minutes, but the high from smoking may last only 5 to 10 minutes. In order to sustain the high, a cocaine abuser has to administer the drug again. For this reason, cocaine is sometimes abused in binges—taken repeatedly within a relatively short period of time, at increasingly higher rates.[9]

When the effects of cocaine wear off, the user experiences a coke crash. There is a sudden drop in liveliness, while depression, irritability, and fatigue set in. To prevent this crash from occurring, the cocaine abuser will use the drug over and over until his supply of drugs is exhausted and/or his money runs out. This behavior leads to psychological dependence.

The intensity of the cocaine high remains stored in the user's memory, which is why, after years of cessation, environmental cues can spark pleasurable memories of prior cocaine experiences that are so commanding and enticing that powerful urges to use cocaine are triggered. This explains why so many cocaine addicts return to consuming the drug after extended periods of sobriety.

Amphetamine

Amphetamine was discovered in the 1880s, but it was not introduced to the public until 1932, when Benzedrine, a nasal inhalant, was marketed. Amphetamine was routinely used during World War II by armies on both sides of the European theater to prevent fatigue. Hitler is believed to have received daily amphetamine injections. When the war ended, soldiers introduced the drug to the United States culture. Amphetamine is considered to be a Schedule II drug since it has some medical value, such as treating narcolepsy and ADHD. Students will use amphetamine for such nonmedical purposes as increasing short-term stamina, which allows them to cram for exams all night. Truck drivers use the drug so that they can drive for extended periods of time. Many people use amphetamine to control weight since it suppresses appetite, which accounts for the prevalence of amphetamine abuse by models.

Amphetamines include drugs such as dextroamphetamine, Benzedrine, and Ritalin. The effects on the central nervous system and other body systems are similar to cocaine, and the body builds a tolerance to it. This means the user must keep using more and more to avoid the crash of withdrawal.

Since amphetamine speeds up bodily functions, parents should be on the alert. If your young person displays excessive energy, is overly confident, or has a heightened sense of well being, consider amphetamine use. Youth who are high on amphetamine will telegraph the fact that they are using this stimulant drug, so be alert for these telltale signs.

Methamphetamine

The next stimulant drug we will look at is closely related chemically to amphetamine, but it provides a much more intense pleasure state. Methamphetamine is taken orally, by snorting, or intravenously. Street names for methamphetamine include *speed, meth, ice,* and *glass.* This drug is made in clandestine labs through a process that can be volatile and dangerous. You might have seen news clips of your local authorities entering a house dressed in hazardous chemical outfits in order to clean out a methamphetamine lab. NIDA has a very excellent website that summarizes methamphetamine:[10]

Methamphetamine is a central nervous system stimulant drug that is similar in structure to amphetamine. Due to its high potential for abuse, methamphetamine is classified as a Schedule II drug and is available only through a prescription that cannot be refilled. Although methamphetamine can be prescribed by a doctor, its medical uses are limited, and the doses that are prescribed are much lower than those typically abused. Most of the methamphetamine abused in this country comes from foreign or domestic superlabs, although it can also be made in small, illegal laboratories, where its production endangers the people in the labs, neighbors, and the environment. . . .

Methamphetamine is a white, odorless, bitter-tasting crystalline powder that easily dissolves in water or alcohol and is taken orally, intranasally (snorting the powder), by needle injection, or by smoking. . . .

Chronic methamphetamine abuse significantly changes how the brain functions. Noninvasive human brain imaging studies have shown alterations in the activity of the dopamine system that are associated with reduced motor skills and impaired verbal learning.[11] Recent studies in chronic methamphetamine abusers have also revealed severe structural and functional changes in areas of the brain associated with emotion and memory,[12] which may account for many of the emotional and cognitive problems observed in chronic methamphetamine abusers.

Repeated methamphetamine abuse can also lead to addiction— a chronic, relapsing disease characterized by compulsive drug seeking and use, which is accompanied by chemical and molecular changes in the brain. Some of these changes persist long after methamphetamine abuse is stopped. Reversal of some of the changes, however, may be observed after sustained periods of abstinence (e.g., more than 1 year).[13]

To control the effects of this drug, the methamphetamine user takes drugs called *downers*, which slow the body. One such group of downers is tranquilizers. When this drug is used, muscles become more relaxed, anxiety is decreased, and reflexes are slowed. Another downer drug category is barbiturates. As mentioned earlier, they are designed to assist with sleep as well as decrease anxiety and tension by slowing down the central nervous system. Often, barbiturates are referred to as *sleeping pills*. Because these drugs produce a state of calmness and relaxation, they decelerate the effects of amphetamine and methamphetamine, which are referred to as *uppers*. The practice of mixing uppers with downers is unhealthy, as it interferes with the body's natural operation and, over time, will produce harmful effects.

Just as cocaine has crack, methamphetamine has ice, which is street slang for a very pure, processed, smokable form of methamphetamine. It appears as clear crystal chunks that look like ice. It is smoked, snorted, or injected. Its effects are similar to those of cocaine but last much longer.

Club Drugs

There is a craze among our youth called rave parties, which are all-night gatherings often held in warehouses and known for their nonstop music, intense dancing, and drug use. The drugs that are popular at these venues are collectively referred to as club drugs. In this section, we will focus upon the more commonly used club drugs, Ecstasy and the animal tranquilizer ketamine. We will also touch upon the date rape drugs Rohypnol and gamma-hydroxybutyrate (GHB), since they are used in social settings our youth frequent. We will begin by discussing the popular drug Ecstasy.

Ecstasy/MDMA

Ecstasy, or MDMA, has many names, including *E, XTC,* and *Adam*. It is a designer drug, which means it is a new substance that was created by changing the molecular structure of an existing drug. Designer drugs are created in underground laboratories, and Ecstasy is often imported from overseas. The drug comes in tablet form and often is marked with such insignia as a Playboy bunny, the Nike swoosh, or the letters CK. It is a Schedule I drug, which means it is illegal, has a high abuse potential, and has no known medical value. MDMA was first produced in 1912 by Merck, a German pharmaceutical company, and was intended as a weight-reduction drug. In the 1980s, MDMA became popular in Texas bars and quickly spread nationwide as a recreational drug. Its use is now widespread.

Users of Ecstasy enjoy the drug because it produces a feeling of well-being and provides pleasant sensory distortions. MDMA is popular at rave parties since it allows the partygoers to remain alert and awake all night. The drug also promotes intense pleasure even when doing nothing more than moving about and touching. Some users describe the sensations produced while under the influence of Ecstasy as the best feelings they have ever experienced. Women who attend rave parties appreciate the drug because it causes a lack of interest in sexual intercourse by men. This allows for the pleasure of dancing and heightened sensations through physical contact with men, but without the pressure to engage in sex, which makes for a far more preferable social setting than the singles bar scene. Due to the peacefulness produced by the drug, pleasant feelings and easy sociability occur, a valued effect of Ecstasy. "E" has become a threat to the bar business in England, and in Northern Ireland, rave parties were one of the few places where Catholic-Protestant barriers temporarily dissolved.[14] Ecstasy is favored by those in their teens and early twenties as a popular club drug.

The Office of National Drug Control Policy points out the following health effects of Ecstasy use:

> In high doses, MDMA can interfere with the body's ability to regulate temperature, sometimes leading to a sharp increase in body temperature (hyperthermia), resulting in liver, kidney, and cardiovascular system failure, and death. MDMA users also risk increases in heart rate and blood pressure, and symptoms such as muscle tension, involuntary teeth clenching, nausea, blurred vision, faintness, and chills or sweating. Psychological effects of MDMA use can include confusion, depression, sleep problems, drug craving, and severe anxiety. Additionally, these problems can occur during as well as sometimes days or weeks after using the drug.[15]

Because "E" stimulates the central nervous system and causes hallucino-genic effects, some MDMA users wave glow sticks to heighten the sensations that Ecstasy produces, while others suck on a baby pacifier to stop the teeth clenching that was mentioned above. Ecstasy depletes serotonin, a neuro-transmitter chemical in the brain that regulates mood, sleeping, eating, thinking, sex, aggressive behavior, and pain sensitivity. Serotonin also keeps an individual from being depressed, and as Ecstasy depletes the body's serotonin, a severe state of depression sets in. Ecstasy also elevates the person's energy level to such a peak that partygoers continually dance, which leads to exhaustion and dehydration. Some "E" users end up being rushed to the emergency room due to heatstroke, which is why users often have bottles of water available. The health effects of this drug should be of concern to every parent.

Due to the heightened sensations that Ecstasy produces, youth throw caution to the wind, ignoring the negative effects of this drug in favor of a sensational experience. This obligates parents to educate their sons and daughters about the dangers of this drug and closely observe them for pos-sible signs of Ecstasy use. Do you know exactly where your son or daughter parties and what that party actually consists of?

Ketamine

Veterinarians administer ketamine as a tranquilizer for their four-legged patients, while humans use it for its enticing psychedelic effects. Referred to as *Special K* or *Vitamin K*, this drug is found primarily in the club scene. Ketamine is a central nervous system depressant. There are side effects of ketamine use that should be of concern to every parent. The Office of National Drug Control Policy summarizes them as follows:

> The use of ketamine produces effects similar to PCP and LSD, causing distorted perceptions of sight and sound and making the user feel disconnected and out of control. The overt hallu-cinatory effects of ketamine are relatively short-acting, lasting approximately one hour or less. However, the user's senses, judgment, and coordination may be affected for up to 24 hours after the initial use of the drug. Use of this drug can also bring

about respiratory depression, heart rate abnormalities, and a withdrawal syndrome.[16]

Drug users mix "Special K" and "E" to create a powerful and highly appealing combination. I saw the impact of this mixture one Sunday morning while working an inner-city emergency room. There had been a rave party nearby, and the ambulances were rolling in with kids suffering from medical problems arising from drug use at the party. Among the patients was a young man in his late teens who had been mixing "E" with "Special K." Once the doctors stabilized him, I was sent to assess his mental health status. During that evaluation, I asked if he was aware what "Special K" was, and he answered that he knew that it was a "cat tranquilizer" but he quickly added that it "was kicking" when mixed with "E." I pointed out to him that this "kicking" mixture had nearly killed him and asked if he'd allow me to work with him to help him stop abusing drugs. He responded, "If you ever took 'Special K' and 'E,' you would know how dumb that question is. It is like nothing you'll ever experience."

The next two drugs included in this section are used primarily in clubs and leave men and women open to rape and sexual assault. These drugs, GHB and Rohypnol, are often dropped into a person's drink while at a bar or social event and immediately depress the central nervous system to such an extent that complete relaxation and partial to full amnesia results. When dropped into a drink containing alcohol, the consumer of the drink becomes incapacitated and unable to resist sexual assaults. The Office of National Drug Control Policy warns:

> The tasteless and odorless depressants Rohypnol and GHB are often used in the commission of sexual assaults due to their ability to sedate and intoxicate unsuspecting victims. Rohypnol, a sedative/tranquilizer, is legally available for prescription in over 50 countries outside of the U.S. and is widely available in Mexico, Colombia, and Europe. Although usually taken orally in pill form, reports have shown that some users grind Rohypnol into a powder and snort the drug.
>
> GHB, available in an odorless, colorless liquid form or as a white powder material, is taken orally, and is frequently combined

with alcohol. In addition to being used to incapacitate individuals for the commission of sexual assault/rape, GHB is also sometimes used by body builders for its alleged anabolic effects.[17]

Take time to share this information with your sons and daughters. Warn them that they must closely guard their drinks at all times, especially if the drink contains alcohol. Instruct them that should they happen to leave their drink alone, even for a brief moment, throw it out, get another cup, and pour a fresh drink. It only takes a split second for Rohypnol or GHB to be dropped into a drink, and since they are colorless and odorless, detection is virtually impossible.

Psychedelics

Psychedelics are psychoactive substances that produce hallucination; distort perceptions in time, space, and orientation; and alter reality. Hallucinations are caused by unfortunate internal brain malfunctions or through the ingestion of certain brain-altering substances that cause these malfunctions. Psychedelics open up the unconscious, which permits pleasant and unpleasant thoughts to rise unchecked into the conscious. The effects are unpredictable, and the user has no way of knowing whether the experience will be pleasant, terrifying, or mixed. Psychedelic drugs include those grown by nature and those created by humans. Some of the more commonly used psychedelics that we will discuss are psilocybin ("magic mushrooms"), DXM, LSD, and PCP. Psychedelics became popular in the 1960s through the work of LSD advocate Timothy Leary.

Psilocybin (Magic Mushrooms)

Psilocybin is obtained from certain mushrooms found in South America, Mexico, and the southwestern section of the United States. They have long, narrow stems topped by caps with dark gills and are referred to by those abusing them as *shrooms, caps,* and *magic mushrooms.* Psilocybin can also be synthetically produced, so the drug is not limited to the southwestern area of the United States. Usually eaten, these mushrooms can also be brewed in tea or added to food to mask their flavor.

The Office of National Drug Control Policy advises us that the "physical effects of psilocybin are usually experienced within 20 minutes of ingestion and can last for 6 hours. Negative physical symptoms of psilocybin use can include vomiting, muscle weakness, drowsiness, and panic reactions. Frequent use of this drug can result in the development of tolerance."[18]

DXM (Dextromethorphan)

DXM is the cough-suppressing ingredient in many over-the-counter cold and cough medications and is sometimes referred to as "robo." For those who take cough syrup as directed, the desired relief is safe, but when an individual consumes large amounts of DXM, dissociation similar to PCP and ketamine occurs. If you happen to find empty bottles or excessive quantities of cough syrup containing DXM in your home, talk to your son or daughter. Parents are surprised to learn that this commonly used over-the-counter medication is so widely abused.

LSD (Acid)

LSD is classified as a Schedule I controlled substance, which means that it has no medical use and possesses a high potential for abuse. It was discovered in 1938 and made popular among youth in the 1960s, when Timothy Leary advocated that people discover their inner and spiritual selves through LSD. Commonly referred to as "acid," LSD is marketed as tablets, capsules, and occasionally in liquid form, but it also is added to blotter paper—absorbent paper that is divided into small decorative squares. It can be taken orally, licked off blotter paper or, if it is in liquid form, put in the eyes. LSD is usually taken orally since it is odorless and its taste is not too bitter. It is relatively inexpensive, with a dose that costs only a few dollars lasting up to twelve hours. It has many side effects, as shown from this quotation from the Office of National Drug Control Policy:

> The effects of LSD are unpredictable. They depend on the amount of the drug taken; the user's personality, mood, and expectations; and the surrounding in which the drug is used. Usually, the user feels the first effects of the drug within 30 to 90 minutes of ingestion. These experiences last for extended periods of time and typically begin to clear after about 12 hours.

The physical effects include dilated pupils, higher body temperature, increased heart rate and blood pressure, sweating, loss of appetite, sleeplessness, dry mouth, and tremors. Sensations may seem to "cross over" for the user, giving the feeling of hearing colors and seeing sounds. If taken in a large enough dose, the drug produces delusions and visual hallucinations.[19]

Odorless, colorless, and small in size, this drug is less likely to be found by parents (unless it's on blotter paper), but you can detect LSD usage through the just-cited behavioral and physical change indicators. Because of its ability to transport the user into a world that is vastly different from the real world, the LSD experience is referred to as a *trip*. A *bad trip* refers to an LSD experience that has severe, adverse reactions. Parents can detect a bad trip through the panic, confusion, anxiety, suspicion, and loss of control that leaving reality produces. LSD users sometimes experience a spontaneous recurrence of a trip as a response to environmental cues or stress, a phenomenon called *flashbacks*. While "tripping," the user will experience multiple feelings and sensations that change unpredictably and sensationally. Delusions and hallucinations occur while orientation to time, space, and self are dramatically altered. Some users report intense colors and sounds, the vanishing of boundaries, and feelings and thoughts that leave the user terrified and fearful of losing control.

Given the perceptual distortions that can occur with a "bad trip," the experience can be an extremely frightening. For some users of LSD, a trip can turn fatal not from internal complications, but from perceptual irregularities. With orientation distorted, falls from buildings, drownings, and other fatal acts can and do occur. LSD users should have someone nearby so that the user doesn't do anything fatal.

PCP (Phencyclidine)

Created initially in the 1950s as an intravenous anesthetic, PCP produces feelings of detachment, and often the user becomes out of control. Its effects are unpredictable, and often violent, as the drug gives the user extreme strength. People high on PCP can become so powerfully violent that it takes several large men to restrain one person. Bizarre behaviors are common, and high doses can cause hallucinations and disconnection with the environment. Thinking is also impaired, and delusions are common. When ingested, PCP's effects can be felt for hours and, since the drug is stored in fat cells for days after ingestion, physical exertion can activate the stored PCP, causing the person to engage in behaviors typical of someone who has just ingested the drug.

This drug is dangerous, and anyone encountering a person high on PCP should not attempt to deal with the individual alone. Get help so that you can safely bring the user to an emergency room, where treatment for the drug's effects can be undertaken. Once the person is in the hospital, special precautions are set in place, since the individual can become violent or suicidal. The user is kept in as calm a setting as possible and is never left alone, despite the cost involved in maintaining extra staff. If hospitals must take these special precautions, parents should never be foolhardy enough to attempt to deal with a son or daughter who is high on PCP without help. Call 911 and get professionals involved.

The Office of National Drug Control Policy provides a very informative but concise statement about PCP:

> PCP (phencyclidine) was developed in the 1950s as an intravenous anesthetic, but its use in humans was discontinued in 1965, because patients often became agitated, delusional, and irrational while recovering from its anesthetic effects. PCP is now being illegally manufactured in laboratories. It is a white crystalline powder that is readily soluble in water or alcohol. It has a distinctive bitter chemical taste. PCP can be mixed easily with dyes and turns up on the illicit drug market in a variety of tablets, capsules, and colored powders. It can be snorted, smoked, or ingested. For smoking, PCP is often applied to a leafy material such as mint, parsley, oregano, or marijuana.[20]

NIDA lists the following adverse effects of PCP:

> At low-to-moderate doses, physiological effects of PCP include a slight increase in breathing rate and a pronounced rise in blood pressure and pulse rate. Breathing becomes shallow; flushing and profuse sweating, generalized numbness of the extremities, and loss of muscular coordination may occur.

At high doses, blood pressure, pulse rate, and respiration drop. This may be accompanied by nausea, vomiting, blurred vision, flicking up and down of the eyes, drooling, loss of balance, and dizziness. PCP abusers are often brought to emergency rooms because of overdose or because of the drug's severe untoward psychological effects. While intoxicated, PCP abusers may become violent or suicidal and are therefore dangerous to themselves and others. High doses of PCP can also cause seizures, coma, and death (though death more often results from accidental injury or suicide during PCP intoxication). Because PCP can also have sedative effects, interactions with other central nervous system depressants, such as alcohol and benzodiazepines, can also lead to coma.[21]

CHAPTER 8

Turmoil Following Discovery:
More about Bill and Susan

Let's continue with Bill and Susan's story. Based on personal experience, Bill figured that teenagers who run away from home usually return within a few days, their prohibited exploits fulfilled. Fully expecting to hear that Sean had returned, Bill called Susan as soon as he got home from a week on the road. He was prepared to set up a meeting with her and Sean, but he was not prepared to hear, "He is still out there somewhere."

"You haven't heard from him at all?"

"Not a word." Sean was proving to be an exception to Bill's theory.

"If you don't mind, I'll be over." There would be no further procrastination.

"You are always welcome. But I don't think I'll be much company."

"Give me ten minutes to get into something comfortable."

"Take your time. You want some coffee?"

"I could use a cup of java. See you in ten."

Supportive concern may have been appropriate last weekend, but now it was time to introduce what Bill believed to be Sean's real problem—substance abuse. To continue avoiding this subject would not only be damaging to Susan and her son, but it was contrary to all that he knew he should be doing if their friendship was truly genuine. Silence was incompatible with the support he felt obligated to extend—the same support he received from other similarly situated parents during his daughter's drug years. He was indebted to those parents who had upheld him, and this evening he vowed to uphold Susan and provide her the support she needed. He owed it to her.

Bill knew that he was embarking upon an uncomfortable undertaking, but he was determined not to be handicapped by the memories that assailed him last Sunday. He had spent the week confronting his uneasiness by getting honest with what he was truly responsible for—himself. With guilt relegated to his emotional trash can, Bill was free to draw upon the experiential advantage of his own family trauma, beginning with that horrible day when he learned of his daughter's addiction from another parent. Since then, Bill had helped many parents who were new and not so new to the world of addiction. Tonight, however, would be different, for those parents were visitors in his life, unlike Sean and Susan. He had grown close to Susan and her family.

He had to validate his suspicions first. He needed proof that Sean was not merely going through one of those adolescent phases.

Susan greeted him at the door, "Thanks for coming over, Bill."

Walking into Susan's disorderly living room, he exchanged a waiting cup of coffee for the list of Unlucky Thirteen behaviors in his hand. "I'd like you to go over this and see how many of these behaviors Sean has been displaying," he said.

Plopping herself onto the couch, Susan scanned the papers. "What's this?"

"It's a test that may help us get clarification with what is going on with Sean." Susan gazed at the paper while Bill said, "Just check the behaviors he has been displaying lately."

Silently, Susan rummaged through her purse for a pen. Her depression was too deep to protest or question him further. Bill decided to take advantage of her sluggishness to conduct an environmental search. "While you're doing that, I'd like to go through Sean's room and see if there is anything that can help us figure out what's going on."

Removing a pen from her purse, she stared vacantly at Bill. "I've got the door closed. I just can't bear to look inside it."

Bill walked up the steps, passing framed photographs of Susan's two sons, mementos of happier times. Opening the door to Sean's room, he was instantly assailed by grotesque images that covered every wall. Just like his daughter during her drug days, Sean had become captivated with drug-centered rock groups. *They're still as awful as I remember them,* Bill thought before offering a prayer of thanks that those days were finally behind him. Then he remembered that relapse could happen to anyone at any time, so a more appropriate invocation was offered: *Thank you, God, for another day that Barbara is clean and sober.*

His daughter's years of drug use had taught him well. Like an experienced narcotics agent, Bill began foraging through Sean's bedroom. Under the loose corner of the wall-to-wall carpet, he removed a small brown envelope containing remains that he assumed to be marijuana. Hidden in a book, he discovered a half-empty pack of cigarette papers. In Sean's dresser, concealed within an untidy pile of T-shirts, he uncovered the instruments of a drug user—a butane lighter lying beside a fire-scarred kitchen spoon. In a rolled-up pair of socks, he found a bag of crack. *Sean must have fled the house so quickly that he didn't have time to retrieve his stuff,* Bill thought.

Bill left to inspect the bathroom, concern for Sean's welfare escalating with each step. Knowing that a drug user is never separated from his drugs for very long, he wondered what could have happened.

In the bathroom, buried deep in a corner of the vanity, Bill located a vial containing an unknown liquid. Susan arrived as he was setting the vial on the edge of the bathtub. "What's that?"

"Most likely some kind of drug," Bill responded factually. There was no easy way to answer that question.

"Drugs!" Susan exclaimed.

"Found it hidden deep inside your bathroom vanity." Bill tried to remain as matter-of-fact as possible.

Susan's face turned pale. Fearful she would faint, Bill suggested, "Why don't we find a place to sit down?"

Bill led Susan to Sean's nearby bedroom, where she collapsed on the bed, her eyes gazing emptily on the poster-burdened wall. Bill leaned against the dresser. Slowly, Susan's desperate eyes turned toward him. "Please don't tell me that Sean is using drugs."

Bill opened the dresser drawer and presented a butane lighter and fire-scarred spoon. "These are the tools of a drug user. Notice the burned underside of the spoon. He's been using the lighter and spoon to cook his drugs."

Feeling like a sadist, Bill laid the T-shirt and its contents on top of the dresser. He looked at the cigarette papers and the small bag containing crack. He decided to hand her the bag of crack. "This was also hidden in Sean's room. Looks like crack."

Slowly, Susan extended her arm, reluctantly taking the bag into her hand. She gazed at the crystalline nuggets for what seemed like an eternity before dropping the bag. As the bag of crack met the carpeted floor, Susan's face collapsed onto her open palms. Bill debated whether he should reach out to her now or give her a little space to process. Deciding to leave Susan alone for the moment, Bill picked up the behavioral test that she had dropped on the bed. A quick scan revealed that at least six categories merited "plus" scores, while all the others earned a check. Sean was definitely involved in the drug scene.

Bill turned his attention back toward Susan. Distraught brown eyes fixed upon Bill. "He's really on drugs, isn't he?" It was a reluctant, anguished admission, validating her secret fears. Surrounded by proof of a potentially fatal illness that threatened all that was meaningful in her world, Susan collapsed into a grief-stricken heap on her son's bed.

You, like Susan, may have been thrust out of the deceptive world of denial following your own investigation. If this book has led you to the unsettling and painful awareness that your son or daughter is using drugs, I wish it were possible to say everything will quickly return to normalcy. Bill truly desired to offer Susan that same assurance, but that would have been misleading and fallacious. The truth is that Susan was entering an emotional firestorm of rare proportions. Susan would search in vain for answers to the unsettling questions she uttered last weekend: "What did I do wrong? How did I fail?"

No one wants to acknowledge substance abuse in a loved one, especially a loved one who is your own flesh and blood. It is heartbreaking to realize that the infant you nourished, protected, grounded, and loved has evolved into an addict or alcoholic.

As parents, we believe it is our primary obligation and responsibility to present to the world a young adult who is well adjusted and responsible. When a son or daughter enters adulthood addicted to brain-altering substances, all parents can offer is an undependable, unpredictable, irrational, irresponsible, and unstable drug user. Without a well-adjusted and dependable young adult, parents view themselves as failures in the number one endeavor of their lifetime. It, therefore, should not surprise anyone that parents of substance abusers are overwhelmed by feelings of guilt and shame, emotions that cripple and render them too paralyzed to act constructively.

Before accepting the guilt, it is only fair that parents come to an authentic understanding of the true nature of addiction. An objective and honest appreciation of the disease of addiction goes a long way toward objectively and accurately judging the extent and appropriateness of parental responsibility. When parents come to a realistic and genuine understanding of addiction, an honest awareness of their true level of accountability is realized. With this knowledge, the shackles of guilt are loosened, freeing them to function in an effective, sane, and balanced manner. They can again assume their roles as capable, wise parents!

Today, Bill will be available to support Susan as she begins her emotional journey. He will educate his good friend about the truth of addiction, just as the upcoming chapters of this book will educate the reader. Like Susan, the reader will develop an appreciation of the repercussions drugs have upon the entire family. Liberated from guilt, sanity returns to the family and the marriage as parents begin to appropriately parent their addicted young person.

Parents, please be fair to yourselves! Before guilt overwhelms you, take time to learn the truth about addiction. Knowing the truth will go a long way, and you will once again be able to be the strong, savvy parent your addicted young person so desperately needs at this critical period in his or her life.

Bill extended his arm toward Susan, prompting her to rise from the bed. "Let's go downstairs and talk. We've got something else in common: drug-addicted kids."

"But yours is doing okay."

"Today Barbara is. I have no assurance that it will be that way tomorrow."

"Do you think Sean will ever be himself again?" she asked, accepting Bill's outstretched hand.

"I didn't think Barbara would ever get her act together, but she did. If my kid is any example, it's quite possible. But before that can happen, there is a lot you will have to learn, and changes you will have to make, just like I had to do."

Rising, Susan purposely declared, "Show me what I have to do."

⚜

Section 2

Understanding
Addiction

CHAPTER 9

The Truth Shall Set You Free

Truth is a liberating thing. When parents learn the truth about addiction, they find themselves free of the shackles of ignorance and misleading beliefs. By learning the truth about addiction, parents come to realize the truly limited role they played in the development of an offspring's addiction, a liberating experience that not only breaks the bondage of false guilt, but also significantly reduces shame and self-defeating thoughts. Knowledge about addiction allows parents to operate from an informed position.

The need to know the truth about addiction isn't limited to parents. Young people addicted to drugs are often also chained by ignorance about addiction. With guilt arising from the hurt they've heaped upon family and friends, they believe they will be forever isolated and alone. After months or even years of antisocial, disruptive, harmful behaviors, youthful addicts are convinced that they are worthless, corrupt, immoral, and never worthy to be loved or forgiven again. Worried that they may have damaged their mind and ruined their health, they feel their hope for the future is further darkened. Since they no longer can function without a regular infusion of drugs, addicts persist in pursuing a drug-centered existence despite a growing desire to quit. But informed parents can do much to displace these unhealthy feelings. By educating themselves, they are liberated enough to objectively share the truth about addiction with their substance-abusing young person, a potentially liberating experience for the addicted young person.

To support our goal of understanding the truth about addiction, we will focus on certain key words and phrases that capture the fundamental essence of what it means to be addicted to brain-altering substances.

Addiction is an *out-of-control urge* to engage in harmful *behaviors* that *progressively increase* despite the *adverse consequences* that are experienced physically, mentally, socially, and spiritually.

Out-of-Control Urge

With the regular use of drugs—brain-altering substances increasingly coming to dominate, control, and demand gratification—a tolerance develops. The need to find and use drugs demands satiation, or else the mental and physical discomfort (withdrawals) that occur when drugs are absent from the addict's body will increase irritability, illness, and agitation. These powerful urges must be placated regardless of how it's done—a dynamic that manifests itself through impulsive, out-of-control, irresponsible, and at times antisocial behaviors. Your young person does not want to steal from you, but drugs are in control, and they are demanding. Any opportunity that can satiate those urges will be taken advantage of. That forty dollars you inadvertently left on your dresser disappears as out-of-control urges take over.

As the parent of an addicted young person, you must acknowledge the behaviors you have been witnessing for what they truly are—out-of-control urges that come from a brain that has been altered by substances and is centered upon satisfying those drug cravings. The values, morals, and norms that you conscientiously instilled into your son or daughter have been lost to the drug-altered brain and cannot compete with those out-of-control urges. Brain-altering substances are in charge—not you, not your young person, and not your years of teaching and guidance.

Behaviors

Addicts become proficient in carrying out behaviors necessary for acquiring and using drugs, such as lying, conning, stealing, cheating, and manipulating. Over time, these drug-centered behaviors combine with other drug-related behaviors, such as irresponsibility, rudeness, coldness, isolation, deception, and immoral and antisocial actions. Combined, they constitute a disturbing repertoire of drug-induced and drug-centered behaviors.

In my work with addicts entering recovery after years of active addiction, I have yet to encounter anyone who didn't acknowledge the vast difference between the person they were prior to the regular use of drugs and the person who walked through the doors of the drug treatment facility. These seasoned addicts openly admitted that the behaviors they acquired were a consequence of their psychological and physiological dependency on drugs. They also acknowledged that, over time, the behaviors acquired in seeking and using drugs became such an integral part of their daily activities that their entire way of conducting themselves was significantly altered.

This admission is an essential early step in the recovery process because, if sobriety and a drug-free life are to be sustained, there must be an acknowledgment that those acquired behaviors are drug related and therefore must be exchanged for positive, sobriety-centered actions. This is why recovering addicts and alcoholics are constantly reminded in Narcotics Anonymous (NA) and Alcoholics Anonymous (AA) that they must "change people, places, and things." Those in recovery from brain-altering substances require behavioral changes, such as meeting and acquiring new sober friends, hanging out at drug-free places, and engaging in activities that do not involve the use of brain-altering substances.

When the addict becomes drug free, major lifestyle changes are necessary to sustain his sobriety, and if parents intend to support their child's early recovery, they must acknowledge the close relationship between addiction and behavior. They must make certain that he changes his friends, hangouts, and activities as well as any behaviors that are the byproducts of drug involvement, such as irresponsibility. It is a parental responsibility that can neither be ignored nor neglected.

Should parents fail to appreciate the intrinsic relationship between addiction and behavior, they will succumb to the common fallacy that all the addict has to do is to stop using, and the drug problem will cease. Such a mind-set is a major disservice to sons and daughters who are starting life in recovery and a setup for a return to active substance use. You must acknowledge that maintaining a drug-free life means much more than merely stopping drug use. Recovery from drugs and alcohol cannot be sustained unless behavioral changes occur—a process that parents must encourage and support—but this will not happen unless parents have an authentic understanding and appreciation of addiction as a behavioral problem.

Progressively Increase

Addiction is not static. The sought-after euphoric experience—the high—cannot be sustained by the original dosage because of growing tolerance. Due to tolerance, a drug user eventually progresses to more frequent use and more potent drugs. In my years of working with addicts, I found few addicts who began their adolescent drug use with "hard" drugs such as psychedelics, heroin, or stimulants. Most began with marijuana or alcohol, while others started with prescription medications and inhalants. These developing addicts eventually realized that the desired euphoric state, the initial "high," couldn't be sustained by maintaining the original dosages, so they increased the frequency of use, increased the amount used, and eventually changed their drug of choice to "harder" substances that eventually were used more frequently and in larger amounts. They also readily admitted that negative behaviors became worse as their addiction progressed.

The drugs that are most commonly involved in early experimental use must never be minimized. Marijuana, while illegal, is commonly used, and many question why it is illegal. Do not buy into this mind-set. This drug is a substance that decreases motivation and introduces your young person to the bliss that comes with being "high," a feeling that can lead your young person progressively into addiction. Likewise, do not minimize the behavior of getting high or "wasted" on alcohol. This must not be seen as a rite of passage. Rather, it's a dangerous activity that directs the young person to seek out more opportunities to get "wasted." Inhalants can permanently destroy brain cells, and parents must be on the alert for signs of their use. Illicit prescription pill use is an entrée for your young person to become another statistic in the rapidly growing number of pill addicts.

The recreational stage begins with "partying" and having fun while using drugs, but eventually the drug user becomes so fascinated with it that she becomes increasingly focused on the upcoming party. Mental fixation intensifies as the developing addict dwells on prior weekends when "having fun" was equated with "getting high." This mind-set leads to daily consumption. With the mind focused on getting high, daily use is inevitable unless treatment is initiated.

When the addict progresses to the preoccupation and powerlessness stages, her life is so completely centered on acquiring and using drugs that parents have no choice but to seek help. Lacking pleasant natural interactions within the brain due to a deficiency of "feel-good" neurotransmitters, the addict must have her fix or drink before she can begin the day or, to use street slang, "Get out the gate." Several times during the afternoon and evening, she must consume her drug of choice or she will become ill. Her life is now a constant search for ways to find money to buy drugs, to locate and purchase her drug, and to safely use the substances she finally located. If she fails in this endeavor, she will experience an onslaught of mental and physical distress (withdrawal). That coveted, euphoric, enjoyable high is now an event that dwells only in the foggy past, despite the fact that consumption of drugs has significantly increased. With the use of brain-altering chemicals no longer an enjoyable activity, the use of drugs and alcohol is now a necessary action exclusively designed to keep the misery of withdrawal at bay and to try to maintain some semblance of normalcy.

Adverse Consequences

Physically

No one can continually ingest drugs and not suffer adverse consequences. We have already seen some of the physical consequences of regular drug use: pallid skin tone, sickly appearance, increased infections, digestive and respiratory problems, decreased appetite, and weight loss. In addition, there is the risk of STDs through careless sex associated with drug use and the drug-centered lifestyle. The sharing of needles by intravenous drug users contributes to the acquisition of HIV and hepatitis C. Longtime addicts present as pathetic copies of human beings with their open sores, swollen limbs, sad eyes, and thin frames. For these addicts, death, the final stage in addiction's unyielding progression, is not far away.

Alcoholics are not immune from the physical deterioration that consistent and excessive consumption brings. Among alcohol-related illnesses are chronic gastritis, cirrhosis of the liver (a very common ailment for long-term alcoholics), fetal alcohol syndrome, hypoglycemia, impotency, brain and heart problems, and pancreatitis.

Mentally

The mental consequences of using brain-altering substances are significant. Talk to anyone who works in the psychiatric ward of your local hospital, and they will tell you that a large percentage of their patients are "dually diagnosed"; that is, they have two illnesses: the disease of addiction along with a coexisting mental illness such as depression or other mood disorders, schizophrenia, anxiety, or psychosis. Many of these patients enter the hospital because the interaction of mental illness and addiction manifests itself in suicidal ideation or an actual suicidal attempt necessitating the secure, safe, therapeutic setting of a hospital. Others enter the hospital because of excessively wide mood swings, hallucinations, and/or delusions that have been caused or exacerbated by the use of brain-altering substances. In the hospital, these dually diagnosed patients are detoxified while receiving therapeutic intervention through the initiation, restarting, or adjusting of psychiatric medications so that depression, suicidal ideations, anxiety, various mood disorders, hallucinations, and delusions are reduced. Unfortunately, all too often the hospital is prohibited from completing treatment prior to discharge because of insurance restrictions, a situation that often leads to another expensive inpatient hospital stay.

When discussing addiction and mental illness, it often is asked, "What came first, drugs or mental illness?" Did the individual have a preexisting mental illness that was worsened by the use of drugs, or did drugs cause the mental illness? The answer varies from individual to individual. For those who have a preexisting mental illness and use illicit drugs, the mental illness is exacerbated. The practice of using illicit drugs to treat the mental illness is called "self-medicating," and initially it does provide relief, but this relief is short-lived and has the long-term consequence of worsening the mental condition and the development of dependence upon brain-altering substances.

Others entered onto the pathway to addiction without any mental illness, but over time the alterations in the brain, as well as the negative social, psychological, and physical effects of drugs, impact the individual's mental health. A person can deal with the negative consequences of drugs for only so long before various mental illnesses such as depression, mood disorders, and anxiety develop. Regardless of which came first, mental distress is now a reality that the addict treats through self-medicating instead of utilizing legitimate, therapeutically sound interventions.

Don't minimize the problem of dual diagnosis. It is a major problem and parents need to be cognizant of its prevalence. Make sure that mental illness is addressed as well as the substance abuse. On its website, NAMI (National Alliance on Mental Illness) addresses the frequency with which mental health disorders and substance abuse disorders are concurrent:

How often do people with severe mental illnesses also experience a co-occurring substance abuse problem?

There is a lack of information on the numbers of people with co-occurring disorders, but research has shown the disorders are very common. According to reports published in the *Journal of the American Medical Association (JAMA):*

➡ Roughly 50 percent of individuals with severe mental disorders are affected by substance abuse.

➡ Thirty-seven percent of alcohol abusers and 53 percent of drug abusers also have at least one serious mental illness.

➡ Of all people diagnosed as mentally ill, 29 percent abuse either alcohol or drugs.

The best data available on the prevalence of co-occurring disorders are derived from two major surveys: the Epidemiologic Catchment Area (ECA) Survey (administered 1980–1984), and the National Comorbidity Survey (NCS), administered between 1990 and 1992.

Results of the NCS and the ECA Survey indicate high prevalence rates for co-occurring substance abuse disorders and mental disorders, as well as the increased risk for people with either a substance abuse disorder or mental disorder for developing a co-occurring disorder. For example, the NCS found that

➡ 42.7 percent of individuals with a 12-month addictive disorder had at least one 12-month mental disorder.

➡ 14.7 percent of individuals with a 12-month mental disorder had at least one 12-month addictive disorder.[1]

The high prevalence rates for co-occurring substance abuse and mental health disorders is verified by the ECA Survey, which found that

> ➥ 47 percent of individuals with schizophrenia also had a substance abuse disorder (more than four times as likely as the general population).
>
> ➥ 61 percent of individuals with bipolar disorder also had a substance abuse disorder (more than five times as likely as the general population).
>
> **Continuing studies support these findings, that these disorders do appear to occur much more frequently than previously realized, and that appropriate integrated treatments must be developed.**[2]

If you have determined that your son or daughter is abusing brain-altering substances, acknowledge that there is a strong likelihood that your young person may also have a mental health disorder that needs to be treated. Don't limit your efforts exclusively to substance abuse treatment. Have a mental health professional evaluate your young person to see if she has a co-occurring disorder, and, if she's found to be dually diagnosed, follow the advice offered and treatment plans developed by professionals.

Socially

Drug use comes with a high social price tag. For adults, it may mean estrangement from spouse and children; loss of job, car, or housing; and possible legal problems. For the young addict, alienation from the family, dropping out of school, an inability to function properly in normal social circumstances, and job loss are a few of the social consequences drugs offer. Normal social interactions, family relations, and other social activities that are typical of emerging young adults become irrelevant. The isolation, remoteness, belligerence, and acting-out behaviors that you are witnessing are directly attributed to substance abuse and the antisocial existence that drugs bring.

Spiritually

Anyone addicted to brain-altering substances cannot help but have a spiritual void in their lives. Addicts and alcoholics are typically empty of positive feelings, animation, and vitality. Rare is the addict who smiles, laughs, or enjoys life unless he is high, and even then the happiness is very transitory. Operating with a brain whose natural "feel-good" interactions have been exchanged for temporary, artificially induced highs, it is virtually impossible for the young addict to experience excitement, cheerfulness, and vitality. This alteration in the brain explains the emptiness that you observe whenever you gaze into the eyes of your addicted son or daughter. It also explains your addicted son's or daughter's listlessness and sluggishness, which for many parents is a major concern. Without the healthy, normal interactions within the brain that promote good feelings, the addict can only present as a sad, dispirited shell of a human being.

The term *spirituality* also implies a belief in God or another higher power in whom people place their faith, trust, and reliance. Your addicted child may have had a belief system based upon rudiments of faith acquired through religious teachings, or at least possessed a set of values and a sense of right and wrong. But after surrendering to the power of drugs, he abandoned the faith of his upbringing and switched to new gods. He began worshipping at the altar of the next drink, hit, fix, shot, smoke, or snort—but these new gods offer inconstant assurance, fragile conviction, and very temporary relief. Yet he continued to live for his new gods.

When your young person ceases drug use and enters recovery, his spiritual void will be an issue that needs to be addressed. For many recovering addicts, this void is filled through the Twelve Steps, which instill a new lifestyle based upon "a power greater than ourselves" and "God as we understood Him." The Twelve Steps of Alcoholics Anonymous, the centerpiece of many treatment programs and self-help groups, provide a road map to the restoration of spirituality. Notice, as you read these Twelve Steps, the spirituality that is woven throughout:

1. We admitted we were powerless over alcohol—that our lives had become unmanageable.

2. Came to believe that a Power greater than ourselves could restore us to sanity.

3. Made a decision to turn our will and our lives over to the care of God *as we understood Him.*

4. Made a searching and fearless moral inventory of ourselves.

5. Admitted to God, to ourselves, and to another human being the exact nature of our wrongs.

6. Were entirely ready to have God remove all these defects of character.

7. Humbly asked Him to remove our shortcomings.

8. Made a list of all persons we had harmed, and became willing to make amends to them all.

9. Made direct amends to such people wherever possible, except when to do so would injure them or others.

10. Continued to take personal inventory and when we were wrong promptly admitted it.

11. Sought through prayer and meditation to improve our conscious contact with God *as we understood Him,* praying only for knowledge of His will for us and the power to carry that out.

12. Having had a spiritual awakening as the result of these steps, we tried to carry this message to alcoholics, and to practice these principles in all our affairs.[3]

In Summary

We began this chapter with the proposition that by coming to understand addiction, parents can be set free from the crippling chains of guilt. Understanding the truth about addiction is indeed liberating. When parents come to realize that drugs propel the addict to engage in behaviors that are irrational, extreme, and incompatible with parental standards, they are not only freed from paralyzing guilt, but are liberated to begin treating that addicted son or daughter rationally and effectively. Accountability begins falling on the shoulders of the addict and her addiction—which is where it belongs.

How can you honestly hold yourself accountable for what is beyond your control? Drugs are ruling, not the morals and value systems that you faithfully instilled. Accept it: Your influence has been usurped by the power of brain-altering substances and, if you are honest with yourself, you will admit that you cannot hold yourself accountable for the alterations brought about in your young person.

Become emancipated. Stop holding yourself accountable for things that are beyond your control and have overpowered any positive influence you once had. Accept the definition of addiction and eradicate that crippling, false guilt that has overtaken your life. Drugs have taken control and addiction has gained its foothold. Behaviors became drug controlled and induced. The values and standards you've worked so hard to instill have been usurped. So stop owning what isn't yours to own.

⚜

CHAPTER 10

The Disease of Addiction

Remember when your child was young and managed to acquire one of those numerous childhood illnesses at the most inconvenient times? Do you recall how you responded? If you were like most parents, you *diagnosed* the illness by taking her temperature and examining the symptoms. Once you gained a basic knowledge about what was afflicting the child, you began to *treat* her by administering an appropriate commercial or homemade remedy. This you did in order to help your child feel better and return to normalcy. Occasionally, you found the illness was too serious or critical to treat yourself. When this occurred, you didn't give a second thought to *seeking out professional help*. You called the child's pediatrician or rushed to an urgent care clinic or emergency room. No matter the cost or inconvenience, seeking immediate and efficient treatment for your child was your paramount concern.

Just because your child is older and the illness happens to be addiction to brain-altering substances, there is no reason to shy away from that tried and proven methodology. This same method—diagnose, treat, and seek out professional help when necessary—can still be advantageous in treating your addicted young person.

In 1956, the American Medical Association (AMA) declared alcoholism to be a disease. Since it is an AMA-recognized disease, approach this illness as such: *diagnose* through an environmental inspection and the Unlucky Thirteen Behavioral Test, *treat* by using techniques that will be found in the third section of this book, and *seek out professional help* by consulting with your doctor or a substance abuse counselor and, when necessary, enrolling your young person in an appropriate treatment program.

By considering addiction to be a disease, you accept the AMA's declaration and turn your back on conventional untruths. Declaring alcoholism to be a disease ran contrary to the cultural mind-set of 1956's society, and more than a half a century later, conditions are not that much different. Like Americans living decades ago, today's culture still clings to the view that alcoholics and drug addicts are social deviants, undesirables, and morally defective people—a powerful societal and cultural stigma that taints a parent's ability to properly appreciate and understand addiction.

By viewing addiction as a stigma, parents become emotionally twisted and lash out at the ill person instead of seeking professional help and adhering to prescribed disease treatment procedures—something they did so expertly in the past. When parents fail to accept addiction as a disease, they sentence themselves to an aimless, irrational, frustrating, and anxiety-ridden existence with no likelihood of providing meaningful help to their young person at this most critical time in her life.

When your preschooler became ill, you didn't blame your child for becoming sick, even if it was due to her failure to wear proper clothing or do as you directed. Your sole focus was on getting the child healthy, so you gave the ill youngster what she needed most—parental love and a pledge that the prescribed treatment regime would be adhered to. You knew addressing behavioral concerns would have to take a backseat to treating the illness, and that's where your focus remained. Today, that same loving concern you exhibited toward earlier illnesses must be resurrected. Do not succumb to the stigma. Your addicted young person may exhibit all kinds of unhealthy traits, but you must remember that she is afflicted with a disease that has altered her mind and, in turn, her behaviors. She needs that same loving support you so expertly offered in the past. If you fail to do this, she will continue to believe she is unworthy and incapable of doing better, and she will shun accepting treatment and turning her life around.

When your child was ill, your love and concern also led you to do painful things in the name of treating the disease. You held the screaming infant while the nurse poked a needle into her arm. At home, you forced nasty-tasting medicine down your child's throat. You remained steadfast in keeping that young person in bed and indoors until her health improved, even though you thought you'd go crazy. You demonstrated your ability for self-discipline because you believed that this was in the best interest of your ill child.

The disease of addiction demands that you continue that self-discipline. You are familiar with enforcing prescribed treatment while demonstrating a proper attitude. By following therapeutically sound treatment plans, you demonstrated your care and concern. You've done it before. You've already "walked the walk." You are fully cognizant of what it takes to treat any serious disease. You have a solid record of success, so treat the disease of addiction as you treated other serious illnesses.

Thanks to the AMA's declaration, not only can you deal with addiction through a familiar means, but you have the added benefit of being able to describe the disease, a powerful tool for anyone hoping to counter addiction. Being able to describe the disease allows substance abuse counselors to develop intelligent and effective treatment plans. These descriptors also allow parents to further understand addiction and thereby enhance their ability to intelligently, skillfully, and effectively implement sound treatment.

Our first disease descriptor is the term *compulsion*. When we view the addiction as a compulsion (that "out-of-control" urge we spoke about earlier), we understand the ill person to be someone who is governed by urges. Behaviorally, compulsion is seen through inappropriate, unpredictable, excessive, and impulsive activities. An essential component of addiction, this descriptor allows parents to view those disturbing, unusual, unpredictable behaviors that they have been witnessing for what they really are—results of the addiction, not bad parenting.

The next disease descriptor, *primary*, implies that we treat addiction as the number one problem. It is and must remain the top priority in the life of the addict. By describing addiction as primary, we recognize the fact that addiction must be treated before attempting to address any other issues. This thinking is the reversal of the treatment modality commonly employed prior to 1956. Until the AMA declared alcoholism to be a disease, treatment emphasized addressing the symptoms of alcohol abuse. Treatment providers operated under the mistaken assumption that alcoholism would cease once its symptoms were addressed. Addiction was viewed as a secondary issue, and since the treatment focused on other issues, it was generally ineffective.

Today, addiction is viewed for what it is—primary. The physician knows that he must treat the disease of alcoholism before he can effectively treat alcohol-related ailments. When treating an alcoholic for gastritis, for instance, the doctor must initially concentrate his attention upon the patient's drinking. Until the drinking ceases, no long-term, effective medical intervention will be successful, no matter how skillful the doctor.

The mental health worker must also recognize the primary nature of addiction. A depressed person who chooses to self-medicate her depression with illicit drugs cannot effectively treat the depression until the use of brain-altering substances ceases. Until the depressed addict undergoes detoxification and her neurotransmitters are restored to normal functioning, it is impossible to effectively execute any treatment modality for depression. In fact, clearing the body of drugs must occur before it can be determined whether the depression is substance-induced or an ongoing, long-term mental disorder.

The primary character of addiction has wide-ranging implications for parents as well. Before parents can address social problems, physical illnesses, or possible psychological disorders, they must first address the young person's substance abuse. For instance, they cannot expect the school to effectively address failing grades until the use of drugs ceases. The doctor can't begin to cure any digestive problems until their son stops polluting his body with drugs. Parents must also realize that social interaction problems cannot be successfully addressed until drug use is treated. Unfortunately, far too many parents waste an enormous amount of money, energy, and time in fruitless attempts to "fix" other issues first.

The next descriptor focuses upon the *predictable and progressive* course a disease will follow. Each disease has a tendency to run a predictable course, something you realized when your pediatrician presented you with the expected course childhood illnesses would follow. The doctor explained the symptoms you could expect to see, pointed out anticipated indicators of the illness's advancement, and identified markers that would announce the ending of the illness. In other words, the doctor presented you with a predictable course, just as this book has introduced you to addiction's predictable and progressive course: experimental, recreational, preoccupation, powerlessness, and finally the terminal stage. Act appropriately before addiction progresses any further.

Chronic, the fourth disease descriptor, reminds us that addiction is a lifelong disease that cannot be cured—but is treatable. Some diseases are temporary, transient illnesses, while others are lifelong conditions. For instance, being sick with the flu is a temporary condition, but other diseases, such as diabetes, remain for the duration of the individual's life. These chronic diseases cannot be cured, but they can be treated and managed as long as the diseased person receives proper care and follows the treatment. As a matter of fact, individuals with chronic diseases usually live a full and valued life if they remain faithful to their prescribed treatment regimes. Unfortunately, many of those who are afflicted with a chronic illness have great difficulty accepting the never-ending nature of their illness. The prospect of having to take medication for the remainder of one's life or living within certain dietary and lifestyle parameters is often met with resistance. No one wants to spend the balance of his life encumbered by treatment, so all too often individuals with a chronic disease stop taking their medications or ignore dietary and lifestyle mandates. Noncompliance with treatment is a major concern for medical personnel.

It's also an ongoing concern for addiction workers. Like others plagued with chronic diseases, recovering addicts often minimize the importance of continuing the strategies that brought them into recovery, such as utilizing a strong support network of recovering addicts or alcoholics, attending self-help groups, working with a sponsor, and so on. Instead, an "I" centered attitude sets in, and the needed peer support, fundamental for effective recovery, is ignored. The recovering addict chooses to depend on self instead of the treatment that has a proven track record of success.

Accepting the truth about addiction means making a commitment to remain linked to recovery supports. It also means forever forgoing the lusty, drug-centered rewards of getting high. For some individuals, this is too much, so they begin denying the gravity and chronic nature of their disease, a dangerous mind-set. They rationalize and justify compromising treatment by experiencing that high "just one more time," which rarely remains at one dose. Relapse, an ever-present danger that ominously hangs over every recovering addict or alcoholic, is cunning, subtle, and influential, which is why the majority of those entering detoxification relapse within ninety days. Addiction is chronic and it must be continually viewed as such. This disease descriptor cannot be ignored or minimized, neither by parents nor those who are addicted.

The next disease descriptor, *terminal,* means that something ends, it ceases to be—it dies. Addiction is considered to be a terminal disease because it can and will claim a person's life unless it is treated. But before this occurs, any hope for a celebrated and fulfilled life will certainly be terminated. One can't continue to abuse the body and brain and expect to live a full, accomplished, successful life. Using drugs is more than a bad habit or an unacceptable lifestyle; it is a premature ending to a meaningful life.

The bumper sticker asserts that "Drugs Kill," and drugs do kill—a truth that is not limited to adult substance abusers. Many an addicted young person has been cut down by the violence associated with the drug culture, driving drunk, overdoses, and substance-induced suicide. Others waste away in institutions and jails with no purpose or hope left in their lives. Some young addicts meet a fate similar to what happened to a young, intelligent college student whose situation is all too common. Doing extremely well in school, he had a brilliant future awaiting him until one night when, at a college party, someone gave him some "bad drugs." Today he exists, unable to make important decisions for himself, but he is progressing; he is now able to function in the community but still needs regular supervision and support.

The final descriptor, *treatable,* reminds us that there is hope for an accomplished, satisfied life. While addiction can never be cured, it can be treated. And those addicts who remain faithful to their treatment can enjoy long, fulfilled lives. These recovering addicts come to realize that hope is achievable and a triumphant life is reachable, but only as long as the individual remains committed to following established treatment expectations. Treatment options are multiple and often involve combining different modalities. One treatment option, for example, would be for the individual to initiate his recovery by enrolling in an inpatient treatment program where he is detoxified and introduced to the Twelve Steps, a way to view and live his new life of sobriety. When he completes the residential program, he returns home, where his recovery is sustained by maintaining regular, consistent association with his hometown recovery community. By interacting with this community, he is able to share with others in similar circumstances, and through this supportive environment, he finds the strength, courage, and motivation needed to sustain and strengthen his recovery. By regularly attending self-help meetings, he demonstrates a personal commitment to remain clean and sober while receiving the crucial, ongoing support that is so essential for maintaining a drug-free life.

Parallel self-help group support is also needed for parents. Two such groups are Al-Anon and Nar-Anon, both of which are based upon the same Twelve Steps that AA and NA observe. These groups provide support, comradeship, encouragement, motivation, and strength to sustain parental resolve—things parents desperately need as they struggle to remain strong and focused. Disciplined love, adherence to firm guidelines, the ability to allow natural and logical consequences to occur without interference—these and other difficult yet essential strategies demand that parents be supported if they are to remain steadfast. Without the strong, sustaining support from those who have learned firsthand how to deal with an addicted loved one, parents tend to compromise treatment expectations. Over time, parents experience reduced determination manifested through such rationalizations as *It hurts to see my daughter suffer so much,* or *She is doing so well now, we can soften up a little.* Unless parents have the support of experienced, insightful parents who have "been there, done that," they will find it difficult to maintain and uphold needed treatment expectations and actions. Even with support, they may falter—but at least their chances improve when they have supportive peers.

When parents are actively involved in a parallel recovery modality, a commonality is shared. Parents not only learn to live the Twelve Steps upon which much of their young person's recovery is based, but they demonstrate a commitment to understanding and appreciating their addicted young person's situation. Seeing Mom and Dad in the "rooms"— a recovery term referring to the rooms in which Twelve Step meetings are held—the young person's recovery program cannot help but be strengthened and inspired.

Parental involvement in support groups can also accelerate a substance abuser's entrée into recovery. Through involvement in these self-help groups, parents learn tactics, techniques, maneuvers, and strategies that can hasten the day when their youthful addict will enter into treatment. Until that day occurs, participation within these groups provides parents the strength and support they need to steadfastly and meaningfully address the young person's active addiction in a sensible, effective manner.

Involvement in self-help support groups is a winning proposition. While going to meetings does consume time and energy, the payoff is vastly more beneficial than the effort expended. Thanks to the upholding assistance and camaraderie that Al-Anon and Nar-Anon offer, parental resolve to avoid reverting back to enabling and codependent behaviors is enhanced. It can also be a personally rewarding experience. Surrounded by others in like circumstances, parents find themselves welcomed and accepted without judgment or explanation. They find support and social interaction through which a meaningful life and hope for the future is restored. Being a parent of an addicted youth should not be a lonely, solitary, miserable existence. Social fulfillment and pleasure can be found and reclaimed.

Recovery is a lifelong process and requires a day-by-day commitment in which the addicted person strives to overcome the desire to get high, to yield to cravings, and to escape from the stress of life by retreating into drugs. That's why those in recovery frequently use the slogan "One day at a time." Staying clean and sober is indeed a day-by-day process. At times it is an hour-by-hour or even minute-by-minute process. Parents must also realize that they are no different. Every day will be a battle not to enable, not to prematurely yield treatment parameters and boundaries, not to weaken or compromise, and to keep codependent tendencies in check. Just as support from knowledgeable and concerned individuals is essential in sustaining the addict's recovery, so is the essential upholding support that parents receive through their self-help support groups. Without that sustenance, it is likely that parents will "relapse" into former behaviors.

Understand and appreciate the disease concept of addiction. It will give you clarity and insight into your son's or daughter's behaviors. It will also give you the insight you need to positively interact with your addicted child as well as help you to be the parent your young person so desperately needs. Ideally, understanding addiction will also motivate you to reach out and gain support from other parents in similar situations—something that is so essential for peace of mind, serenity, and restoration of your life.

CHAPTER 11

The Roles We Assume

Addiction brings havoc and turmoil to every family it touches. It spares no one. It doesn't care about age, gender, or race. It negatively affects everyone in the family. To understand its impact, let us begin with a definition of *family:* "Family is an intimately connected unit composed of changing alliances that impact each individual positively and negatively while uniting members for the purpose of presenting a favorable public image."

Within this closely knit entity, lives are enriched through shared love and concern while successes strengthen members. When, however, expected love, emotional sustenance, and reciprocal support are interrupted and family successes are replaced with failures and tribulations, each member is negatively impacted. When addiction enters the family, the addict's behaviors compel parental attention to be focused onto the addict, leaving the other family members deprived of encouragement and love. Unable to receive their individualized nurturing, the other members are obliged to find ways to protect themselves from being further emotionally wounded. Assumed roles provide this protection both internally and externally, as well as maintain the delicate equilibrium within the family.

Internal self-protection: Assumed roles shield each individual family member from the inevitable downward spiral that any serious illness within the family brings. Through these assumed roles, novel ways are found for each family member to protect himself or herself from internal emotional pain. With the assumed roles come new adaptive behaviors. A new meaning to life, coping skills, and the prevention of further emotional deterioration are some of the by-products of assumed roles.

External family protection: Publicly, the family's good name must be safeguarded. No matter how much internal deterioration the family may experience, a favorable external appearance must be maintained and protected. The assumed roles that various family members adopt provide innovative and often very effective ways to meet this expectation.

Maintaining family balance: Role assumption is underpinned by the development and adoption of rules that are unspoken but clearly understood. These rules exist to maintain some semblance of balance within the dysfunctional family unit. As you look at a sampling of these rules, you see how they are designed to avoid conflict. Some of the rules include not talking about the problem (the addict and his addiction), never confronting the ill person, never baring emotions or feelings, and never taking care of yourself, as it selfishly distracts from the welfare of the overall family. While not good for the family members' mental health, these rules do facilitate basic family functioning. They also underpin the assumption of false roles.

As these unspoken, unwritten rules take over, everyone learns to act like everything is okay. Feelings, needs, and sensitivity toward each other can no longer be safely expressed, which causes an incredible amount of harm. These rules are especially detrimental for the addict, who needs confrontation as motivation to enter treatment—but, unfortunately, the rules prohibit such confrontation, so the addict's substance abuse remains unchallenged.

With the unwritten family rules in place, assumed roles appear. There are five basic roles, none of which are static. These roles were developed by Sharon Wegscheider-Cruse. Some family members adopt a mix of roles, while others switch roles from time to time. In a small family, it is common for a member to assume more than one role, while within larger families more than one member will take on the same role. It should be stressed that the role an individual assumes is less a function of personality than it is the result of their chronological position within the family. For instance, the oldest nonaddicted sibling in the family, regardless of whatever personality she normally displays, usually assumes the Hero role, while the youngest sibling generally assumes the role of the Mascot. We will begin our discussion by first looking at the assumed role parents usually adopt.

The Enabler

There isn't a single chemically dependent person who hasn't had their addiction aided by an Enabler, a person who is emotionally attached to the addict and, out of love and concern, engages in behaviors that foster instead of confront the addiction. Enablers include such caring individuals as parents, relatives, teachers, friends, and some employers—individuals who, out of authentic concern, tend to conceal, ignore, lie, or assume responsibility for the addicted person. Parents enable their young person by excuse making, covering up, doing for, and refusing to confront. Relatives enable when they counter parental sanctions by providing support and money. Teachers enable when they overextend themselves instead of holding the substance-abusing student accountable for his actions or lack of action. Close friends enable by going out of their way to cover up or make excuses, while employers enable by intentionally ignoring behaviors and/or withholding consequences.

The addicted person takes advantage of these sincerely concerned individuals through manipulation, until an environment favorable to the continuation of drug use is developed. When, out of love, Grandpa gives his addicted granddaughter twenty dollars, the addict doesn't see this as a gesture of love, but rather as a new source of money to buy drugs, a resource she will take advantage of or manipulate as long as possible. When Mom and Dad obstruct the consequences of substance abuse by covering up, rescuing, or doing for, the addict sees this as ensuring that she doesn't have to worry about consequences that may befall her. The addict "works" or manipulates Mom and Dad by playing on their guilt and shame so the behaviors can continue.

At the top of the addict's roster of Enablers, there is the Chief Enabler, a person who is very close to the addict and engages in enabling behaviors that promote addiction. For the adult addict, it is normally the spouse, while youthful addicts often find grandparents to be excellent Chief Enablers. These individuals have a deep, authentic love for the addict, and their actions flow from this genuine love, a love that yearns to protect and help the beloved.

Enablers and Chief Enablers are unquestionably motivated by legitimate concern for the addicted person, but often this is not the only motivator. Shame and social status often serve as powerful motivators as parents attempt to protect the good name of the addicted young person, themselves, and/or the family. Fears about *What will my family/neighbors/ friends think?* force an Enabler or Chief Enabler to engage in actions that they would never have considered under normal circumstances.

Some Enablers are terrified of the negative consequences of their loved one's addictive behaviors. In what they consider to be safeguarding actions, they engage in abnormal activities that are perceived as "protecting," such as making excuses, covering up, lying, and doing for. These Enablers feel they have no other choice and justify their behaviors with rationalizations such as *If I don't do this, my daughter will go to jail/be thrown out of school/ lose her job/be harmed/have her life ruined/contract an incurable illness.*

It is a powerful mix: love, concern, social shame, and fear for a loved one's well-being. It is a mix that is strong enough to cause any adult to act irrationally by covering up, lying, rescuing, ignoring, or forcefully confronting anyone who dares to bring the addicted person's behavior into question. As this enabling behavior continues, an environment is created that not only tolerates continued substance abuse, but guarantees prolonged suffering and distress for everyone involved. Inevitably, the addict becomes less and less reliable, to which the Enabler responds by assuming additional responsibilities. Sometimes the Enabler delegates the addict's household responsibilities to other siblings, causing a whole new set of negative dynamics within the family. The Enabler, motivated by the addict's growing deterioration, attempts to further control their comings and goings—unsuccessfully. Over time, the Enabler makes decisions the addict should be making in a futile attempt to control the addict—an impossible goal.

Emotionally, the Enabler seethes with bottled-up frustration and anger, boiling just below the surface waiting to erupt on anyone nearby, which usually happens over a relatively minor incident. The Enabler's appearance and health pay the price for constantly staying on the alert. No one can sustain an intense, hypervigilant state without developing such stress-related conditions as hypertension, digestive problems, and ulcers. Depression eventually takes over, causing further deterioration. The Enabler ceases exercising and eating properly, giving rise to such self-destructive behaviors as excessive smoking, drinking, and the use of tranquilizers.

Socially, the Enabler withdraws. Preoccupied with the addict's behaviors, the Enabler has no time or inclination to interact with others. Even around the home, avoidance becomes the norm as the Enabler tires of constant quarrels and chooses to remain silent and emotionally isolated. The Enabler feels powerless, yet he continues to assume responsibility and do for the addict. Eventually, the Enabler is overwhelmed.

The Hero

Normally the oldest child, or the second in the birth order if the eldest is the addict or rejects this role, the Hero emerges as the shining light, a source of pride for the family. The Hero functions as the conscientious, dependable person both in school and at home. Externally, the Hero appears to have it all together as he steadfastly presents to the world such façades as being a top student and a polite, well-mannered, responsible young man. He fills in for his parents around the home, taking care of the younger siblings and upkeep of the house. The Hero's achievements do bring relief for the family by providing momentary self-worth. After all, who can criticize a family with a son who is responsible, well-liked, and polite?

Eventually frustration sets in for the Hero since the situation at home is not improving, despite his best efforts. The Hero asks himself, *What else can I do?* Without any alternatives, the Hero continues with his overly responsible façade. It is all he knows; yet the Hero continues to find himself in a deteriorating situation. With conditions not improving, the Hero feels inadequate and insufficient, yet he continues with his deceptive mask of responsibility, achievement, and success, hiding the anger and low self-esteem. Despite his best efforts, the family remains dysfunctional, and the Hero feels like a failure.

In addition, the Hero has no social outlets. His resolute dedication toward saving the family from further disintegration doesn't allow time or inclination for a normal social life. Alone, without any social outlets, the Hero feels overwhelmed and hopeless. Steadfastly, the Hero does the only thing he knows to do, continue his Hero image and continue to proclaim to the world, "I'm a good person, therefore my family is good."

Living the role of a Hero has long-term negative repercussions. Unable to fully fix things, the Hero comes to believe that if only he did just a little better, goal fulfillment and satisfaction could be achieved. As a result, the Hero enters adulthood believing that he can never achieve personal satisfaction unless things are done "just a little bit better." He never experiences peace of mind, nor is he able to fully engage in positive social relationships. His adult life is marked by excessive work and an inability to accept criticism or admit that he is wrong. As an adult Hero, he assumes responsibility for everyone, and even in marriage he tends to choose a spouse who is dependent and in need of "help."

All, however, is not lost. If the Hero learns to accept failure and become responsible for self, peace and serenity can be achieved. Having lived his life as a high achiever, the adult Hero will enter adulthood with practiced skills and attributes that offer the chance to be successful in whatever undertakings he chooses.

Parents, give permission for the Hero to make mistakes. Emphasize to him that none of us is perfect and it is okay to be imperfect. Stop holding the Hero to higher than necessary standards (a few "B" grades are healthy). Let the Hero know that he can't always fix things and isn't expected to fix things. Around the home, take over the tasks and responsibilities that he has assumed. Encourage him to enjoy life, develop a social life, be imperfect, make mistakes, welcome our imperfect world, have fun, and above all—be a kid again.

The Scapegoat

The Scapegoat is usually found after the Hero in the family birth order, although some first-born choose this role. Most Scapegoats tried the Hero role, but since they lacked the maturity and experience to compete with their older sibling, they surrendered that role. With the Hero earning whatever is left of parental praise and attention, the Scapegoat chooses to separate from the family, become emotionally distant, and seek companionship outside of the home. Frustrated and angry at parental neglect, her addicted sibling, and the attention-grabbing Hero, the Scapegoat learns that her anger and frustration can be discharged through highly charged, peer-centered, and trouble-making behaviors. Mom and Dad may be preoccupied with the addicted sibling, but the Scapegoat has found a way to get her needs satisfied. In very short order, the Scapegoat finds herself mired in regular acting-out behaviors. For these behaviors, the Scapegoat is punished, a form of parental attention that may not be desirable, but sure beats being ignored. Meanwhile, the family benefits by placing blame for its deteriorating situation on the Scapegoat child—thus the name *Scapegoat.*

A duality sets in. The Scapegoat doesn't like what she has become and doesn't want to keep living the role of the troublemaker, but there is seemingly no way out, so the lifestyle continues. Unless intervention occurs, the Scapegoat will grow up believing that the only way to gain attention is by acting out. Without a change in parental approach, it is possible that the Scapegoat will encounter difficulties in work, school, and relationships.

All, however, is not lost if parents show the Scapegoat she is loved and accepted by paying attention to her positive actions. It is suggested that parents of Scapegoats conscientiously provide positive rewards for acceptable behaviors. The more you consistently connect positive actions, both small and large, with rewarding consequences, the better your chances of reprogramming or "conditioning" the Scapegoat to engage in righteous behaviors. Offering the rewarding consequences of acceptance and belonging—which is all the Scapegoat wants—can bring that wayward son or daughter home, since home is now an increasingly attractive place. The process of becoming a Scapegoat did not happen overnight, and bringing her off the corner and back home will take time. But persevere, for the rewards are worth all the effort.

If the Scapegoat receives parental nurturing and support, as an adult she will acquire courage and a high level of social competency (skills she started acquiring in order to survive within her acting-out peer group). To remain an integral member of the peer group, she had to learn how to ingratiate, win over, and impress her peers, which meant she had to become highly skilled in successfully navigating challenging relationships.

Experienced in interacting with problematic people, the Scapegoat enters adulthood able to successfully interact with just about anyone.

The Lost Child

With all the chaos in the family, the next chronological child finds himself forgotten. Crowded out by the Hero's acclamation, the Scapegoat's acting out, and the addict's out-of-control behaviors, there is no room left to receive any of Mom and Dad's attention, so he retreats into his private world and becomes "lost" to the family and society.

The Lost Child is a loner who takes care of his own wants and needs. Turning inward, he finds peace in a world entirely of his creation. At a time when he should be discovering and acquiring social skills, the Lost Child exists in a world without any meaningful social relationships. Lacking social skills, he deliberately avoids social situations, and for a while he replaces social interaction with video games or toys. Over time, the Lost Child discovers that it is impossible to go through life alone, so he occasionally attempts to be social, but doesn't know how to give and take with his peers. Lacking these essential social skills, friendships become difficult to initiate and maintain, so warmth and human closeness remain foreign experiences. Loneliness and isolation become familiar and consistent companions.

Unless things change within the family, the Lost Child will become a Lost Adult who cannot communicate competently and interact confidently in the adult world. Unable to initiate and maintain significant commitments and socialize, the Lost Child is destined for a miserable adult life, substituting material objects for positive relationships and feelings. A new car, a fully loaded computer, the latest electronic gadget, or the finest stereo substitutes for companionship. Surrounded by material possessions, the adult version of the Lost Child continues to silently suffer rejection and loneliness.

If the Lost Child's parents conscientiously draw him into openness, such as spending quality, one-on-one time with him, he will emerge as an adult who is talented, creative, imaginative, and capable of being socially interactive. That creativity and highly tuned imagination, which shaped his invented world, can lead to success and personal fulfillment in many careers, but only if the Lost Child receives parental love, time, and attention.

The Mascot

This final role is generally reserved for the youngest child in the family, but youngsters of "special status," such as the only male in a family of females or a youngster with a disability, may also assume the role of a Mascot. This is the child whom the family protects from tragedies. Instead of explaining how a sibling's addiction is affecting the family, the youngster is assured that all is well, even when, instinctively, she knows that things aren't right. The family's good intentions create confusion and distrust. Knowing something is wrong, but unable to learn what is going on from those whom she should trust, the Mascot becomes confused.

Unsure of herself, the young sibling seeks to find a niche within the confusion and uncertainty created by the addicted sibling. Over time, she learns that delighting and entertaining the family can bring desired attention, so she assumes the role of the "family clown" or the "cute one." Through these behaviors, she becomes the center of attention. She has found a reliable way to gain attention, but the Mascot also becomes known for her irritating attention-seeking actions. In younger children, squirming, interrupting, and engaging in bothersome acts are common manifestations of this assumed role. The Mascot is often improperly diagnosed as hyperactive and placed on drugs. Within the school setting, she is often considered to have a learning disability and/or a short attention span.

The Mascot whose parents do not change the way they interact with her will enter adulthood as an immature, lonely, and fearful individual—characteristics that she hides behind her comic mask. No matter how often the Mascot may receive applause for her amusing cleverness, insecurity and loneliness remain. As she enters adulthood, her insecurities, which she still hides behind her comic mask and outgoing personality, hamper her ability to handle stress and lead to the development of stress-related illnesses such as ulcers. When the Mascot marries, she tends to find a spouse who has Hero attributes. Should, however, the Mascot receive meaningful help from parents, she can emerge into an adult who is well-balanced, popular, enjoys life, and is able to take care of herself while possessing an excellent sense of humor and being a pleasure to be around.

Create an environment that shows the Mascot she is accepted without resorting to the mask of humor or cuteness. By showering the Mascot with attention when she is not playing the role of the comic, parents deescalate annoying traits and in time bring the Mascot to a developmental point where she can enter adulthood as a balanced person with whom it is a delight to interact. You might want to consider giving your Mascot attention by working with her on her homework. Around the house, you can make sure that you immediately give her your approval and loving mindfulness when positive, nonclowning behaviors occur. Over and over, demonstrate to the Mascot that she is accepted, appreciated, and liked without having to put on the mask of the clown. That enjoyable but annoying Mascot needs your help if she is to ever experience proper social development, so give her that which she needs—attention and positive affirmation.

In Summary

Addiction is a family problem and requires family treatment. Nonaddicted siblings need an atmosphere where they can sort things out, gain perspective, be educated about what is going on within the family, and experience the benefits of parental love and concern. The addicted young person will have an addiction problem for the rest of her life (remember, addiction is a chronic disease), but her siblings need not spend the rest of their lives suffering the negative consequences. Intervention by parents following some of the suggestions in this chapter can go a long way toward averting an unhealthy adulthood.

In addition, you might want to turn to Alateen. Based on the Twelve Steps of AA, Alateen meetings are designed for teenagers with an addicted family member. Understanding, insight, support, and encouragement received in these groups help the nonaddicted teen to deal with the craziness that accompanies addiction in the family. Sometimes Alateen meetings are held at a site where an Al-Anon meeting is simultaneously scheduled, which allows parents to get support while their sober sons and daughters receive meaningful help. Check to see if your community has such a coordinated set of meetings.

At home, parents can do much to curtail and address the devastating impact that addiction has upon the family. Regardless of the role a son or daughter has assumed, time, attention, and one-on-one interactions can go a long way toward bringing normalcy to each sibling. You may feel burdened by the addicted sibling, you may even feel overwhelmed, but you cannot be so beleaguered that you relinquish your responsibilities toward the other children in your family.

CHAPTER 12

Becoming an Actor instead of a Reactor

Most parents of addicts and alcoholics tend to find themselves surrendering their self and independence. This surrendering is referred to as codependency and, according to Melody Beattie, whose best-selling book *Codependent No More* brought the term into prominence, a codependent is an individual "who has let another person's behavior affect him or her, and who is obsessed with controlling that person's behavior."[1]

Looking at this definition, we see two key properties of codependency:

1. The codependent permits another's behavior to influence his life; yet,

2. The codependent continues to be obsessed with attempts to control the other person.

The tendency to engage in codependent behaviors affects nearly every parent of an addicted young person. To counter this tendency, parents must understand exactly what codependency is. I am indebted to *Codependent No More*, where much of the following summarized material is found. We begin our discussion by looking at the factors that must be present for codependency to be birthed and matured.

1. *The presence of a serious illness.* Without the backdrop of a serious illness, codependency cannot develop or flourish. The development of codependency demands an environment so harshly stressed by a severe illness that it significantly alters traditional relationships within the family.

2. *The presence of unspoken rules.* As codependency develops, unspoken rules emerge, supporting the family's efforts to maintain a precarious but necessary balance. These rules manage to maintain that balance, but they also exact a tremendous emotional price on each family member. We have already briefly touched on the existence of these rules, but here are some of the more common ones: no divulging or talking about the family's "problem," no honest expression of feelings, never admit vulnerability and imperfection, you must remain "strong," taking care of yourself is viewed as "selfish" and puts you above the family's needs, do nothing that contributes to "selfish" personal growth, and don't trust anyone in the family, including yourself.

3. *Awareness that violating these rules will result in censure.* Since violation of these unwritten rules will upset the delicate family equilibrium, all family members instinctively know the importance of conscientiously adhering to them and are fully aware of the harsh censure that violating these rules will bring.

These rules are not limited to families with substance abusers, for they can be found in families plagued by other compulsive disorders involving overeating, shopping, sex, gambling, or workaholism. They can also be found in families where sexual, physical, and/or mental abuse occurs. The presence of rebellious teenagers, criminal activity, or a serious mental or physical illness within the family also opens the family toward adherence to these rules.

To help you understand codependency, here are some of the characteristics codependents often display. As these are briefly summarized, see if any of them describe you.

1. *Codependents are responsible people.* Actually, they are overly responsible. They feel responsible for everyone and believe they have to be the responsible person since everyone else is so irresponsible. They see the world as plagued by an epidemic of irresponsibility, and they have no choice but to step forward and fill the void by being continually responsible—but they will not step up and take responsibility for their own needs and lives.

2. *Codependents are very dependable people.* Actually, codependents are too dependable. You can depend upon them to do anything, except take care of themselves.

3. *Codependents are reliable cleaner-uppers.* The codependent resents people who make messes and then expect someone else to clean them up. They may resent it, but who ends up cleaning up the messes? The codependent, of course!

4. *Codependents are noted for their giving.* Codependents are well known for giving. They consistently give and give and give until they have nothing left to give themselves.

5. *Codependents are caring people.* Codependents authentically care about others, but unfortunately are so preoccupied with their mission of caring for others that they have no time left to care for themselves.

6. *Codependents are good deed doers.* Doing good deeds is their vocation in life. They are so dedicated to this calling that they will do good deeds regardless of the cost involved to themselves.

7. *Codependents are great problem solvers.* Codependents become deeply immersed in problem solving. No matter what the problem, they will respond. Just don't ask them to solve their own problems.

8. *Codependents constantly blame others.* By continually dealing with the problems created by the "irresponsibility" and "stupidity" of others, codependents blame others for everything that is wrong. Just don't expect them to blame themselves for anything.

9. *Codependents are unaware of their surroundings.* Codependents are so absorbed in the problems of others that they fail to see the big picture. With their focus exclusively on the needs and problems of others, codependents operate as if they had blinders on, their attention so narrowly focused on the perceived needs of others that they cannot appreciate or see their own needs nor can they grasp the negative impact they are having upon the situation.

10. *Codependents are martyrs.* Codependents love to play the role of martyr. It is a role for which they are perfectly suited, due to all the sacrifices they make. Unfortunately, they fail to recognize that martyrs often mess things up by getting in the way through their intrusive actions.

11. *Codependents are victims.* Codependents feel like victims, and their feelings are on target. Having spent so much of their time and energy obsessively taking care of others without setting boundaries and limits, they inevitably end up victimized.

12. *Codependents are miserable people.* Burdened as they are by the cares of others, how can codependents be anything but miserable? Yet we must never know of the codependent's misery, so feelings are submerged and covered up by façades. Do not be fooled. Whatever the disguise, underneath lies a miserable person.

13. *Codependents are resentful.* Since codependents will not hold others accountable for their actions, resentment over continued failures eventually takes over. Yet, they continue to fix things despite growing resentment.

14. *Codependents don't feel positive feelings.* Immersed by frustration, disgust, and resentment—the aftermath of being unappreciated—the codependent eventually ceases experiencing positive emotions.

15. *Codependents have poor relationships.* How can they have positive relationships when they are so busy controlling and taking care of others? Besides, they have neither the time nor the energy to

develop truly positive relationships, and if they did, their inclination to control would eventually destroy the relationship.

16. *Codependents have no energy for positive endeavors.* Whatever energy a codependent may have, it is dedicated toward worrying about others, helping them, and figuring out how to save them by controlling them. Expending so much energy in such futile activities leaves no energy for pursuits that are positive and beneficial to self.

17. *Codependents can't say no.* The only time codependents will ever say no is when you offer them a chance to enjoy life, to have fun.

18. *Codependents don't think clearly.* If they did think clearly, they would have to acknowledge the futility of their behaviors and, in turn, begin to make changes. As long as they remain unclear in their thinking, they allow themselves to continue their codependent lifestyle and "reach out" to others—the sole purpose of their lives.

Are you a codependent?

Long-Term Effects of Codependency

Those who are codependent find their life beset by unwelcome problems. Some of the more common problems are the following:

1. *Development of addictive behaviors.* Overwhelmed by tormenting feelings and emotions, the codependent attempts to ignore, cover up, and hide his pain through the use of tranquilizers, drinking, gambling, eating, shopping, and other compulsive acts—a pattern that gives rise to addictions.

2. *Development of depression.* To exist as a codependent is to live life in such a constant state of tension and failure that, at some point, hopelessness and helplessness set in—indisputable signs of depression.

3. *Increased health problems.* Existing in a state marked by constant stress, ailments such as headaches, ulcers, asthma,

and hypertension will inevitably develop. No one can live as a codependent and remain healthy.

4. *Low self-esteem.* Because the codependent is so intimately involved in the life of the addict, all of the addict's multiple failures are viewed by the codependent as his failings. Loss of self-esteem must occur for anyone who has allowed self to be defined in terms of a failure-prone person.

5. *Numbing of feelings.* None of us is able to sustain a constant barrage of painful events, misery, and distress without eventually shutting down and becoming emotionally numb.

Overcoming Codependency

Below are four suggestions for overcoming codependency: exercise detachment, become now-centered, become reality-centered, and improve your attitude and approach. We will now explore these four suggestions.

Exercise Detachment

For our purposes, the term *detachment* means disengaging self from the insanity that the addicted person generates. Basically, this is allowing the addicted person to take full responsibility for the consequences of her behaviors while the recovering codependent takes responsibility for what he truly is responsible for—self. Detachment happens when you don't rush to the police station to post bail or otherwise rescue your daughter after she is busted for possession of drugs. Detachment is when you let her stay in jail so she can experience the full consequences of her actions. Detachment is when you take your daughter to a residential drug rehab program and refuse to yield to her pleas and your heartache. Detachment is when you ignore that powerful parental inclination to rescue, enable, or "help" by compromising your integrity, and instead allow unwelcome consequences to occur.

Detachment was demonstrated in the past when you put your emotions on hold while exercising loving care and faithfully following medical directives—a skill that must be resurrected if you intend to effectively treat the disease of addiction.

Become detached. Stop absorbing and owning the consequences that drug use brings. Step back and allow consequences to fall where they belong—upon the addict's shoulders. Be able to authentically assist your addicted child by acting from a perspective that is rational, realistic, and unclouded by harmful emotions such as crippling guilt.

Become Now-Centered

Being *now-centered* means focusing on the unfolding of your day instead of attempting to control the unfolding of someone else's day. Now-centered parents recognize they cannot manage, plan, and arrange the day-to-day life of others. Unlike codependent parents, now-centered parents focus on themselves and let others, including their addicted son or daughter, deal with their own day. Now-centered parents cease trying to manipulate and control their young person's daily life by focusing on their own lives and savoring the joys their day brings.

Being now-centered also keeps parents from focusing on the past. Now-centered parents don't waste time and energy on something they can't change—the past. Instead, they leave their guilt-ridden yesterdays behind by living today as it unfolds. Now-centered individuals savor the day's adventures and delights. Now-centered parents take time to "smell the roses" and enjoy the large and small blessings that each day offers, something that they lost when addiction, codependency, and feelings of guilt overwhelmed them.

If you truly want to help your addicted young person, begin living your today for all it has to offer. When your focus is centered on your today, you are no longer controlled by guilt over the past and can't be manipulated or controlled by your young person's dramatization and resurrection of the past. No longer subject to the past, you cease being controlled by real and imagined guilt.

Become Reality-Centered

Being *reality-centered* means accepting circumstances for what they truly are. Reality-centered parents admit that their young person is addicted to brain-altering substances and they can't "make" him stop using drugs. Reality-centered parents acknowledge that the cessation of drug use is something only the substance abuser can decide to do. Since reality-centered parents no longer cling to false hopes, they are free from the erroneous proprietorship that occurs when parents "own" the young person's drug-centered insanity. Reality-centered parents are now free to live life again.

Becoming a reality-centered parent is a major accomplishment for any parent of an addict. It requires faith in a higher power as well as the ability to step back and allow the addict to experience the consequences of his addiction, character traits that run directly against the parental instinct to take care of, control, and protect. When parents finally operate from a reality-centered mind-set, miracles happen. With the parent no longer interfering in the life of the addict, the possibility that the addict will enter treatment increases significantly, since he must now deal with the consequences of his drug-centered behaviors without any hope of being "saved," "rescued," or "bailed out" by codependent parents.

Improve Your Attitude and Approach

If you wish to overcome your codependency, an attitudinal change must also occur, which requires trying the following:

Cease Taking Things Personally

Your child's addiction belongs to her—not you. She could have chosen to live a clean and sober life, like many of her peers in similar circumstances. She could have chosen to follow your guidance, principles, and norms—but she didn't choose any of these salutary options. Instead, she chose to use and abuse brain-altering substances, even though she knew of your opposition to such behavior. Her decision to disregard your teachings and wishes was most likely influenced by powerful peer pressures, but it was still a free-will choice that she and she alone must own. Whatever the circumstances, she made an independent choice. At no time did you tie her down or force drugs into her. Her addiction march began with, was strengthened through, and sustained by choices she made.

Even if you agree with this view, you may still feel accountable as you inventory your perceived and real parental failings. If this is you, realize that no matter how lousy, mediocre, or competent you rate your parenting, it was ultimately your young person's choice to use drugs. Unfortunately, many parents cannot get beyond guilt's hold, and they persist in owning the young person's addiction while their young person, suffering from the "blaming disease" of addiction, regularly bombards them with accusations of being "the problem" or "the reason" for her condition. Coupled with our culture's whispered and not-so-silent criticism of parents of addicts, parents can't help but to see themselves as failures, despite the fact that it was ultimately the young person's decision to use drugs.

If you are assailed by guilt-laden messages, practice the suggestions offered in this chapter: become detached, uphold a now-centered attitude, and maintain a reality-centered perspective. Parents who follow these suggestions will remain balanced and objective, recognizing those accusations for what they are—allegations from a brain altered by chemicals and ill with the "blaming disease" of addiction.

Don't Let Others "Push Your Buttons"

You are familiar with this saying. By pushing a button on your coffee maker, you initiate a predictable, anticipated activity, and emotionally we are not much different from an automated electronic device. We all have certain sensitivity points, "buttons" if you will, which when pushed will bring about an expected response. Over the years, your young person has learned not only what your buttons are, but also what behaviors could be expected whenever one of your buttons is pushed.

If you are going to effectively deal with your substance abusing young person, you will have to learn how to control those accustomed responses each time one of your buttons is pushed. You will have to cease automatically *reacting* and instead act in a strategically sound manner. As you come to master the art of *acting* instead of *reacting*, you will discover that not only will you substantially decrease your tendency to engage in codependent behaviors, but you will be able to maintain control whenever one of those buttons is pushed.

Let's say Mom, whom we will call Betty, caught her daughter using the phone after being told not to. From past history, Betty's daughter knows that by pushing the button labeled "disregarding rules," her mother will react in predictable ways: lecturing, ranting, and shouting threats that she most likely will not follow through on. While her daughter doesn't appreciate these expected behaviors, she realizes that they are a small but accustomed price to pay for the drugs she has just located over the phone. By reacting to her daughter's actions with ineffectual, predictable behaviors, Betty hasn't done anything meaningful to address her daughter's behavior.

Now imagine how effective it would be if Betty acted in a composed, positive, effective manner, "I FEEL very upset ABOUT your refusal to comply with my request to not use the phone BECAUSE it shows a lack of respect. I have no choice but to keep your cell phone." (See chapter 15 for more about using this format when interacting with your young person.)

What an effective act! Instead of feeding into another infamous mother-daughter conflict and reacting with predictable and accustomed behaviors, Betty has maintained control. She avoided having her button pushed by acting in a manner in which the emphasis remains upon her daughter's behavior. By not erupting into one of her expected, irrational, emotional, reactive responses, Betty chose instead to use assertive communication tactics. Betty prevented her daughter from engaging in "blaming disease" rationalizations such as *No wonder I get high. There is no way I can deal with my mom's screaming and shouting unless I'm high.* Due to Betty's action, such rationalizations lose credibility, and her daughter is forced to take responsibility for her behavior, which she cannot deflect onto her mother.

What are your buttons? How can you *act* instead of *react* when those buttons are pushed?

Maintain Your Comfort Level

Retaining control when substance-induced insanity attacks you requires that you maintain your comfort level. If you are ill at ease, if you are uncomfortable, then you will do and say things you shouldn't. Ill at ease, you are vulnerable to the various manipulations and machinations your addicted young person practices. Ill at ease, you are emotionally troubled, and your discomfort will be obvious. Uncomfortable, you become confused, and when you interact you will operate without a firm, sensible, objective plan of action. You will *react.*

When your young person acts out, delay responding to him until you have achieved a safe comfort level. Saying and doing as little as possible is a form of acting. Being silent is an extremely effective tactic that more of us should use. Silence allows you the space to compose yourself and thereby retain control. Silence allows for a quiet "time-out" respite that can provide you the opportunity to calm down and analyze what is really occurring so you develop a sensible plan of action. It also helps you control the emotional turmoil seething within you.

There is nothing wrong with taking a few moments to calm down, evaluate the situation, and take care of yourself. A solitary walk around the block to clear your head and calm your emotions can bring many benefits. Retreating to your porch, bedroom, or backyard, where you can quietly collect your thoughts, is a much more beneficial action than emotionally, impulsively, angrily reacting. You might want to take a page out of your addicted offspring's repertoire of drug-centered behaviors and retreat to the bathroom, where privacy is assured. Only instead of getting high in the bathroom, you use your isolation to regain your composure and evaluate your options so that you can determine the best course of action. A few minutes acting by retreating to a quiet place, composing yourself, and developing a sensible, strategic plan of action is so much more effective than time spent reacting in an emotionally charged way.

Resurrect Those Activities That Once Brought You Pleasure

Maintaining a proper attitude when dealing with a substance-abusing young person cannot occur unless you live a satisfying life. Living with an addicted young person is traumatic, distressing, and agonizing—but it should not keep you from enjoying life. You don't have to be miserable just because your kid is addicted. You can and should take time out to enjoy life. When parents begin enjoying and savoring life by engaging in activities they enjoy, their attitudes and approaches can only improve. So rediscover those personally pleasing activities that once made your life so enjoyable. Ask yourself, *What things brought me pleasure in my B.C. (before children) days? What is holding me back from enjoying them again? Why don't I restart them now?*

You might want to consider initiating an exercise program or setting aside an evening each week for you and your spouse to spend together. You could revisit those activities that brought both of you so much pleasure and enjoyment. Consider taking time to return to those hobbies and activities that you once enjoyed or to reconnect with old friends. Overcoming codependency need not be a miserable experience.

When you begin to enjoy life again, you will be surprised at how quickly such acts impact your addicted young person. What better motivation to seek recovery from drugs than to realize that your Enablers have abandoned their codependent ways and are again enjoying life? Mom and Dad are *acting,* not *reacting!* They are enjoying life! What a great way to motivate someone to consider entering treatment—Mom and Dad enjoying life while the addicted offspring suffers in his or her addiction, wishing for a way out.

Admit Your Powerlessness

You cannot heal yourself from the harmful effects of codependency, nor can you effectively parent your addicted kid, until you admit that you are powerless to stop her drug use. Whether your son or daughter is in active addiction or recovering from addiction, admitting your powerlessness is a necessary early action step. Acknowledging that drugs powerfully control an addict is the first step in the Twelve Step program of NA and AA. Other self-help support groups, such as Co-Dependents Anonymous (CoDA), have adopted these same Twelve Steps, which begin, "We admitted that we were powerless over . . ." The placement of these words at the beginning is not accidental. It is an affirmation of the fact that before any recovery occurs, an authentic admission of one's powerlessness must take place.

Admitting to powerlessness is more than an intellectual acknowledgment of your young person's use of drugs. Circumstances and events have most likely led you to intellectually acknowledge the presence of addiction within your family, but this doesn't necessarily mean that you are fully admitting powerlessness. You may have intellectually admitted to your young person's drug use, but emotionally, do you still develop schemes designed to end drug use through manipulation and by retaining control of the addicted young person? Or are you embracing rationalizations, intellectualizations, minimizations, and excuse making—all ways we try to retain our power, authority, and control? Removal of these harmful tendencies must occur if there is to be a full admission of your powerlessness over drugs.

To admit that you are powerless is a terrifying act that becomes even more daunting when you realize with horror that anyone addicted to brain-altering substances is basically an irresponsible person and is predisposed to act in a compulsive, impulsive, dangerous, even fatal manner. It is an *act,* made even more gutsy when you realize that there is no guarantee that drug use will cease, nor is there any assurance that a devastating, possibly fatal, drug-centered event will not occur.

It is also an act that recognizes and appreciates the fact that you must cease your useless enabling and codependency, which you may do in the name of safekeeping, but actually produces nothing positive. Admitting that you are powerless is a truly frightening act since the progressive nature of addiction may eventually lead to a state in which your young person, worn down and pillaged by brain-altering substances, finally loses everything—possibly even her life. Admitting to powerlessness is an act that acknowledges the truth about addiction and your proper role in addressing it.

You love your child, drugs and all. It is a love that cries out and yearns to reach out and rescue her from the clutches of addiction. Unfortunately, the nature of addiction limits what your love can do because you are powerless over the command addiction holds. Yet all is not lost. There are things you can do. You can, for instance, allow the natural and logical consequences of addiction to flow unimpeded. Should your child persist in running away, you have the power to go to court, try to have the judge declare her "out of control," and place her in one of the state's programs and facilities (section 3 will tell you how this process works). You can accept your powerlessness by allowing the juvenile authorities to deal with your out-of-control, substance-abusing young person. If the police find your runaway daughter with drugs on her, you can acknowledge your powerlessness by letting her experience the logical consequences of her action by remaining in detention on drug possession charges, and by shunning the inclination to hire an expensive lawyer. You keep your powerlessness in the forefront when your young person returns home from a drug rehab program and you steadfastly maintain treatment parameters and consequences, both negative and positive. You acknowledge your powerlessness when you enforce treatment plan consequences because she violated treatment plan expectations. You show you accept your powerlessness whenever you allow your addicted young person to experience the full force of the consequences of drug use.

Get Support for Yourself

Having the opportunity to process events and feelings with a trained therapist or counselor can be a tremendous blessing for the troubled parent. Getting help from a professional who offers group, individual, or family therapy is one of the most beneficial things you can do for yourself, for your family, and for the addicted young person. You, however, are urged to carefully screen potential therapists and counselors in order to ensure they are familiar with both codependency and addiction. Not every professional is well practiced in these areas, and the professional's level of expertise will greatly impact the quality of treatment your family receives.

You are also strongly encouraged to consider the world of self-help groups. These groups serve as excellent supplements to the professional help therapists and counselors offer. For many parents, these groups provide sufficient support in and of themselves. They are less expensive than professional help (no fees), and they provide the important benefit of offering relevant support anytime that it is needed. For those who have strong codependent tendencies, Co-Dependents Anonymous offers excellent support. For a listing of CoDA groups in your area, look in your phone directory for "Co-Dependents Anonymous." For more information and a listing of local meetings, go to www.coda.org and click on "Find a Meeting."

If you are someone who grew up in an alcoholic family, you most likely have codependency issues. If this is your story, you are encouraged to seek out Adult Children Anonymous or Adult Children of Alcoholics. These groups should be listed in your phone book or in your local newspaper's community events calendar. If your local resources fail you, request a meeting location list from www.adultchildren.org.

Nar-Anon and Al-Anon are two other excellent resources for those with addicted loved ones. The focus of Nar-Anon is on those whose loved ones are addicted to drugs, while Al-Anon focuses on alcohol. Since both are based on the same Twelve Steps, you could access either organization. These organizations should be listed in the front of your local phone book, in your community newspaper's events calendar, or on the Internet—go to www.al-anon.alateen.org or www.nar-anon.org to find meetings in your area. You can also write directly to Al-Anon:

Al-Anon Family Group Headquarters
1600 Corporate Landing Pkwy
Virginia Beach, VA 23454

This address is a worldwide clearinghouse for Al-Anon families and, if you ask, you will receive a list of local meeting locations. You can also correspond with them regarding any special problems you may have. If you call your local Al-Anon or Nar-Anon, remember that the people answering the local Al-Anon and Nar-Anon phones are volunteers, so the number may not be staffed full time. Leave your phone number, and you will receive a return call. Most volunteers use their home phone number as the contact number.

The beauty of being involved in these self-help groups is that you get to interact with others in similar situations, and through these interchanges, you learn how they handle addiction within their families. You also have the opportunity to share your experiences and feelings with those who have personal expertise in dealing with the pain and misery of addiction and codependency. Talking with these experienced individuals about what you are going through can be quite advantageous and, given the personal history of individuals within these groups, you need not feel uncomfortable interacting with them. You will quickly discover that the nightmares of your life are most likely mild in comparison to what others in these self-help groups have endured.

Some people fear that the people in these groups might be judgmental, but this is not the case. Rather, you will find participants in these support groups to be warm, open, and inviting. How can they be otherwise, having personally experienced the powerlessness and insanity of addiction? Give yourself a break and try these groups. See if you don't also experience the warmth, camaraderie, and support that only similarly situated individuals can provide. Unfortunately, many people reject this invaluable help with excuses such as "I don't want to open up to strangers" (you don't have to); "I don't want to have my family's business all over town" (these groups honor anonymity, and you are encouraged to share only what you are comfortable revealing); or "I don't feel like spending an hour listening to someone talk about their tale of personal woe" (inspiration, support, and hope predominate in these groups). Give yourself a break and begin to network with self-help groups. You shouldn't be without meaningful support.

Do not judge these groups with your first encounter. Rather, try different groups until you locate one you are comfortable with. My own first Al-Anon meeting was a disaster. Held in the basement of a church, it could have been mistaken for the church's sewing circle. The group consisted mostly of women who were older than I. That group may have been relevant for those ladies, but I couldn't relate—and I didn't want to, either. Unfamiliar with the benefits that Al-Anon could offer, I saw Al-Anon as an inconvenience my young person's treatment program was forcing upon me. It should also be said, in all fairness, that I hate having people force things upon me (such as attending meetings), so I was looking for an excuse to avoid future meetings. The "sewing circle" gave me a great excuse to avoid Al-Anon, but the treatment program insisted I attend Al-Anon meetings, so I tried other groups. In short order, I found a group that was relevant and comfortable for me.

I got connected, and once that happened, attending Al-Anon no longer was something being forced upon me, but rather it became an activity that I looked forward to. As my appreciation and acceptance of Al-Anon grew, it became the centerpiece of my recovery from the craziness that addiction had brought into my life. Through Al-Anon, I discovered support and gained needed insight into not only how to deal with my addicted offspring, but how to regain my own independence. I even found a racquetball partner, and together we vented our frustration on that little, hard rubber ball. I became involved in various Al-Anon activities and gained many friendships that were deep and genuine. My Al-Anon group joined with local AA groups to throw some of the most enjoyable New Year's Eve parties I have ever attended. Through Al-Anon, I found unconditional love and constant support, as well as many opportunities to socialize.

In Summary

It is possible to recapture and regain control over your life. When you begin acting in your best interest instead of reacting, codependency will be replaced by independence and freedom from the insanity your substance-abusing young person has wrought. Defeating the insanity of addiction and its expected aftereffect—codependency—is possible, but this will happen only when you make the decision to *act* by taking charge of your life and cease *reacting*.

What is your decision? Will you act by working to overcome codependency by following the suggestions in this chapter? Will you become detached, now-centered, and reality-centered, and improve your attitude and approach through the suggestions offered? Your son's or daughter's life could very well hinge on your response!

CHAPTER 13

The Causes of Addiction

Now that you understand the fundamentals of what it means to be addicted to brain-altering substances and the impact that addiction has on everyone in the family, it is time to focus on the main factors that lead to addiction. As we begin this exploration, it must be stressed that there is no single, universally acknowledged causative factor that explains the development of addiction. Without an all-embracing theory for drug use, it's important to examine the main causes. The secondary goal of this exploration is to provide parents who remain crippled by guilt another opportunity to further discern their true role in the development of addiction and hopefully diminish their guilt.

Genetic Predisposition

The first causative explanation for the development of addiction, genetic predisposition, states that a genetic trait exists that makes certain individuals predisposed to succumb to addictive behaviors. This explanation is akin to the genetic link to various diseases such as cancer and heart problems. Proponents cite numerous studies that demonstrate the presence of this inherited trait, and while these scholarly reports are interesting and well worth your time to study, you might want to consider a more personal form of research. Create a family tree and then highlight family members known to have problems with alcohol, drugs, gambling, and other compulsive disorders. A pattern, if it exists, will become clear through this exercise.

If you discover a genetic predisposition within your family, please do not yield to pessimism. Predisposition isn't predetermination. Your family tree may indicate the presence of addiction, but it also shows that not all family members are addicted. Having the trait in your family doesn't mean all your offspring are destined to be addicted, but it should motivate you to see this as a wake-up call. You should, for instance, begin making your children aware of the presence of this genetic vulnerability, which personalizes the dangers of experimenting with brain-altering substances. As you share this information, take care to explain that, unlike many of their peers who may have a different genetic orientation, your children's genetic predisposition can easily "hook" them into a life controlled by drugs. Be sure to emphasize the danger of an "I can take it or leave it" attitude. Of course, educating your youngsters about genetic predisposition doesn't guarantee that your children will abstain whenever they encounter brain-altering substances, but it does serve as a powerful tool in your preventive arsenal.

The need to educate and warn your family of a possible genetic predisposition also requires parents to critically review their own lifestyles. What is the model that you present? To warn your offspring of a genetic predisposition while drinking in front of them, abusing prescription medications, or smoking marijuana not only delivers a contradictory message, but it negates a powerful, highly personalized message.

Acceptance of genetic predisposition as a causative factor can bring some degree of solace, as it directly confronts the commonly held, yet very erroneous, assumption that addicted youth are the result of faulty parenting. By viewing an offspring's addiction as genetically rooted, parents can approach their young person's addiction without the burden of stigma-induced guilt.

Viewing genetic predisposition as a causative factor also has a positive impact on the youthful addict. Torn by guilt over numerous offenses committed in his pursuit of drugs, realization that his actions were, at least in part, the result of a genetic predisposition can go a long way toward lessening that guilt. This is not to make excuses for the addict or exonerate his actions. Rather, it is an acknowledgment of a highly regarded causative factor that helps the addict more accurately view his addiction, and thereby diminish his inhibiting guilt—and with diminished guilt comes the possibility of a greater readiness to get help.

Conditioning

The second causative factor, conditioning, is based on the works of behavioral theorists such as Ivan Pavlov, who observed that behavior could be adjusted by connecting a specific stimulus with a rewarding or punishing outcome. Pavlov found that when a stimulus is associated with a rewarding outcome, the subject will choose the pleasure-producing stimulus and avoid the stimulus associated with pain. As the subject continues selecting the rewarding stimulus, the subject becomes *conditioned* or, to use a modern technological word, *programmed* to choose the stimulus associated with a rewarding outcome. Over time, the subject becomes so conditioned that whenever the reward-producing stimulus is presented, the subject will with minimal, if any, reflection seek out the rewarding stimulus.

Conditioning has everything to do with the pleasurable, highly rewarding, euphoric state that we refer to as the "high." Your emerging adult experienced the pleasurable results of the stimulus (drugs), savored its gratifying, rewarding outcome (the high), and repeatedly sought out the reward-producing stimulus (drugs). That lusty, intense, drug-induced high compelled the individual to repetitively consume the stimulus, which over time created a programmed or conditioned response to use the stimulus whenever it is presented.

In chapter 4, the reader was introduced to the limbic system—the unconscious, emotional part of the brain, its pleasure system. With each pleasurable experience, the limbic system becomes more and more programmed to respond to cues offering potentially pleasurable experiences. The frontal lobe—the seat of reasoning, judgment, and intellect—attempts to control or modify the unconscious limbic system. When drugs are involved, the frontal lobe becomes handicapped by damage from drugs. This makes the limbic system more likely to override the damaged frontal lobe and the programmed response to use drugs more likely to occur.

With regular stimulus satisfaction through the limbic system, there naturally follows a negation of social taboos, moral teachings, family values, and anything else that stands in the way of accessing the pleasure-producing stimulus. Social and moral standards, as well as conformity to family values, become less and less relevant to a mind that has been conditioned, thanks to a strengthened limbic system and a damaged frontal lobe.

Parents must realize that parental teaching and training cannot begin to compete with the seductive allure of the substance-induced high. The power of a drug-induced high should never be underestimated or minimized, and to expect parental values, training, and influence, as well as ethics and morals, to successfully compete with the magnetism of a substance-induced high is a senseless and preposterous notion. As conditioning takes hold, those commendable personal characteristics, which parents diligently instilled, are thrust into the hidden recesses of an altered brain (think drug-damaged frontal lobe) that is now focused on habitually seeking out the stimulus (drugs) and experiencing its reward (the high), regardless of the behaviors demanded.

Eventually, nothing matters but stimulus satisfaction, which is pursued impulsively and compulsively. The strength of conditioning becomes so powerful that the pursuit and consumption of the stimulus becomes all-consuming. Lying, cheating, stealing, engaging in antisocial behaviors, and any other actions that ensure stimulus satisfaction are used. Stealing from parents, changing friends to drug-using peers, seeking out drug-centered activities, running away, skipping school—these are just a few examples of the behaviors the conditioned brain sanctions so that it can achieve stimulus satisfaction. Such is the power of conditioning.

Psychologically Induced Use

The next hypothesis maintains that addiction is a direct response to psychological trauma, which often has its roots in early life events. Addiction is often referred to as a *disease of the feelings* because users of brain-altering substances consume drugs to avoid mental and/or physical distress. Feeling bad, suffering from unresolved abuse or a history of neglect or abandonment? Having trouble coping with today's stressors? The disease of the feelings tells the addict that he can cope by turning to brain-altering substances. The individual comes to depend on drugs to deal with emotional turmoil, and with this comes an increase in tolerance, which results in drugs being used in increasing amounts and more frequently.

We are all exposed to various traumas, and the innocence of childhood does not immunize anyone from being traumatized. The death of a significant person in a child's life can generate substantial emotional turmoil and leave the child emotionally wounded with feelings of abandonment and loneliness. Abuse, regardless of whether it is physical, sexual, or mental (verbal), profoundly traumatizes. Parental blunders, both in the form of omissions and commissions, leave the individual hurt, troubled, and emotionally scarred. As the young person journeys from childhood to adulthood, these traumas demand notice and resolution. Some adolescents reach out to a caring and supportive adult, but others don't—and these youth flounder, unable to address their issues. For these youth, brain-altering substances offer an effortless and reliable way to submerge the pain, hurt, and anguish of earlier trauma(s), albeit temporarily. This prevents the difficult task of learning social coping skills from occurring, since the addict chooses the easy, painless escape that drugs offer.

The psychologically induced hypothesis has the potential to intensify the crippling effects of guilt for parents. When they view their actions as having adversely affected an offspring, and perhaps causing him to turn to drugs to cover up parental-induced pain, they feel a sense of responsibility. Should this be your situation, take time out for some rational introspection. Understand and accept the fact that, from time to time, all of us make mistakes. Realize that none of us is perfect and each of us occasionally does things that, with the advantage of hindsight, we recognize weren't in a person's best interest, even though the actions were made with the best of intentions and may have been conscientiously processed. Being a parent doesn't earn anyone immunity from making unhealthy decisions. You may, for instance, have unknowingly chosen sitters who you later discovered were abusive, or you may have inadvertently placed your children in neighborhoods that, over time, proved to be damaging to them. These were apparently good decisions that produced unforeseen negative consequences.

For some parents, decisions may have been made hastily, in a moment of anger or during periods of emotional turmoil. For other parents, societal, environmental, physical, and mental pressures created the need to act without proper forethought. Certain parents possessed personality traits that led them to become easily frustrated, angry, upset, or prone to other impulsive reactions. Some parents became addicted to drugs, alcohol, gambling, or other behaviors that resulted in significant emotional loss and neglect for their children. Others, desiring to provide only the best for their sons and daughters, become so caught up in their careers that they became workaholics and left the child's nurturing needs unmet.

Sometimes children are hurt because families are overtaken by circumstances beyond their control. From time to time, all families are affected by situations that are unanticipated and over which they have little or no control. Divorce, an unexpected job loss, job transfers, recessions, requiring your youngster to be a latchkey child, downsizing, increased violence perpetuated upon our youth— these and other modern-day conditions are so commonplace that it is not unusual for youth to be polluted with emotional wounds. In addition, some families are faced with a mental illness such as depression, while others are afflicted with a major physical illness. As we have seen, havoc is created with the introduction of any serious illness within even the best of families, resulting in the eradication of normal, healthy family dynamics. In these homes, the warmth, support, and nurturing that all children are entitled to and need are lost. For youth from these families, psychological distress is to be expected, and many not only assume foreign roles but also turn to drugs as a quick and easy escape from the chaos and emotional pain generated through serious family illnesses or crises.

If your young person is using drugs, you very well may feel culpable. You see yourself as having failed your youngster and hold yourself responsible (at least partly) for her addiction to brain-altering substances. If this describes your state of mind, get some perspective by realizing you have one of two choices: You can forgive yourself, thereby allowing you to operate as a parent who is liberated from guilt, or you can permit guilt and regret to overwhelm you, making you unable to effectively address your young person's addiction. Will you choose self-forgiveness and release yourself from guilt and the powerlessness it brings, or will you choose to wallow in self-flagellation and the impotence that brings? Will you choose reliving mistakes from the past and thereby rendering yourself ineffectual as a parent, or will you choose to leave the past behind by forgiving yourself so you can again be the effective parent your young person so desperately needs? I hope you will choose forgiveness.

Experience the freedom of self-forgiveness. Accept and embrace your true role in addiction's development, and then sincerely forgive yourself for your faults and mistakes. Acknowledge that whatever you may have done is part of your past and not your present. Realize that it makes no sense to burden yourself today with the "sins" of the past. Recognize that you must release guilt's burden. Most religions present God as merciful and forgiving, and if you are a believer, seek his merciful forgiveness. Be humble and acknowledge that you are not perfect as you would like to be. Release your pride so that you can enjoy true peace of mind. Forgive yourself so you can honestly say to your addicted son or daughter, "I may not have been the greatest parent, but I've forgiven myself and I ask your forgiveness. And now that I've forgiven myself, I am prepared to be the parent you need."

Societal Pressures

Another factor to take into account when considering causes for substance abuse is the impact that our society has upon today's youth. Society sanctions the use of brain-altering substances in very powerful yet subtle ways, such as with its promotion of instant gratification, a mind-set that characterizes today's youth. Growing up in a culture of microwave dinners, instant potatoes, and high-speed Internet, our youth believe that everything can be received immediately, an attitude validated through marketing strategies such as "Charge now and pay later." Our youth are told that instant relief from pain and discomfort is not only worthy and desirable, but something to be actively sought. Barraged by TV ads that tell us that if we are feeling ill, are in pain, or have a headache, all we have to do is pop a pill for instant relief, our youth come to believe that instant relief is the norm, the expected. Growing up in such an environment of instant gratification, is it any wonder that our youth adopt an instant-relief, pill-popping mind-set that easily transitions from over-the-counter, rapid-acting remedies to illicit brain-altering substances?

Our society also encourages the use of brain-altering substances by connecting the use of alcohol with fun. Watch advertisements for beer on television, and you can't miss the unashamed message being promoted: Use this brain-altering substance, and you'll have fun. Beer companies have successfully indoctrinated our youth, as demonstrated by the all-too-common high school and college parties where bingeing and heavy drinking frequently occur. You might want to review the statistics about alcohol abuse presented in the introduction to this book. But this isn't enough. The entertainment industry has also been offering music that brazenly promotes and glorifies drug use as acceptable and cool. Take time to listen to the lyrics that your young person absorbs daily, and you will come to realize that within the noise assaulting your young person, there are messages being conveyed that skillfully validate drug use and counter the values you instilled in him.

When your young person walks out your front door, she is entering a world that offers guitar-playing junkies as role models, equates the use of brain-altering substances with fun, encourages immediate self-gratification, and promotes instant relief from whatever is painful or troublesome. How can the values, training, and morals that parents instilled compete with this omnipresent societal propaganda? Operating within such an environment, the adolescent peer culture finds its cues. If instant gratification and rapid cures are okay, why shouldn't I seek instant relief? If having a good time and alcohol are linked together in the adult society, why shouldn't I imitate adults and have fun with alcohol? If musical idols use drugs, why shouldn't I follow their lead?

The peer culture, which gets validity for its values from the larger society, directly influences what your adolescent chooses to make a part of her life. If your teen wants to be accepted (and all teens do), conformity to the peer group's standards is imperative. The types of clothing worn, the terminology used, and the norms embraced are all determined by what the peer group dictates. Visit any middle or high school and study the social scene, the culture, and the many cliques. You will see powerful testimonies of the power of the peer group and the high level of group conformity it demands. Unfortunately, not all teens find acceptance in the more desirable peer groups. For the teen who is rejected by the preferred cliques, there is always the clique of last resort, the one that is always willing to accept one more person—that drug-using crew whose only criteria for admittance is a willingness to use brain-altering substances.

Many a journey down addiction's progressive pathway began only after being rejected by the "better" social groups. The homely girl finds acceptance in the drug-using crowd, as does the awkward, uncoordinated boy. The student with a learning disability is able to enjoy acceptance, as is the young person who is too insecure to be comfortable with any other group. The drug-using group does not care what kind of grades you earn or how ill-favored your features or attributes are. If you are willing to use drugs, you are welcome. Want to belong but can't find a group who will accept you? Turn to the clique that is ready and willing to embrace one more outcast soul, the drug-using crew who, in consort with society at large, provides a milieu that sanctions and encourages the use of brain-altering substances.

Despite the impact of societal pressures, all too many parents ignore the role society plays in initiating and fostering addiction. Instead of looking at the societal factors that contributed to an offspring's substance use, these parents turn inward and ask those troubling questions, *What did I do wrong? How did I fail?*

Look around your world and ask yourself, *What did society do wrong to my kid? How did society fail my kid?*

An Eclectic Approach

While there is no single causative factor by which addiction can be explained, I hope these factors have shed some light on your particular situation. Maybe there exists a genetic predisposition toward addiction within your family. Maybe your child developed a conditioned response that led to addiction. Maybe your kid was emotionally distressed by events in her life and discovered brain-altering substances helped in coping with the pain and discomfort. Maybe she succumbed to societal pressures. Maybe a combination of two or more causes contributed to your young person's addiction. An eclectic approach, which combines various theories to explain your child's addiction, could very well be the answer to the guilt-ridden query, *What did I do wrong? How did I fail?*

No two addicts are the same. No two people follow the same pathway toward acquiring addiction, for every addict has a unique, highly individualized story about his journey down addiction's pathway. In resolving the need to know why your child engaged in drug use, you might find that a multiplicity of causes offers the most viable explanation. Your young person is a complex being, and multiple causes may account for your multifaceted young person's addiction to brain-altering substances.

CHAPTER 14

Preparing Your Arsenal

Ever since President Nixon first used the term in a speech on June 17, 1971, the U.S. Government has been claiming it has been waging a "War on Drugs," an assertion that is debatable considering the insufficiency of government resources assigned to battle the massive onslaught drugs have made upon all aspects of our society, the obvious lack of any well-thought-out strategy, and the intolerable results demonstrated to date. Had World War II been conducted with the same lack of resolve that the government extended in its forty-year-old War on Drugs, we would be speaking a different language and celebrating different holidays. Lacking any true passion to confront the alarming encroachment of drugs on our society, our leaders have spent the last four decades allowing brain-altering substances to gain a solid foothold in our society, especially among our youth. Because of the failure of this War on Drugs, every socioeconomic stratum of our society has been laid open to the destructive invasion of drugs. Poor inner-city communities lie destroyed by drug-induced violence, thievery, and fear of youthful drug gangs who thrive on drug sale profits. Respectable, hardworking citizens, who are unable or disinclined to flee their neighborhoods, find themselves spending nights huddled behind locked doors and barred windows. With daylight, their children cautiously venture out to play while Mom combs the playground for used needles and keeps a watchful eye out for youthful gangs who won't hesitate to engage in senseless gunfights, with stray bullets hitting innocent children. Overwhelmed and victimized by violence, death, and the discriminatory jailing of inner-city youth and adults—all needless casualties of our failed, self-proclaimed War on Drugs—our urban communities lie ravaged after forty years of this badly run war.

Prosperous neighborhoods haven't escaped our government's failure to successfully wage its War on Drugs either. Middle-class and moneyed youth succumb to the seduction of brain-altering substances daily, while formerly intact and functional families fall victim to the dysfunctional life that drugs bring. Communities of impressive homes with professionally landscaped lawns may appear to be safe havens, but behind those manicured lawns are more youth who have yielded to brain-altering substances (especially prescription medications) than can be found in the poorer communities across town. Parents may have thought that buying a home in that well-to-do community would provide children with opportunity, but it couldn't protect youth from falling victim in our half-hearted War on Drugs. Many well-off parents have belatedly discovered that their $400,000 home wasn't a guarantee that their sons and daughters wouldn't become addicted, nor could it protect their family from being fractured and devastated by brain-altering substances.

Regardless of your zip code, the War on Drugs has extended its battle zone to your neighborhood, and if your beloved son or daughter has made the choice to use brain-altering substances, your home and family have become its latest front line. Unlike the government, you cannot enter this war indifferently, because you will be fighting for your family. Your battles will not be detailed on the front page of your newspaper, debated in the halls of Congress, or fought on foreign soil. Instead, they will be fought entirely within your home, and they will be fought only with the skills and weaponry that you take the time to learn and master. You will come to realize that the only resource you can rely on will be the weapons presented to you in the next section of this book and your willingness to become skilled in using them. Any governmental assistance and support that you may receive will reluctantly appear only after you have undergone substantial devastation and considerable expenditures in time, money, and energy. For all practical purposes, your war will be a private undertaking, for which, at this time, you are poorly prepared, poorly equipped, and poorly trained to win.

If you intend to save your loved one, you must begin your preparations now. You must become knowledgeable and skilled in using weapons with the capability to triumphantly snatch your young person from addiction to brain-altering substances. Hopefully by the end of the next section you will have gained sufficient insight and knowledge to strategically utilize the weaponry presented. In each chapter, you will be introduced to another weapon that, if conscientiously mastered, will allow you to skillfully engage the enemy of addiction. But first you must commit yourself to learning about and mastering the weapons taught in the upcoming section.

You have now been educated about the disease of addiction. You understand the truth about addiction and are aware of its basic concepts and components. You are cognizant of the impact addiction has upon all members of the family, and you are aware of the need to counter the parental tendency to be an Enabler and live as a codependent. You have sufficient wisdom to begin your own lifesaving personal "war on drugs."

Regard the upcoming section with the same mind-set you would view the training you'd receive in a marine boot camp. The powerful armies of addiction have already conscripted your addicted young person. It is imperative that you begin your war preparation with dedication so you can become sufficiently skilled to win your young person back from their mighty forces. To do this, you must totally commit yourself, and you must conscientiously prepare yourself. It is possible to emerge victorious over the forces of addiction—but if you wish to realize that victory, you must earnestly prepare yourself now.

※

Section 3

Basic Training

CHAPTER 15

Gaining the Advantage by Using Feelings

You've learned about the addict's practice of using drugs to cover up, submerge, and suppress painful, distressing, disquieting feelings. Subduing unwelcome feelings with brain-altering substances has short-term benefits but negative long-term consequences, since it prevents the acquisition of necessary social coping skills. For parents, this deficiency offers a unique advantage whenever they interact with their substance-abusing kid on a feelings level. Unfamiliar and unskilled in relating to feelings, the addicted young person is highly vulnerable whenever parents choose to interact on this level. Consider the difference between "I FEEL scared ABOUT your behavior BECAUSE you are doing things that can only harm you" and the all-too-typical interactions of most parents: angrily standing nose-to-nose, hands on hips, uselessly arguing in a loud, angry tone with an immature, brain-altered person.

If you choose to interact with your substance-abusing son or daughter by sharing feelings and maintaining a feelings interaction, you should be able to retain control. If you become practiced in expressing your feelings in the manner suggested here, you will significantly improve your communications outcome while disarming your substance abuser. Your young person simply doesn't know what to do when confronted with feelings, since he is only skilled in practiced *reactions* to your traditionally *reactive* behaviors: screaming, shouting, lecturing, and making threats that most likely will not be enforced. The addicted young person has no idea what to do when you share your feelings. He may be highly skilled in mentally shutting down your lectures, preaching, and irrational reactions, but he doesn't know how to functionally counter your feelings-based exchange. Parents, use this vulnerability!

While involved in a family treatment program nearly twenty-five years ago, I learned to use a format that I have been using ever since and teach to my clients. It is effective since it allows parents the opportunity to capitalize upon the substance abuser's lack of experience in dealing with feelings. When properly executed, it allows parents to keep their interactions on a level that produces uneasiness and confusion within their addicted offspring, while granting parents the ability to maintain control throughout the interaction. The format is: "I FEEL _____ ABOUT _____ BECAUSE _____."

Try this proven format to express yourself when your fifteen-year-old is being enrolled into a rehab program. Imagine the impact that the following will have upon her: "I FEEL hopeful ABOUT enrolling you in this rehab program BECAUSE it gives all of us a second chance to pull things together." This is vastly superior to the more common statements "If you don't take advantage of this program, I'm giving up on you," or "Your mother and I have had it with you. If you don't work this program, there will be nothing left between us."

These latter statements are all-too-common examples of communication that is counterproductive because the focus is switched from the immediate issue—drug treatment—to the troubled parent-child relationship. Any opportunity to emphasize the value of treatment and express hope for the future is lost. Instead of sending their child off with a positive, hopeful statement, the parents' words sanction the young person to view her placement in a drug rehab program as another example of excessive, unilateral, controlling, punitive parental actions.

By beginning with an "I" statement, the focus remains on the speaker, not the substance abuser. Because the speaker keeps the focus on his feelings, the substance abuser is less defensive and more receptive to what is being said. By using this format, Dad leaves his daughter with no option but to focus on self, an advantageous mind-set and an excellent mental construct to have as she enters treatment. Because Dad used the feeling format, the addicted young person is thrust into an uncomfortable, unfamiliar arena (having to deal with feelings) that leaves her without a practiced counter. She is just too inexperienced in dealing with feelings. By taking the interaction to a feeling level, you keep accountability on the real issue, drug treatment, while avoiding any opportunity for her to shift that focus onto the ongoing parent-child power struggle or resort to various "blaming disease" thoughts and statements.

Your feeling statement may be met with an angry look, a sigh, a "whatever," or even a curse, but do not be fooled. That feeling statement is being felt, and it will be remembered. Your young person simply doesn't know how to respond on a feeling level, so she responds by doing what she does best—resorting to belligerence, opposition, or stony silence. You can rest assured that once she is settled into the treatment program, your statement of hope for the future will be meaningful. It will weigh heavily on her, especially once the treatment has progressed beyond detoxification and into personal valuation.

Another thing to keep in mind when dealing with an addicted young person is that emerging adults have no established value system because they are still constructing their values and standards. The evolutionary process of sifting, testing, sorting out, discarding, and eventually deciding on what he will claim as his value system is incomplete. Parents may have consistently instilled values and morals into their young person, taking him to church, synagogue, mosque, or temple regularly. They may have taught him "right from wrong," but it was parental values that were catechized. They are not your young person's values, and until he refines, tests, and compares parental values with dissimilar values, whatever values parents have instilled cannot and will not be owned by the emerging adult. Every young person must go through the adventure of self-discovery, and part of that process involves testing parental values while experimenting with new values acquired by curiosity, peers, and society. One day the emerging adult will have his own set of values, and parental influence will have played a significant role in determining that set of values, but today your young person's value system is evolving. It is still under construction.

Since parents have established value systems, they are handicapped whenever they attempt to interact with a person who lacks an established value system. So act wisely. Use the feeling format and you will maintain the upper hand, even when dealing with someone without a fixed value system. Applying the feeling format brings your interactions into an area that is uncomfortable and foreign, where the addict is vulnerable. Think about how difficult it is for the altered brain to counter when it hears, "I FEEL scared ABOUT your drug use BECAUSE it is corrupting all that is good in you."

Your young person can't effectively argue, rationalize, or offer excuses. She is less likely to counter with a nasty remark or aggressive behaviors (if she should choose to resort to these actions, they will be much less extreme) since you have assertively maintained control by bringing her into an uncomfortable, foreign situation.

When you begin relating to your addicted young person by expressing yourself through the suggested feeling format, you will most likely experience a sense of awkwardness and stiffness, especially if you have historically resorted to the more traditional parental approaches of screaming, shouting, lecturing, dispensing unilateral punishments, and making empty threats. Being proficient and comfortable in executing this technique requires considerable practice, so imagine various scenarios that could happen, and then mentally create an appropriate feeling response: "I FEEL _____ ABOUT _____ BECAUSE _____." You can also practice this form of communication on co-workers and others with whom you regularly interact. No matter whom you interact with, you will be pleasantly surprised at the results you get when you begin expressing yourself through this format.

Successfully waging your personal war on drugs requires that you be able to maintain control over situations. You cannot surrender any advantage to your addicted son or daughter. There will be numerous future clashes and battles, of this you can be sure, but if you wish to emerge victorious, the skillful utilization of this strategic and practical weapon will be essential. So begin to practice this most powerful weapon: "I FEEL _____

ABOUT ________ BECAUSE ________." When the combat becomes intense, your well-rehearsed familiarity with this form of communicating will allow you to maintain control and increase the probability of a good outcome.

Many readers will resist adjusting to this communication style. Admittedly, it is awkward and uncomfortable until you gain a familiarity with it, but do not give up on it. Expressing yourself through an "I feel" statement is a powerful technique that keeps you in control, no matter what is going on—and that includes interacting with an addicted young person. So practice, practice, and practice until you can utilize the format in any emotionally distressed communication.

CHAPTER 16

Assertiveness—It Works

All significant interactions between individuals occur through one of three forms of communication: passive, aggressive, or assertive. When an individual chooses a specific form of communication, he establishes how his rights and the rights of others will be respected, as well as the regard each person will be given in the interchange. This is because each form of communication transmits a specific imprint that determines the nature of the interaction. When, for instance, an individual chooses to communicate passively, he surrenders his rights to the other person and allows that person to dominate him. If he chooses to be aggressive, he rolls over the rights of others and dictatorially controls that person, leaving the other individual angry, frustrated, and resentful. When an individual employs the assertive form of communication, he connects in a manner that takes into account the rights of others and thereby creates an atmosphere that fosters a respectful interchange. Tragically, assertive communication is underutilized, especially by parents entangled in an emotionally charged, stress-filled exchange with a substance-abusing son or daughter.

For parents who are trapped in the trenches as they wage their personal war on drugs, assertiveness is an invaluable weapon. Without it, parents will eventually be overrun by numerous substance-induced skirmishes. If parents choose to interact passively, their addicted young person will roll over them and leave them angry, frustrated, and resentful, as well as feeling overwhelmed, hopeless, and helpless. If parents elect to use the aggressive form of interaction, they will provoke their young person into even more destructive and combative encounters.

Should parents decide to assertively interact with their addicted young person, they will foster a respectful, healthy atmosphere and greatly enhance the chance that they will be able to disarm or at least neutralize their addicted young person. By assertively interacting, parents relate in a straightforward, sincere, truthful, yet respectful manner that acknowledges their offspring's rights as a human being. They demonstrate that they respect her as a person, despite what drugs have done to her. This sets the stage for further interactions that are positive, beneficial, and advantageous.

Once mastered, assertive communication is a skill that not only enhances the possibility of snatching a son or daughter from addiction's grasp, but also offers the benefit of productive communication in other aspects of life. As is true with the feeling format of interaction just discussed, once parents begin to assertively communicate, they are surprised at the widespread positive results that it produces.

To prevent confusion, let us take a moment to differentiate between *assertiveness* and *aggressiveness*. An aggressive individual takes charge of an interchange through such behaviors as bullying, disregarding the rights of others, taking advantage of others, pushing others around, and manipulating others in order to fulfill his needs and agendas. He expresses himself through threatening, offensive, demanding, and hostile interactions; disregards the rights of others; takes sole responsibility for making decisions; ignores the feelings of others; and uses sarcasm, insults, and put-downs to belittle others and their opinions. Aggressiveness demands rather than requests, resorts to labeling, and imposes ideas without regard for the feelings or beliefs of others.

The assertive person also takes charge, but he does it by respecting those with whom he is communicating, by honoring the other person's rights, feelings, and opinions. The person practicing assertiveness values the feelings, needs, and rights of all involved in the interaction—including self. He shows concern and respect by abstaining from name-calling, labeling, sarcasm, and put-downs. The assertive person assumes his rightful share of responsibility in decision making and is able to say no to requests without feeling guilty.

Let's use an example to contrast each of the three behaviors. On a hot, muggy afternoon in early June, Dad's business appointments put him close to his home. Deciding that a refreshing shower on an oppressively hot day would be in order, he turns his car toward home. Expecting his son to be attending his final week in school, he opens the front door of his home to be greeted by the sweet aroma of marijuana and the sight of his son and two of his friends sitting in the middle of the living room, a cloud of smoke hanging over their heads as the boys clumsily attempt to hide their pipes.

Should Dad choose the passive form of communicating, he will ignore the cloud of smoke, the distinctive smell of marijuana, and the obvious presence of drug paraphernalia. He will quietly head upstairs to take his planned shower, stuffing his feelings and avoiding confronting or mentioning what is occurring within his home. By choosing this form of interaction, the passive dad fails to exercise his legitimate authority, doesn't stand up for his rights as a father, fails to express his feelings, and delivers an unhealthy message to his son. By passively reacting, Dad transmits the impression that he no longer has concern for his son and/or licenses his son's behavior.

Why would any parent react in such an acquiescent manner? Actually, there are reasonable explanations. Dad may be so worn down by constantly dealing with one substance-induced incident after another that he has exhausted any desire, energy, or resolve to confront one more event. Such resignation is not all that uncommon for those who, over time, have been beaten down by their young person's continual, drug-crazed behaviors. Tired of winless confrontations, Dad may have decided that avoiding another unwelcome confrontation is a far more preferable option than engaging in another futile conflict. There is also the possibility that Dad is patiently waiting for that magical day soon when his son turns eighteen and he can legally toss him out of the home. After all, why get into another conflict when that emancipating birthday is only a few days away?

Many readers may find such behavior by a father to be reprehensible, yet passively reacting to substance-induced behaviors is common for parents who have given up, are "burned out," or are overwhelmed by feelings of hopelessness and helplessness. If conditions within your home have not deteriorated to such a state, say a prayer of thanks and be nonjudgmental. One day, especially if you endure year after year of insanity, you very well may come to see passive behavior as a viable survival option.

At the opposite end of the continuum is the aggressive dad who, upon entering his house, rages, "What the hell do you think you're doing? Get these pothead bums out of here. You are the most useless thing I've ever met. Clean this mess up, you worthless good-for-nothing. I ought to whip you."

Any parent walking into such a situation should rightly be incensed. Dad is completely justified in being upset and angry, yet his aggressive behavior is not justifiable. Regardless of the situation, interacting with his son in a belittling, insulting, threatening manner is inappropriate and ineffectual. Nothing is accomplished, save Dad venting his frustration and anger. The son turns inward, embarrassed by being put down in front of his peers and upset at his father's words. He knows he was wrong, but because of Dad's aggressive behavior, he is empowered to shift the focus from his behavior onto his father's actions and words. Instead of forcing him to deal with his substance-induced behavior, his father's actions give him permission to twist his focus onto Dad's fury. With the son incensed at his father's aggressive behavior, any opportunity to address drug use in a meaningful manner is totally obliterated.

Unlike the passive or aggressive father, the assertive dad neither rolls over nor bursts into irreparable rage. Instead, he firmly plants himself in the center of the smoke-filled room and declares, "I FEEL very upset ABOUT your using drugs in my home BECAUSE it shows a total disregard for what your mom and I stand for. I FEEL scared ABOUT where drugs are taking you BECAUSE it looks like you don't care anymore. Your friends need to leave and we need to talk."

The assertive dad directly and honestly expresses himself without belittling or threatening. The manner in which he keeps responsibility for the pot smoking on his son frustrates any opportunity for the son to shift the focus away from it. While legitimately angry and upset, Dad chooses to assertively address the situation by utilizing the feeling format, which allows him to maintain self-control while immediately addressing the situation in a manner that doesn't violate his son's basic rights as a person. In the absence of any provocative words or inciting actions by his father, the son cannot twist the focus onto his father. He cannot avoid accountability, nor does he have a viable justification to shut the door to communication. He has no other option but to be open and amenable to Dad's follow-up talk. Once the drug-using friends are gone, the stage will be set for Dad to communicate: "I FEEL fearful ABOUT what drugs are doing to you BECAUSE it appears that drugs are controlling you. I'd FEEL hopeful ABOUT things if we could talk BECAUSE we need to figure out how to end the control drugs have gained over you."

What an effective opening for quality communication, and it might even initiate treatment!

Each of the three behavioral approaches has a specific impact. The dad who elected to use passive behavior stored up his feelings and allowed tension to grow unchecked. Repressed feelings and emotions remain trapped and suppressed until they eventually explode, often violently, and usually over a relatively insignificant event. The passive dad also avoids communicating with his son, a reaction that further damages their relationship by conveying confusing and mixed messages. By not receiving the needed and expected leadership, guidance, and authority that all young people want (even though they will rarely admit it), the son feels rejected and frustrated by the lack of parental guidance and loving leadership that he so desperately needs.

The aggressive dad experienced a release of his anger and maintained his position of authority within the family. His venting of emotions may have provided instant relief and indulgence, but in expressing his anger he generated additional emotional harm and animosity with his son by stepping on and over his son's rights. Yes, that's right—his son has rights even in such a situation. At the very least, he has a right to be treated as a human being, but Dad ignores his humanity by belittling and embarrassing him in front of his peers, which only fosters the potential for retaliatory and aggressive behavior in the future. He also exacerbates ongoing parent-child hostilities and power struggles. Because of his aggressive approach, Dad creates an atmosphere in which arguments, shouting, striking back, revenge seeking, and an increasingly tense father-son relationship can be expected.

The dad who elected to engage in assertive behavior related to his son in a direct, honest, and open manner by genuinely expressing his feelings and concerns. Outside of the energy expended in exercising self-control, there were no costs for the assertive dad. By expressing himself in a manner that was respectful, Dad treated his son as someone who is important and has feelings and rights worthy of note—despite his behavior. By respecting his son and not putting him down, the assertive dad set the stage for open and honest communication that can only effect positive outcomes, something neither the passive nor aggressive father was able to do.

Despite the reported advantages that conducting oneself in an assertive manner offers, many parents feel ambivalent about adopting this approach. No one likes to make changes in their life, and changing to an assertive pattern of interacting while trying to cope with an irrational, acting-out addict is often perceived as awkward, uncomfortable, and even ludicrous. It is so much easier to react with authoritarian methods such as aggressiveness, lecturing, and issuing sanctions and commands. Years of conditioning may have established these customary patterns of acting—but these habitual behaviors must be changed if you expect to positively interact with that addicted offspring. This is an enormous adjustment for some parents, but if these changes are made, the results are very effective. Begin the process now to eradicate those old *reactive* behaviors and start practicing the art of *acting* in an assertive manner.

Assertiveness is successful in many situations: at home, on the job, socially, and in the family. Imagine the difference between "I'd FEEL very happy ABOUT you doing the dishes tonight BECAUSE I have spent an hour on my feet cooking dinner and I'm tired" and the all-too-common "Do the dishes right now and shut that TV off."

Assertive communication is not always a guarantee that the desired result will occur, but it is surely more advantageous than the other two forms of communicating. Assertive communication does not promise the TV will be turned off and the dishes done, so Mom may have to revisit the impasse. Consider the difference between harshly declaring, "I told you to do the dishes. Now shut that TV off and get into that kitchen" and evenly stating, "I FEEL hurt ABOUT your unwillingness to do the dishes BECAUSE it shows you have no regard for me." Which form of communicating do you think will most likely achieve cooperative compliance with Mom's requests and decrease future problems?

Assertively relating enhances all communications, even in relationships that are troubled and highly charged. When you honor your rights as a human being while respecting the rights of another human, you promote the continuation of advantageous communication, something that cannot occur with the aggressive and passive forms of interacting. By remaining respectful in your communications, you create an atmosphere in which all parties find it easier to interact in a positive manner. By showing respect, the assertive individual jams open the door to effective communication by maintaining an openness that allows the other person to enter without feeling overwhelmed by fear, guilt, or intimidation. In addition, people come to respect you (since you are respecting them), eventually resulting in communication based on mutual respect, honesty, and openness.

For those unfamiliar with assertive communication, especially those who historically have used aggressive communication, it should be clarified that interacting in an assertive manner in no way implies tolerating or condoning acting-out, antisocial, destructive, drug-centered actions. Rather, by its nature, assertiveness validates the rights of both people to be treated as a human regardless of the behaviors displayed, which forces the addict to question her behaviors. You convey to the addict that, despite everything she has done, you still regard her as a human being with certain inborn rights, which sets up a situation that increases the addict's discomfort with her behaviors. By being assertive, you have maintained respect and honored the rights of all parties, a far more preferable situation than those based on the unproductive reactions you formerly engaged in.

Because assertiveness places a heavy emphasis on respecting the rights of others, disrespect decreases while respect increases. This phenomenon applies equally to addicts as well as clear-thinking, rational individuals. For some readers, the idea of being assertive with a youthful addict may seem like a fantasy, yet it actually does work if you give it a chance. It sets the stage for easier repair of damaged relations, and when the day finally arrives that drugs are removed from your son or daughter, assertiveness will make it much easier to mend family ties. This is in stark contrast to the time and effort it will take to repair relationships damaged by aggressive or passive behavior.

In order to help you become assertive and to maximize the impact assertive behavior can have, the following suggestions are offered. You are strongly urged to process these suggestions and incorporate them into all your interactions.

Become Assertive as Soon as Possible

Timing and choosing the proper moment are crucial if you are to optimally utilize assertive communication, so the rule of thumb is to be assertive as soon as feasible. Waiting for the "perfect" moment (it will never come) or the "right" words (which you always figure out too late) only hinders implementing assertiveness, and this delay is tantamount to surrendering a valuable weapon in your war arsenal. It is better to address a concern, even if the moment or what you say is less than optimal, than it is to delay addressing the situation. The longer you delay initiating assertive communication, the harder it will be to effectively utilize this very valuable tactic.

Delay is usually interpreted as passivity with all the unhealthy implications carried with it. In the recently cited example, it was proper for Dad to immediately interact with his son. Even though Dad didn't have time to prepare and rehearse what he would say, he knew the situation required him to immediately do and say something. He did this without hesitation by asserting himself through the use of the feeling format. Once you become skilled in utilizing this mode of interacting, you too will be able to immediately act without fear of saying or doing the wrong thing, since this form of communication supports a positive exchange.

Take Time to Control Your Thoughts and Feelings

It was proper for Dad to delay initiating an in-depth discussion. His son's friends needed to leave, and Dad, unnerved by what he had just witnessed, needed time to process his emotions and collect himself and his thoughts. If Dad immediately began an in-depth father-son dialogue in the presence of his son's friends, he would have violated his son's rights by unnecessarily embarrassing him before his peers. And his son wouldn't feel free to share his feelings.

Assertiveness produces optimal benefits when everyone can give their undivided attention to the conversation. In the scenario we have been looking at, Dad assertively speaks and then disappears upstairs to shower (his original plan, and a great way to calm himself down). By taking a strategic time-out, Dad is setting the stage for a positive interchange. Once the house has been emptied and both father and son have taken a few minutes to collect themselves, he can constructively interact with his son under more favorable circumstances.

Be Honest in Your Interactions

Remain honest in all that you say. Being assertive requires that everything you say should be credible and genuine. There is nothing worse than dishonesty to destroy any hope for an effective and beneficial interaction. In our example, the assertive dad immediately made his point in as straightforward and honest a manner as possible, sharing his feelings and concerns by honestly expressing them. "I FEEL fearful ABOUT what drugs are doing to you BECAUSE it appears that drugs are controlling you. I'd FEEL hopeful ABOUT things if we could talk BECAUSE we need to figure out how to end the control drugs have gained over you," negates any opportunity for his son to sidetrack the situation. Since Dad remained honest in his communication, only positive results can follow. Honestly expressing how one feels sets the stage for an open and straightforward interchange.

Become Skilled in Using the Feeling Format

Expressing yourself through the feeling format may seem stiff and foreign, but regardless of the level of your discomfort, you must persevere. Sticking to this format will pay off, just as it did in our example. Dad's effective use of this communication model could only have occurred after considerable practice and rehearsal, preparation that produced the effective response we saw. Because he had taken the time to become comfortable with the feeling format, our distressed dad was able to adhere to the feeling format and thereby create an environment that prohibited the son from evading positive communication or diverting the focus from his actions.

Avoid Labeling or the Use of Put-Downs

Be careful not to label. There is nothing wrong with mentioning the behavior, but labeling the behavior can be destructive. Our assertive dad addressed the unacceptable conditions he found in his living room, but not once did he label his son or his friends with such derogatory terms as *junkies* or *potheads.* Unlike the aggressive dad, he avoided derogatory remarks, and in turn set the stage for effective communication. He also avoided put-downs and sarcasm. Such behaviors are always aggressive and accomplish nothing except to eliminate the possibility of having a healthy and beneficial interchange.

Listen to What the Other Person Is Saying

Check yourself from time to time to make sure you really are hearing what the other person is saying. Listening closely and attentively to the other person is a trait every assertive individual possesses, but unfortunately, far too many parents tend to dominate and lead the conversation or force it into a predetermined course. It is a well-practiced habit that can be difficult to overcome, so parents must force themselves to closely listen to what their children are saying and resist the tendency to control the conversation or plan their next response.

While the example we are considering doesn't record the follow-up dialogue, it is fairly safe to assume that when father and son sit down to talk, the assertive dad will remain focused on his son's words. He will periodically take time to check himself in order to make sure that he is attentively listening to what his son is actually saying and avoid those old habits of lording over, monopolizing, and leading the conversation.

Be Concise

When talking, avoid excessive wordiness. Refrain from lecturing and long-winded discourses. These may be long-standing practices that you have utilized for years, but you must admit that they usually turn youthful listeners off and halt any opportunity for meaningful dialogue. To ensure that your words are concise, relevant, and to the point, faithful utilization of the feeling format is imperative. Keep the "BECAUSE" statement to one brief sentence.

Use Appropriate Body Language

We speak volumes with our bodies, and when the body is not in conformity with what we are saying, our words come forth as superficial and void of credibility. Standing with clenched hands as you declare that everything is okay will come forth as incongruous. If you are angry, you might as well verbalize how you feel because your body is going to say it for you anyway. The other person will observe how you are truly feeling, so be honest and say, "I FEEL angry ABOUT your drug use BECAUSE it's hurting me, you, and our relationship."

Stated feelings must be in accord with what the body is saying, so when your eyes are showing anger and frustration and your fists are tightly clenched, honestly declare, "I FEEL furious ABOUT your damaging my car BECAUSE you didn't have my permission to drive it. Furthermore, I FEEL angry ABOUT you taking my car without my permission BECAUSE you have violated my trust in you."

By keeping your stated feelings and body language congruent, you have protected your rights, you have honored the other person's rights (being honest with him), and you have placed the responsibility for the act upon the other person without resorting to demeaning, damaging words. In harmony with your body, honestly express your feelings and lay the groundwork for future action: "I FEEL confident ABOUT getting my damaged car fixed BECAUSE I have insurance and you have a job. I also FEEL assured ABOUT getting my car repaired BECAUSE you can either pay me for the cost of the car's repair or I can call the police and have the court make you pay for it."

Assertive communication, effective use of the feeling format, and applying natural and logical consequences—it's a combination that maintains control even in highly charged situations. It certainly is much more effective than your former reactive behaviors!

Here are a few helpful tips to ensure that your body language is appropriate. When speaking, face the person directly. If you don't, you imply indifference, disinterest, or a lack of concern on your part. People who are truly concerned about each another face one another and maintain good eye contact. They also avoid aggressive acts such as pointing a finger or standing too close, behaviors that are perceived in our culture as aggressive, intimidating actions. Some gestures can be passive, such as looking down or away, mumbling, and whispering. These forms of communication bespeak fear, discomfort, and a sense of inferiority and insecurity. To ensure that you don't fall victim to any of these body language mistakes, remain upright, keep your arms down, maintain good eye contact, and, if you are sitting, be sure to lean slightly forward to indicate interest.

In Summary

Parents, you will need to have every armament available to you so that you can successfully engage the enemy of addiction. Assertiveness is an important weapon that you will have to deploy over and over in your personal war on drugs. You cannot afford to be passive or aggressive, for both behaviors only provoke needless conflicts that unnecessarily delay the day when your beloved young person seeks treatment. Begin now to master assertiveness. Replay prior interactions in your mind, exploring how you could have been more assertive, and then mentally practice appropriate assertive responses. You might want to also imagine future scenarios and how you could assertively address these events. You are urged to interact assertively in all areas of your life by practicing the feeling format as often as possible. Be assertive with your spouse, neighbor, co-worker, boss, and close friends, which will not only give you practice being assertive, but will also enhance your social interactions.

Remember, "I FEEL _____ ABOUT _____ BECAUSE _____ " keeps your interchange on an assertive level. By keeping the interchange centered on feelings, you safeguard your rights as well as the rights of others. You also prevent passive behavior and vanquish the tendency to engage in an aggressive interchange. All of us, including substance abusers, appreciate someone who respects our rights and humanity, so respect that addicted young person by being assertive.

CHAPTER 17

Unimpeded Consequences

Parents have always imposed mandates, codes of conduct, standards, and expectations upon their children. This domineering model of parenting was widely accepted for generations, and given the social context of earlier decades, it operated as a functional style of parenting. Today, however, parents find themselves raising sons and daughters in a society that is still reeling from the rapid and dramatic cultural transformations of the past half century. Fear of being investigated by child protective services, while operating in a fluid society that increasingly diminishes past morals and values, leaves today's parents understandably bewildered and confused. Parents legitimately ask, "What am I supposed to do? The old methods simply don't work!" A solution to this quandary lies in the work of social psychiatrist Alfred Adler, whose doctrine of natural and logical consequences postulates that a person can expect certain consequences to happen whenever a specific action occurs. These consequences proceed directly from the act and have the potential to render beneficial learning outcomes. Since consequences are much more meaningful and powerful than any parental sanctions, parents are urged to allow consequences to flow unimpeded. Natural and logical consequences also allow parents to step back and thereby avoid parent-child struggles while leaving the addict to struggle with the consequences of her drug-centered actions.

A distinction between natural and logical consequences must be made before we can continue our discussion. Natural consequences are those consequences that flow directly from the nature of the act. An example of a natural consequence would be a toddler who touches a hot stove, despite parental warnings. The painful consequence of being burned teaches a powerful, painful, and unforgettable lesson to the toddler, one that is far more meaningful than anything Mom can say or do.

Logical consequences flow not from the natural order of things, but from standards and regulations that society designs so that our social order can be maintained. Being pulled over by the police and getting a ticket for running a red light is an example of a logical consequence. The need for traffic safety requires laws and consequences when the established principles are violated.

Stepping back and allowing consequences to flow would seem easy to do, but for most parents, getting out of the way and/or doing nothing while a loved one suffers discomforting consequences is contrary to all that is instinctual—an instinct that begins when their child is an infant. Because children need to be protected from immature and impulsive actions, a strong parental tendency develops to intervene in the name of safeguarding the child. This tendency is strengthened daily as parents respond to the baby's needs. When the infant grows into a toddler, parents find safeguarding the child requires more and more time, energy, and alertness. At times, the need for protection necessitates a swift and authoritative response, such as when a child suddenly dashes toward the street. Immediately rushing to grab the youngster, Mom obstructs the consequences of dashing into the street, thereby safeguarding the child from harm. This is a totally appropriate and laudable action, but this mandate to protect the child conditions Mom to habitually interrupt consequences, even consequences that could offer beneficial learning without any physically harmful outcomes. This tendency to thwart consequences becomes so deep-seated that parents *react* without taking time to distinguish between behaviors presenting imminent danger and those offering beneficial learning opportunities.

Let me illustrate this with an incident that is initially free of any drug-related overtones. A second grader, Johnny, leaves the house to catch the school bus and forgets to take his lunch. Finding the forgotten lunch on the kitchen table, Mom has three options. First, she can personally take the lunch to Johnny's school, inconveniencing herself but ensuring Johnny gets his lunch. Second, she can call the school and ask them to advance Johnny lunch money that she will pay back the next day. This option offers less inconvenience, and still ensures that Johnny gets lunch. Finally, Mom has the option of doing nothing and thereby allowing her son to experience the consequences of his irresponsibility.

Many mothers, uncomfortable with the idea of Johnny missing lunch, will choose one of the first two options. Some mothers, however, will do nothing, and through their inaction they will allow Johnny to experience minor hunger pains, a natural consequence of his irresponsibility. For each of these options, the question must be asked, "What have you taught Johnny by the choice you made?" For those mothers who made sure food was delivered to Johnny, the answer is that Johnny learned absolutely nothing except what he already knew—Mom will rescue me. If Mom chooses the third option and permits her son to go without lunch, will Johnny face serious harm? Of course not, but he will experience some minor hunger pangs and, more important, develop an appreciation for the need to be responsible—a lesson learned without any effort on Mom's part.

How many forgotten lunches do you think it will take for Johnny to make sure he takes his lunch to school each day? By allowing him to experience the natural consequences that flow from forgetting his lunch, a valuable lesson about responsibility has been taught, something that couldn't occur if Mom goes out of her way to make sure he gets lunch.

While this example may seem like a small event in the grand scheme of things, it does illustrate the power of consequences as a teaching tool that promotes healthy maturation. Let Johnny feel the consequences of being irresponsible. Let him appreciate the discomfort and hunger that comes from irresponsibility. Let him experience this consequence so that an invaluable lesson about responsibility is learned in an effective manner.

Fast-forward a few years. Mom is checking Johnny's jacket pocket prior to putting it in the washing machine when she finds a bag containing crystals she suspects to be crack cocaine. Mom has a few options to choose from. She could throw the crack away and say nothing to her son, rationalizing that someone borrowed the jacket and forgot to take the drugs out when he returned the jacket. She has another option of choosing to talk with Johnny about the perils of drug use. Mom knows that keeping lines of communication open is important, and after gazing at the bag of crack she concludes, *Parent-child talks are useful, and besides, we haven't sat down and talked in a while. This will give me an opportunity to talk to Johnny about drugs.*

Mom also has the choice to impose sanctions. She could restrict her son to the house as punishment. She could even add a secondary punishment by having Johnny clean up his room. *After all,* she reasons as she looks at his disorganized bedroom, *this room is a mess. As long as Johnny is confined to the house, he might as well do something constructive.*

Other options available to Mom are to allow Johnny the opportunity to experience the logical consequences of involvement with drugs. At one end of the spectrum of logical consequences, she could call the community health center, her HMO, or her health insurance carrier and have her son evaluated for outpatient drug treatment. Midway along the spectrum of available options, she could place him in a residential drug treatment program where Johnny could get more intensive help for his substance abuse, a logical consequence that directly and profoundly addresses the issue of drug use and is very appropriate for advanced-level drug use, which is what crack use is. At the far end of the spectrum, Mom could concede that her son had violated the law and call the police, a rather drastic consequence, but one that flows logically from society's laws.

Let's look a little more closely at Mom's choices. The option of tossing the bag away and saying nothing has the benefit of avoiding confrontation while preserving Mom's denial. This is much more appealing than confronting her son and exposing every parent's secret fear—that a child may be using drugs. If she chooses this option, the question must be asked, "What benefit will this be for Johnny?" Of course, the answer is nothing, but Mom avoids an unpleasant, accusative encounter. Mom is also able to maintain her denial and prevent her naiveté from being further challenged.

If Mom chooses to have a talk with her son, the question must again be asked, "What benefit will this be for Johnny?" If she is honest with herself, she will admit that there is very little that she could say that he hasn't already heard from his peers or teachers. There is nothing that she could say that would magically stop him from using drugs. Parental talks are necessary, and they are a very effective way to address and even deter drug use, but if Johnny's addiction has progressed to the level of crack use, he needs more than Mom's talk. Engaging in meaningful talks with an experimental substance abuser can be helpful, but for an addict who has advanced beyond the experimental stage, something more than talking is needed. Mom may justify this as keeping the lines of communication open, but given his advanced level of drug use, what can she say to stop it? Johnny will most likely offer empty promises and make superficial commitments that he never intends to keep. If Mom wants to help Johnny stop his advanced drug use, more will be needed. Communication must always remain consistent, but as a sole response to advanced drug use, it is inadequate.

If she chooses the option of confining Johnny to the house and making him clean up his room, the question must again be asked, "What benefit will this be for Johnny?" Again, the answer is nothing that positively impacts upon his drug use. Putting him on house restriction and making him clean his room is an arbitrary punishment that is not logically related to crack use. Confining Johnny to the home may be a logical consequence if she had already prohibited him from associating with certain peers, but this is not the situation. Johnny's consequences must reflect the advanced level of drug use that crack exemplifies. Unless Mom intends to be attached to him twenty-four hours a day, her son will find a way to procure his supply even under these illogical restrictions.

By imposing punishment that is not a logical consequence of advanced drug use, Mom will further disrupt her life because she must now contend with Johnny and his antagonistic behaviors. Johnny can deflect the focus from his drug use onto the punishment, which he sees as one more unilateral and arbitrary punishment Mom has imposed upon him. A mind-set is created that promotes further antagonistic behaviors and justifies Johnny not dealing with his drug use.

Mom could avoid the ineffective responses above by initiating drug treatment, which is an appropriate and very logical consequence for drug use. If Mom chooses community-based treatment, Johnny's use of drugs is confronted and professionally challenged. Within the family, he will be labeled as the one who has to see a counselor, the one who is in trouble, and the one who must spend his free time attending a counseling program—all appropriate, meaningful, and valuable consequences that flow directly from his drug use.

A more appropriate option for advanced drug use would be to enroll Johnny in a residential drug rehabilitation program, an option that strongly confronts his use of brain-altering substances and more intensely forces Johnny to focus on his drug use. Because he has chosen to use drugs, Johnny will lose his freedom, be repeatedly confronted about his drug-centered behaviors, and, depending upon the extent of drug use and the type of drugs used, endure the anguish and pain of withdrawal. At the very least, Johnny's drug-centered life will be significantly disrupted while Mom will get a well-deserved break from her son's substance-induced craziness. If she chooses this consequence, Johnny will be forced to deal with the logical consequences of drug use in a very significant way.

Calling the police, another logical consequence for engaging in an illegal activity, raises the consequence of drug use to a significantly higher level. Now Johnny will have to deal with the police. He will be bombarded with a lot of questions, including from whom he got his drugs. He will be pressured to snitch on his drug-using friends as well as his drug supplier, and he may have to deal with lawyers and judges, not a pleasant undertaking for any young person. Johnny may also have to endure the humiliating process of being fingerprinted and booked, with the possibility of spending time in a correctional facility.

The impact of any of these last three logical consequences is positive. Drug use now has unacceptable and unwanted penalties. Unwanted exposure to drug treatment professionals, possible involvement with additional authority figures, loss of freedom and his ability to use drugs with abandon—these are some of the consequences that loudly speak to Johnny. By keeping consequences centered on his use of drugs, the impact is powerful, is meaningful, and directly addresses the abuse of brain-altering substances.

Logical consequences are so much more powerful than any parental sanctions or lectures!

The following points enhance the powerful learning experiences that logical consequences offer. Take time to familiarize yourself with these suggestions.

1. *Consequences must be directly related to the behavior.* If consequences are to be effective, they must be directly connected to the behavior in question. Due to his *driving* while intoxicated, the *driver* experiences established societal consequences, such as fines and legal costs, as he tries to retain his privilege and right to *drive. Driving* while intoxicated leads to logical consequences that are directly related to the act of *driving* drunk. The logical consequences are directly associated with the societal standard violated—*driving* while intoxicated.

2. *Consequences must have a significant meaning to the person.* Consequences can serve as a meaningful learning experience only if they are costly enough to become meaningful for the individual. Driving drunk has high-priced, high-impact consequences, such as expensive fines, time lost attending court, the stress and cost of dealing with the legal system, and the inconvenience of locating and utilizing slower public transportation when the authorities revoke his driver's license. These significant, high-impact consequences are logically related to the act of driving while intoxicated.

3. *Consequences must be established before the person engages in the behavior.* Unless the individual has prior knowledge and awareness of the logical consequences, the consequences will appear as arbitrary and unpredictable. To avoid this, you must make sure that your son or daughter is fully aware of the consequences that will occur should a prohibited behavior happen.

4. *The individual must be able to fully own the choice made.* For logical consequences to be most effective, the individual must have full ownership, which means there must be involvement by all parties in establishing both positive and negative logical

consequences. We live in a democratic society, and your young person is a democratically oriented individual, so consequences should be cooperatively determined and not randomly imposed. Once your democratically oriented daughter assents to jointly established consequences, she owns the decision and operates in full awareness of the consequences, both positive and negative. By involving your young person on the front end, you avoid any possibility that there will be a compromising of ownership by faulting you for being "random" or "arbitrary." It also negates the "blaming disease" aspect of addiction, since there is no one to blame but self.

5. *Consequences must occur as soon as possible after the act.* Logical consequences must be quickly realized, or they lose their value as a powerful learning experience. This is particularly true for today's "now-oriented" youth who learn life's lessons best when they are quickly taught. Youth have always been now-oriented, but for our young people, who have grown up in an instant gratification culture, it is imperative that consequences be quickly acknowledged. For these youth, the old saying "Justice delayed is justice denied" could be changed to read "Consequence delayed is consequential learning denied."

    There are times, however, when it can be beneficial to delay consequences. Here's one example of delaying consequences in order to ensure a more effective outcome. Jimmy habitually leaves his clothing and other possessions scattered throughout the house, and after months of uselessly asking Jimmy to put his clothing away, Mom and Dad decide to utilize logical consequences. They meet with their son and let him know that continued failure to responsibly pick up his things will result in their removal. They explain that such an action flows logically from his being too irresponsible to own and control his possessions. After waiting several days, during which Jimmy continues to drop his clothing and other possessions all over the house, Dad gathers all the carelessly discarded items into a plastic bag and removes them from the home.

For Jimmy, the loss of several days' worth of clothing and possessions is a far more significant consequence than removal of one or two thoughtlessly discarded items, which would have been the case had immediate consequences been enacted. Jimmy may be able to go without a few personal items, but not several days' worth. When, after a couple of weeks, Dad finally returns the carelessly discarded items, Jimmy will have a much deeper appreciation of the need to put things away than if Dad had immediately acted.

6. *Logical consequences should be action centered.* The fewer words, the better. Since kids develop a unique ability to let your "words of wisdom" flow in one ear and out the other, talking doesn't work. This is particularly true of substance abusers, so let the consequences do the talking for you. The effect is dramatically greater.

   Sometimes action means doing nothing, such as when Dorothy is arrested for possession of drugs and her parents decide to allow the consequences of her actions to fall on her shoulders. Her parents do not go to the police lock-up when the arresting officer phones them, a very logical consequence. They do not contact the family lawyer, which forces Dorothy to go through the trouble of acquiring a public defender and being represented by an overworked, underprepared lawyer. They do not post bail, thus allowing their daughter the opportunity to fully experience another logical consequence of drug use—incarceration. By choosing to do nothing (which can be a powerful act), parents conduct themselves in a manner that is much more effective than anything they could do.

7. *Logical consequences must involve joint cooperation by everyone involved.* When determining logical consequences, all those who will be affected should be involved in establishing consequences and claiming ownership of them. Parents, natural and step-siblings, and live-in or nearby relatives must be included in determining the logical consequences and must agree to

stand fast in adhering to them. Without this unification, your addicted young person will find someone who will unwittingly sabotage the logical consequence.

8. *Consistency is crucial.* This final suggestion is probably the most difficult for parents to faithfully follow, yet it is critical if you are to effectively combat addiction. No one wants to see a loved one suffer, so we are predisposed to act in a manner that short-circuits the suffering. Parents are especially vulnerable to the desire to thwart pain, suffering, and discomfort, a tendency that is especially evident when consequences begin to exact their toll upon a loved one, even when it's positive. At such times, Mom and Dad start rationalizing, *My kid is showing signs of trying to turn it around. I ought to cut her a break, and besides, if I show her that I'm in her corner, she'll be more motivated to keep moving forward.*

If Mom and Dad begin compromising what has been working by short-circuiting logical consequences, the addict will view this premature termination of consequences as a victory, a validation of her belief that she can outlast her parents. Indefatigable, youth need only one or two premature terminations of logical consequences to believe that they can outlast their older, wearier, less energetic parents.

In Summary

Allowing consequences to happen allows Mom and Dad to avoid resorting to old, reactive behaviors like lecturing, screaming, shouting, leveling unenforceable threats, and giving arbitrary punishment. When parents step back and allow natural and logical consequences to flow unimpeded, they address substance use and its associated behaviors in a manner that is less taxing and much more effective than traditional parental reactions. By allowing your young person to experience natural and logical consequences, a powerful weapon to combat addiction is deployed. Begin to use it, no matter how heart wrenching it may be. This weapon is the centerpiece of your war on drugs weaponry.

CHAPTER 18

Staying the Course

Natural and logical consequences are at the center of any parent's personal arsenal. Yet this valuable weapon can be easily corrupted. Consequences are distressing for the addict, but they are also torturous for parents. Still, parents must continue to allow disturbing and painful drug-induced consequences to occur, hoping that one day their impact reaches a point where a drug-centered life becomes so tormenting that, to borrow an AA slogan, the addict becomes "sick and tired of being sick and tired." This eventuality is not guaranteed, but parents must continue to make consequences a part of their young person's daily life while they fight the strong temptation to surrender by stepping in, fixing, rescuing, or helping. Not an easy task!

Since youth are protected by various safety nets, parents are often the only ones to allow the natural and logical consequences of drug use to be felt by the user. This leads to a lonely life marked by external criticism and internal misery as parents permit one wretched consequence after another to be felt by their addict. For months or even years, all parents can do is sanction, instigate, and foster more and more misery—without any apparent results. They watch helplessly as drugs continue to dominate despite their best efforts.

Some drug users are easily motivated to stop drug use or enter treatment after just one or two consequential experiences, such as being firmly confronted by parents about their drug use or following a substance-induced, eye-opening event. Some addicts will endure a succession of suspensions from school, encounters with the law, and conflicts at home before they reach the point of seeking help. For others, their individualized, consequential breaking point is so deep that even this is not enough. For these addicts, surviving on the streets, engaging in prostitution, or being jailed or hospitalized will precede any openness to treatment. Heartbreakingly, some addicts are so controlled by substances that not even these events will motivate them to seek treatment. For parents of such addicts, years of frustration and discouragement are their fate, yet they must not give up.

In my years of working with addicts, it never ceases to amaze me when older addicts, who had begun their journey during their teen years, would arrive at the clinic having reached their motivational tipping point after twenty to thirty years of active addiction, thanks to overdue parental action. Although these seasoned addicts may be in their forties and fifties and should have been emancipated from the nest a long time ago, parental enabling and codependency, referred to by parents as "helping," shielded the addict from reaching a motivational point of misery. After years of being used, the addict's codependent and enabling parents, wearied and beaten down, finally cut the addict off from any further support. With the parental safety net gone, the addict plunges downward and soon seeks treatment. If only his parents had acted years ago!

You are probably asking yourself, *How long will I have to go through this craziness of enforcing consequences?* The answer is threefold. First, the process is unique to each person. It depends upon the individual's circumstances, her personality, and whatever situations may impact the addict. Second, the length of the process depends upon how large a safety net your young person has. Safety nets created by programs that service our youth as well as the actions of concerned youth workers and teachers cushion and protect them. How encompassing is your young person's safety net? Finally, the young person's sense of invincibility and level of independence is a factor. All youth feel invulnerable to a certain degree, but for those who stubbornly remain impenetrable and unreceptive to adults and their counsel, the trail of consequences can be long. These youthful addicts go from one consequence to another, hanging on to their drug-centered thinking and behaviors, resisting all efforts to confront their use of brain-altering substances.

You may be one of those fortunate parents with a young person who earnestly enters recovery having suffered only minimal effects of consequences. But should you not be so blessed, prepare for and anticipate a worst-case scenario. Mentally prepare yourself for many turbulent years. Realize that for an unpredictable amount of time, you may have to remain unwaveringly committed to the painful process of allowing the consequences of substance abuse to continue.

Allowing consequences to be felt is an offensive and abnormal undertaking for any parent, and it requires ongoing support from others— especially your spouse. There must be an atmosphere in which spouses cooperatively agree to not interfere with consequences as they unfold. For some couples, this is a fairly easy process, but for others, it can be a difficult undertaking involving the fusion of two perspectives into a unified front. Yet it must be done, so commit to overcoming any differences, no matter how complex and strong they may be. Work to create a unified, coordinated approach. The health and welfare of your son or daughter demands no less than a jointly owned, authentic commitment to not interfere with natural and logical consequences.

Sometimes this means addressing the problem of denial by one parent. It is not uncommon for one spouse to admit to the existence of a drug problem while the other remains in denial, as manifested by rationalizing, minimizing, and intellectualizing. Some parents will both admit to a problem, with one spouse opting to sit on the sidelines, hoping that nothing further happens and somehow things will miraculously clear up. To bring a spouse who is in denial or chooses to do nothing into agreement is extremely difficult. Yet it must be attempted. If this process fails, and it very well may, the other spouse's denial or obstruction will have to be challenged—but this should not be done alone. Differences can quickly escalate into unhealthy, hostile, and unproductive spousal skirmishes. To prevent this, seek out a third party such as a counselor, therapist, or a knowledgeable and savvy member of your support group to serve as a mediator.

Should a spouse reject attempts to work in harmony and develop a unified plan of action, the other parent must resort to operating as if he or she were a single parent. The parent without a cooperative spouse must ask the same questions single parents must ask: *What will I be able to do by myself? What will I do in the face of overt or covert resistance when my spouse (or addicted offspring) recruits friends, neighbors, or relatives to ally with him? Where will I find the support I need since this cannot be a solo endeavor? How will I sustain myself should this become a long, protracted process?*

If you have little or no spousal support, begin to answer these questions now and then process your responses with those who make up your support system. Your concerns involve too many emotions and are too significant for you to address alone, so seek feedback from your supports and remain open to their input. Remember, however, that when spouses are not unified, positive outcomes are seriously jeopardized.

Rose, a recently divorced mother with a seventeen-year-old son named David, attempts to deal with her son's involvement in drug use and trafficking. She allows natural and logical consequences to happen at every opportunity, and she continues to reach out to her ex-husband, pleading for his support and cooperation. He refuses to join forces and will not even sit down to talk with Rose, so she deals with it single-handedly. She enrolls her son in a community-based treatment program, and when it is clear that it isn't working, she seeks out legal advice to get the court system to declare David "out of control." Her ex-husband is furious when he learns the court has taken control of David, but Rose refuses to compromise. In time, David returns home and seems to be a changed person, but Rose faithfully holds him to aftercare expectations, such as daily NA meetings, and she drives him to them nightly. Her ex-husband blames Rose and "her ways" for David's problems and refuses to admit that his son needs NA meetings or even has a drug problem. David picks up on his father's opposition and begins countering Rose, but she remains unwavering and persists in her efforts to hold David to his aftercare program.

One day she discovers a bag of crack cocaine in his book bag, and as a logical consequence, she places him in a residential drug rehabilitation program that was highly praised by her support group. Rose's ex-husband condemns her actions, and David plays on the rift between his parents. He flees the program and arrives at his father's apartment, pleading to be allowed to move in and promising to "behave." His father grants him admission to his apartment, ignoring Rose's pleas. David plays up to his father, appeases him, and creates horror stories about his life with his mother. Meanwhile, David resumes his drug-centered existence, but since Dad remains in denial, the signs of drug use are ignored. Dad excuses away David's behaviors by attributing them to his ex-wife and "her ways," and justifies his actions with rationalizations such as *We're working on developing a strong father-son bond. David needs a man in his life, not a nagging mother. With good male influence, David will be all right.*

Rose, fearing for her son's welfare, threatens to seek custody of David, but Dad springs into action. Exploiting David's falsifications, he goes to court and depicts Rose's tactics and her other antidrug efforts as abusive and neglectful. With Rose unable to afford adequate legal representation, the father is able to depict her as an unfit mother, and the court gives him legal custody of David.

Lacking the financial ability to adequately counteract her ex's slick depiction in court, Rose is forced to communicate with her son by phone, reminding him each time they talk that she is ready and willing to help and support him whenever he is ready to stop using drugs. One parent is living in denial and enabling the son's addiction, while the other is blocked from engaging in proven strategies to lead the son into recovery. Meanwhile, David continues to successfully manipulate parental discord and division while pursuing his drug-centered life unimpeded. Without parental unity, coordination, and shared strategic planning, David continues his drug-centered activities—but his fate is sealed.

Today, David languishes in jail, serving a lengthy sentence for multiple drug charges. Rose has moved back to her home state and is restarting her life. Surrounded by her family of origin and a strong local Nar-Anon support system, she eases her pain by consoling herself with the knowledge that she did everything she could and should have done. Dad falls into a state of depression. No longer able to deny his son's drug addiction, he lives with remorse and regret.

All too often, parents find themselves so torn apart by marital strife that they cannot put aside their differences and hostilities, even to save their child from the clutches of addiction and its destructive outcomes. Divided by spousal discord, they cannot stand as a united front. If this is your situation, continue trying to reach out to the other spouse and attempt to reconcile your differences. If you can, seek help from a professional counselor skilled in family counseling and addictions. You might also consider speaking to those in Al-Anon, Nar-Anon, and other support groups to learn how they were able to address marital disunion. Embrace their experience by being open to the advice and suggestions they offer. If all efforts fail and a unified stance can't be created (this very well may happen, as it did for Rose), you will be forced to enter your war on drugs alone—but you are not really alone. There are support groups ready to help you, if only you choose to utilize them. Being a single parent or married to a spouse in denial is difficult and can seem overwhelming, but hope can be found in support groups such as Al-Anon or Nar-Anon. This doesn't have to be a solo effort.

Also consider enlisting the support of friends, relatives, teachers, and any other significant adults in your addicted young person's life. Even the police can be enlisted, should things deteriorate to that level. You could tell the next officer who appears at your door, "The only way my son will stop using drugs is if the full repercussions of his actions are felt. I'd like your cooperation if you can."

It is imperative that consequences be felt by the addict. It is equally imperative that those consequences are not blocked by a parent—something that can be difficult to prevent in the best of circumstances. To remain faithful to consequential learning, develop as strong and widespread a support system as you can. Ask your supports, and hopefully your spouse, to keep you faithful toward your goal.

⁂

CHAPTER 19

A Ten-Step Plan of Action

In addition to enlisting as much support as possible, there are ten specific steps to take in order to develop an effective strategy of bringing consequences to bear in your child's life. Carefully review these steps, understand them, and implement what you can so that the initial part of your strategic action plan can begin.

Step 1: Ascertain Your Available Resources

Begin by contacting your health care provider to see what substance abuse programs your policy qualifies you for, the extent and types of services available, the allotted hours/days usable for substance abuse treatment, and out-of-pocket costs such as copayments. Don't be afraid to ask as many questions as necessary, take notes, and carefully compare the data obtained over the phone with the informational brochures that your health care provider makes available. Be sure to also learn the process for accessing drug treatment services, since many insurance carriers, especially HMOs, have specific procedures and predetermined entry points.

After you have familiarized yourself with your commercial insurance resources, explore the governmental or nonprofit programs in your area.

You can begin this process by looking in the telephone book under such headings as "Drug Abuse and Addiction." You should also call your local health department and find out what services that agency offers. Ask the same questions you asked when speaking with your insurance carrier: What will be your financial responsibility? How many treatment hours/days are allotted? And what types of services are offered? You should also identify the bureaucratic requirements and procedures to follow in order to access these services. Don't forget to jot down the names, titles, and phone numbers of contact people, and while you are on the phone, get a comprehensive listing of treatment programs your city or county offers.

Step 2: Develop an Early Strategic Plan of Action

Now that you are aware of the various services and programs available, begin organizing your information to intelligently develop a strategically sound, resource-centered plan. Locate all available treatment options and then determine which programs best match your financial capabilities, while offering a treatment milieu that is appropriate for your substance abuser. For instance, if economic resources or health care benefits are limited, you will probably want to start by using an outpatient treatment modality, or you can utilize governmental services by enrolling your young person in a government-sponsored, community-based drug treatment program.

There are several advantages to a community-based approach. Services are offered at a cost that is low enough to preserve money and insurance allotments, resources you will need later if the addiction progresses. Enrolling your young substance abuser in a community-based program also sends a very clear signal to your young person that you are resolved to address her addiction, a powerful consequential message that she needs to experience.

On the downside, you must realize that initial treatment will most likely not be successful, a fact that most parents have a difficult time accepting. All of us want our loved one to quickly enter into and respond to treatment, but most early treatment experiences do not lead to continuous, long-term recovery. Usually, addicts undergo cycles of relapse and enrollment in treatment before they are truly ready to commit to recovery. Reality, therefore, dictates that the true purpose of early utilization of community-based programs should be to demonstrate your intention to address substance abuse. Your young person needs to realize that you fully intend to deal with her substance abuse, doing whatever it takes. In short, enrollment in a community treatment program shows your commitment to allow the logical consequences of drug use to be felt.

Some parents are fortunate enough to have a young person halt her addiction early. For them, placement of a substance-using young person in a community program will serve as an enlightening, jolting experience and may be sufficient. Naturally, every parent wants early treatment ventures to "take," and if your son or daughter enters the world of sobriety and remains drug free through community-based treatment, be grateful to the God of your understanding. Just remember that many youth fail to sincerely enter treatment at this point, so consider your efforts as sensible, early steps that are part of your strategy to help your young person reach that motivational point of misery.

Another low-cost, viable, community-based treatment option is regular attendance at local Narcotics Anonymous (NA) or Alcoholics Anonymous (AA) meetings. These self-help groups are voluntary and function under the premise that those in attendance are internally motivated toward recovery, a premise that may not fit your young person. These self-help groups do, however, offer many benefits, even for the youthful addict who is not fully motivated for change. They can, for instance, expose your young person to individuals who are serious about their recovery and are willing to assist him in living a clean and sober life. Interacting with these individuals may be just what your child needs to inspire and motivate him into a firm desire to become clean and sober (remember, addiction began as a peer activity, so there is no reason recovery can't likewise begin as a peer activity).

When a young person becomes involved in NA or AA, there is an expectation that he obtain a sponsor, a recovering addict or alcoholic who serves as a personal tutor, mentor, and central support for the individual's recovery. The main function of a sponsor is to tutor the newcomer in the Twelve Steps, which are the foundation for living a drug- and alcohol-free way of life.

For parents unfamiliar with the concept of sponsorship, I offer the following standards that I believe should be followed when looking for a sponsor:

1. The sponsor must live the Twelve Steps and have an intimate knowledge of them. It is the sponsor's primary duty to provide individualized instruction in the Twelve Steps, which are principles and guidelines that promote a clean and sober life. This can only be done if the sponsor knows and is living them.

2. The sponsor should have a few years of continuous sobriety. Since it takes considerable time to properly learn the Twelve Steps and begin living life in accord with these principles, a good gauge to determine if a person is properly equipped to sponsor a novice would be to make sure he has at least three years of continuous clean time.

3. Whoever is selected to be a sponsor should be of the same sex, otherwise the emotional closeness that evolves within a sponsorship relationship could corrupt the benefits that relationship offers. In addition, men and women don't see things from the same perspective. We are "wired" differently, and this could be a definite impediment, especially if you deal with intimate or gender-centered issues.

4. The sponsor should also be someone who does not sanction your addict's manipulations. A good sponsor is less a "friend" than she is a demanding, concerned person who is intent on challenging and confronting those subtle behaviors and thoughts that lead a person back into active substance abuse.

5. Family members or old friends who are in recovery should not be considered when looking for a sponsor. While it may seem like a good idea to have someone who knows the individual serve as a sponsor, this can be a terrible miscalculation. There is just too much emotional baggage from the past, as well as family baggage, that will impede the demanding approach that is so necessary to be an effective sponsor. If your child has a

close family member in recovery, this person could serve as an integral part of her support network, but not as a sponsor.

Acquiring a sponsor is an act that significantly affects recovery. Your young person will need that one-on-one, intimate relationship to help overpower obstacles unique to recovery, such as dealing with cravings or those subtle, deceptive thoughts (called "stinking thinking" by the recovery community) that can lead to relapse. Someone who intimately understands the way addicts and alcoholics think is needed to effectively deal with this thinking, namely a sponsor with a strong recovery program.

Attending NA or AA meetings, developing a recovery support network, working closely with a sponsor, learning and living the Twelve Steps—these are excellent suggestions for your strategic planning. If a young person has reached her motivational point of misery, becoming involved in NA or AA may be all that is needed. Unfortunately for most young addicts, this is not the situation. More is needed, but this should not deter you from making NA or AA part of your strategic planning. Twelve Step groups are excellent for confronting substance abuse, and they should definitely be considered as an adjunct for anyone in a community-based treatment program or when your son or daughter returns from an inpatient facility. There are few things more powerful than recovering addicts helping other addicts. Parents would be foolish not to include Twelve Step groups in their strategic planning.

Step 3: Gradual Is Best

We have spent so much time and space talking about the progressive nature of addiction that it seems almost redundant to include this in the ten steps for a good action plan. Yet many parents tend to ignore the progressive nature of addiction in favor of that one-shot, all-out quick solution, a costly and prolonging mistake. Addiction is a progressive illness, and countering it must also be progressive.

Parents will, for instance, overly respond to drug use during the early experimental or recreational stages by enrolling their young person in a costly residential drug treatment program. This all-out response is wasteful and ineffectual, prematurely exhausts resources, and severely handicaps any future efforts to counter addiction. Young addicts who have not had the opportunity to progressively experience the gradual toughening of consequences will spend their residential treatment time scheming how to fool their counselors, while preoccupied with resentments toward parents for overreacting. These youth do the minimal needed to appease staff, and by viewing their placement in a residential treatment program as another example of their parents' excessive attempts to control their life, they display an amazing imperviousness to any rehabilitation. When they leave their treatment program and return home, they are convinced that they have survived the worst of the worst and can withstand anything else coming their way. With such a mind-set, the effectiveness of any future treatment options is seriously compromised.

Gradual is best unless—and this is an important exception—a parent has significantly delayed admitting that the young person has a substance abuse problem and, as a result, the son or daughter has developed a dangerously elevated level of daily drug use. Let's say that by the time the parent finally admits that the daughter is addicted, she is daily injecting a mixture of heroin and cocaine into her veins, a practice called "speed balling." Since she has progressed to such an advanced stage of addiction, it is imperative that treatment occurs in an inpatient facility where detoxification is available, doors are locked, and interaction with the community is minimal and tightly controlled. Given the amount and types of drugs she uses daily, community-based programs definitely will not work since the intense drug cravings will be so powerful they will propel her back to her supplier, the street, and active addiction. As you develop your strategic planning, be sure to remember this important exception.

Step 4: Mental Health Planning

Your strategic planning should also address the mental health problems associated with substance abuse. As has already been pointed out, the continued use of brain-altering substances can either cause a mental illness to develop or make a preexisting one worse. For those who have a substance-induced mood disorder, often no further treatment is needed. Once the body is free of drugs, the signs and symptoms of the illness clear up. For addicts who suffer from untreated childhood trauma, neglect, abandonment, and abuse, follow-up mental health treatment is imperative. Addicts who are tormented by guilt over what they did to loved ones during their active addiction or who suffer from other emotionally crippling past events also need mental health treatment. Failing to address these mental health concerns is to fail your son or daughter. Do not let the stigma associated with mental illness keep you from investigating various programs in your area. Your son or daughter may not need a dual-treatment modality, but prepare in case it one day becomes a necessity. From a statistical point of view, one day you may need a dual-diagnosis program.

The National Alliance on Mental Illness, an organization I greatly respect, offers sound reasons for considering mental health in early strategic planning:

> Adolescents are often referred to treatment for substance abuse but are not referred to a qualified mental health professional for appropriate diagnosis and treatment of any underlying cause for their drug and alcohol abuse. However, many teens have symptoms of a mood disorder that may in fact lead to self-medicating with street drugs and alcohol.
>
> Families and caregivers know how difficult it is to find treatment for an adolescent who abuses drugs or alcohol but also is diagnosed with a brain disorder (mental illness); i.e., ADHD, depression, or bipolar disorder. Traditionally, programs that treat individuals with brain disorders do not treat individuals with active substance abuse problems, and programs for substance abusers are not geared for people with mental illness. Adolescents are often caught in this treatment or services gap.
>
> ### Is dual diagnosis common?
>
> The combination of mental illness and substance abuse is so common that many clinicians now expect to find it. Studies show that **more than half of young persons with a substance abuse diagnosis also have a diagnosable mental illness.**[1]

Although the majority of adolescent drug users have a co-occurring mental illness, as the article by NAMI points out, there is a scarcity of programs that treat both mental illness and substance abuse at the same time. This places an onerous burden on parents to find and locate a program that treats dual-diagnosed clients. Be wise and start the process now. The process NAMI suggests you follow is this:

> The presence of both disorders must first be established by careful assessment. This may be difficult because the symptoms of one disorder can mimic the symptoms of the other. Seek referral to a psychologist or psychiatrist. Local NAMI affiliates are happy to refer families to mental health professionals their members recommend. (Call the NAMI HelpLine at 800-950-6264 for a local contact.)
>
> Once a professional assessment has confirmed a dual diagnosis of mental illness and substance abuse, mental health professionals and family members should work together on a strategy for integrating care and motivating the adolescent.[2]

Plan to get your young person evaluated for both mental health and substance abuse. You might also want to call your local governmental agencies and your health insurance carrier in addition to the NAMI HelpLine. Contact them just as you did in step one of this ten-step process. Learn if they offer dual-diagnosis treatment, and if they don't, ask for suggestions on who you can contact to locate such a program. If you find a dual-diagnosis program, learn what your financial burden will be and what expenses the government or commercial insurance carrier will assume—and be sure to determine the process and requirements that need to be met in order to access treatment.

The just-cited NAMI article also offers some excellent practical advice to parents who have a young person with a substance abuse disorder:

1. Don't regard it as a family disgrace. Recovery is possible just as with other illnesses.

2. Encourage and facilitate participation in support groups during and after treatment.

3. Don't nag, preach, or lecture.

4. Don't use the "if you loved me" approach. It is like saying, "If you loved me, you would not have tuberculosis."

5. Establish consequences for behaviors. Don't be afraid to call upon law enforcement if teens engage in underage drinking on your premises. You can be legally responsible for endangering minors if you do not take timely action.

6. Avoid threats unless you think them through carefully and definitely intend to carry them out. Idle threats only make the person with a substance abuse disorder feel you don't mean what you say.

7. During recovery, encourage teens to engage in after-school activities with adult supervision. If they cannot participate in sports or other extracurricular school activities, part-time employment or volunteer work can build self-esteem.

8. Don't expect an immediate, 100 percent recovery. Like any illness, there is a period of convalescence. There may be relapses and times of tension and resentment among family members.

9. Do offer love, support, and understanding during the recovery.[3]

Before we move from mental health planning, let me say, as a therapist who has worked for years with dually diagnosed clients, that they do get better. Dually diagnosed clients who are involved in and stick with a proper program modality not only become drug free, but they also become emotionally stable. Your job is twofold: (1) find the program that is right for your dually diagnosed son or daughter, and (2) become involved in your dually diagnosed young person's treatment. Parental involvement is crucial to successful outcomes.

Step 5: Identify Which Programs Are Appropriate for Each Progressive Stage of Addiction

In the interest of being proactive, and to assist you in establishing a sound strategic plan, review your listing of area treatment programs and determine which ones are appropriate for each stage of addiction. Community-based programs, for instance, could be plugged in for the experimentation or early recreational use stage, while short-term inpatient programs would be appropriate for advanced recreational use or early preoccupation stage addiction. If your young person has advanced to late-stage preoccupation or powerlessness, you will need longer residential treatment programs. One day, you may have to determine which stage of addiction's progression your son or daughter has advanced to, so prepare now by jointly agreeing upon the most acceptable program for each stage (experimental, recreational, preoccupation, powerlessness).

Before you move on to other weapons in your strategic planning, take time to openly and honestly talk about issues related to this process. Remember, unity between parents is essential, and this unification begins by sharing openly and honestly how each of you would feel if a specific treatment modality were initiated. For instance, will you be comfortable treating your early addiction stage young person at home through a community-based program that is supplemented by Twelve Step meetings and a behavioral contract to govern his movements at home? Will both of you be able to maintain treatment parameters and expectations, and persevere despite whatever hardships are involved?

Should your young person advance to the point where residential treatment is the most appropriate level of treatment, how will you feel about placing your son or daughter in a residential program? How will you feel when friends, neighbors, and relatives inquire about the whereabouts of your young person—and what will you say? When the addicted young person returns home, will you be able to sustain prescribed aftercare treatment programs, such as daily Twelve Step meetings, and enforce behavioral contracts?

How will you feel if your son or daughter is diagnosed with a coexisting mental illness and faces the dual stigma associated with this? Will you be able to consistently maintain treatment expectations at home, such as medication compliance and keeping all therapy appointments as well as NA meetings? Be open and honest as you discuss these issues. Stigma can be a major problem for parents particularly concerned with social appearance. How you intend to deal with dual stigmas is a subject worth exploring now—while it is not too late.

Step 6: Explore Inpatient Drug Treatment

This next stage in your ten-step process requires that, together, you and your spouse take time to explore the various inpatient programs in your area. Since placement in a treatment facility is generally reserved for those diagnosed as dependent on substances rather than those who abuse substances, I would be remiss not to discuss the criteria that professionals use to determine how far your young person's addiction has progressed. In order to assist professionals, the American Psychiatric Association has developed criteria for clinicians to diagnose the progressive state of a client's use of brain-altering substances. These criteria are set forth in the *Diagnostic and Statistical Manual of Mental Disorders,* Fourth Edition, Text Revision (DSM-IV-TR) and are used by counselors, therapists, psychologists, and other professionals.

A trained professional can help you make the final determination, but parents can get a rough idea of the progressive stage of their young person's use of brain-altering substances. The following is the DSM-IV-TR's definition for *substance dependence.*

A maladaptive pattern of substance use, leading to clinically significant impairment or distress, as manifested by three (or more) of the following, occurring at any time in the same 12-month period:

(1) tolerance, as defined by either of the following:

   (a) a need for markedly increased amounts of the substance to achieve intoxication or desired effect

   (b) markedly diminished effect with continued use of the same amount of the substance

(2) withdrawal, as manifested by either of the following:

   (a) the characteristic withdrawal syndrome for the substance (refer to Criteria A and B of the criteria sets for Withdrawal from the specific substances)

   (b) the same (or a closely related) substance is taken to relieve or avoid withdrawal symptoms

(3) the substance is often taken in larger amounts over a longer period than was intended

(4) there is a persistent desire or unsuccessful efforts to cut down or control substance use

(5) a great deal of time is spent in activities necessary to obtain the substance (e.g., visiting multiple doctors or driving long distances), use the substance (e.g., chain-smoking), or recover from its effects

(6) important social, occupational, or recreational activities are given up or reduced because of substance use

(7) the substance use is continued despite knowledge of having a persistent or recurrent physical or psychological problem that is likely to have been caused or exacerbated by the substance (e.g., current cocaine use despite recognition of cocaine-induced depression, or continued drinking despite recognition that an ulcer was made worse by alcohol consumption)[4]

Substance abuse is defined as

A. A maladaptive pattern of substance use leading to clinically significant impairment or distress, as manifested
by one (or more) of the following, occurring within a
12-month period:

  (1) recurrent substance use resulting in failure to fulfill
      major role obligations at work, school, or home (e.g.,
      repeated absences or poor work performance related
      to substance use; substance-related absences, suspen-
      sions, or expulsions from school; neglect of children or
      household)

  (2) recurrent substance use in situation in which it is
      physically hazardous (e.g., driving an automobile or
      operating a machine when impaired by substance use)

  (3) recurrent substance-related legal problems (e.g., arrests
      for substance-related disorderly conduct)

  (4) continued substance use despite having persistent or
      recurrent social or interpersonal problems caused or
      exacerbated by the effects of the substance (e.g., argu-
      ments with spouse about consequences of intoxica-
      tion, physical fights)

B. The symptoms have never met the criteria for
Substance Dependence for this class of substance.[5]

At the risk of oversimplification, let me attempt to compare abuse and
dependency. Abuse is less severe, with drugs having *some control* over the
user of brain-altering substances, while with dependence drugs are *in control*.
They rule, they dominate, and they are the user's life focus.

Is your young person an abuser of brain-altering substances or dependent on them? It is imperative that you know, because if he is drug
dependent and you place him into a treatment modality for those who
abuse drugs, the treatment will not work. Should you place an abuser in a

program designed for those who are dependent, you will most likely experience negative long-term effects. So consult with professionals and determine whether your son or daughter is an abuser of or dependent on brain-altering substances. It is an important distinction that you will need to make, should it become necessary to determine an appropriate level of treatment.

The logical consequence for drug dependency is placement in an inpatient drug treatment facility. Preparation, however, is crucial if you are to effectively execute this consequence, and that begins with visiting the various programs in your area in order to assess the treatment modalities that are offered. To assist you in this process, a discussion of the key elements you should look for when investigating treatment programs is offered in the next chapter. Do not try to assess a treatment modality without first familiarizing yourself with the features and qualifications you should be looking for, as well as becoming familiar with the questions you should be asking. For now, it is important to realize that investigating residential programs is a necessary part of your strategic planning, and that investigation should begin soon. A warning is in order: Don't allow yourself to be talked into enrolling your young person prematurely. You are there to research options, not to be subjected to a sales pitch.

While touring inpatient facilities, if you happen to encounter a person who is intent upon enrolling your son or daughter that day, take a moment to explain that your young person doesn't fully meet the criteria for dependency, but you will keep the program in mind when she does. A little knowledge about the DSM-IV criteria can go a long way toward shutting down an intrusive individual intent on enrolling your young person in a treatment program without considering whether it would be the most appropriate placement diagnostically.

Once you have investigated the programs in your area, take time to compare each one and decide which would be most suitable for your resources. While you and your spouse are considering your accessible resources and treatment programs, take time to openly and honestly discuss whether each of you will be "strong" enough to put your child away in a residential program. This is not an easy task, and many a parent has reneged when the time comes to take a son or daughter to a residential program, even when conditions have deteriorated to such an extent that there was no other choice available. Some parents have become so distraught and guilt-ridden after placing their son or daughter in a residential treatment program that their addicted young person was able to manipulate their guilt into a premature withdrawal from treatment. In order to prevent this from happening and further dividing parents, it is best if feelings, fears, concerns, and other possible impediments, such as unresolved guilt, are openly shared now so that no one is blindsided by an abrupt emotional reaction.

For many youth, placement in a residential program is necessary, but that placement must be owned by both parents and executed in a strategically sound manner. It must not occur too early, should not be undertaken without proper research, and should not be delayed too long. Planning, research, and coming to understand each other's feelings are necessary prerequisites for effectively using inpatient programs. In addition, enrolling your substance-abusing son or daughter in a residential treatment program requires a major expenditure of time and money, factors that make careful preparation, especially the judicious utilization of resources, imperative.

Step 7: Explore Your Legal Options

In addition to residential drug treatment programs, there are other residential options that should be considered. Some of these options involve utilizing the legal system to access treatment programs that would otherwise be unavailable to your young person. Should your young person fail to respond to your efforts to address drug use through substance abuse programs, turning to the legal system could be a viable option.

You could, for instance, go to juvenile court and request that the court assume control and authority over your addicted son. In each state, there is a process that allows you to petition the judge or juvenile magistrate to declare your addicted son or daughter to be "out of control" or a "child in need of supervision." Your state may have different designations for this process, but whatever it is called, you will have to stand before a juvenile judge and prove that you can no longer manage your addicted son or daughter—that you have lost control. This is a troubling and humiliating experience that can make you feel you're appearing like a "wimp" or distraught parent seeking to "dump" a problem child. To avoid such an appearance, demonstrate to the court that you have exhausted every resource at your disposal and are in need of additional assistance. You should, therefore, appear in court with a ledger listing what your son or daughter has done and what you did to respond. It should be presented in chronological fashion and have supporting documents when possible (arrest reports, suspension from school documents, etc). If the court affirms your request, you will have to turn complete authority of your young person over to the judicial system, something few parents can comfortably do. It is therefore imperative that both spouses fully understand how each will react to such a surrendering move. Is each parent capable of turning over control of that young person to complete strangers who will most likely institutionalize her? Do both of you have the ability to remain steadfast, despite the emotional turmoil? Will each spouse be able to support the other during this emotionally tumultuous undertaking?

As with other weaponry, you should research what is involved. Instead of waiting until a crisis is in progress, when you might not be thinking clearly, prepare yourself now by calling the courthouse and inquiring about programs for "out of control" youth. Learn what the expectations are. Be sure to save the names and phone numbers of those to whom you spoke, and keep whatever notes you make when inquiring into the process.

It would also be advisable to contact your family lawyer, if you have one, and inquire about any legal ramifications that may exist, the extent of the parental rights you are surrendering, and any expectations the court will be looking for. Your lawyer should be able to prepare you when you are ready to appear for a hearing, but it is not necessary for a lawyer to be present, as a properly documented ledger should be sufficient. Be sure to also consult with your Al-Anon and Nar-Anon supports. Some of these parents have been forced to declare their sons and daughters "out of control," and they can tell you firsthand what you can expect. Ideally, you will not get to the point of having to engage this option, but if circumstances deteriorate to the extent that this is necessary, you should be prepared. So start now. Develop that chronological listing of incidents and what you did to address the behaviors.

There is another legal option that you can utilize to get help for your addicted son or daughter. You can go to the courthouse and initiate the process of having the court involuntarily remove your son or daughter in order to have a psychiatric evaluation done. In my jurisdiction, this process is known as filing an emergency petition (different jurisdictions have different terms) and is used only when a person presents as an imminent danger to self or others. It begins by filling out a form indicating what exactly is going on, and then appearing before a judge or court magistrate, who will expect you to clearly demonstrate that your son or daughter is currently a danger to self or others as manifested by homicidal and/or suicidal ideation, violence, bizarre behaviors, threats, or actual attempts to harm self or others. This is not a process that is taken lightly, since it impacts a person's basic rights, so you should be prepared to thoroughly justify your allegation that your son or daughter is posing a definite threat to self or others. You should also bring any witnesses you can and be prepared to present any historic documents. Granting en emergency petition is based solely on current conditions, but it doesn't hurt to provide background information to aid the judge in better understanding your son or daughter. Most judges are document oriented, so please take time now to construct your documentation so that you are not trying to pull together a coherent document in the midst of a crisis.

Should the judge determine that your young person is a threat to self or others, the police will be ordered to remove him against his will and to transport your young person to an emergency room for a psychiatric evaluation. Be prepared to see him removed in mechanical restraints.

When the judge signs the emergency petition, attempt to find out which hospital emergency room your young person will be transported to (usually it's the nearest emergency room with the capability of securely containing emergency petition patients). Once you get to the designated emergency room, ask to talk to the mental health professional on duty. Explain that your son or daughter has been brought in on an emergency petition and you would like to speak to the psychiatrist, social worker, or mental health worker on call. All too often, when people are placed in the backseat of a police car, they display an amazing ability to suddenly "pull things together." By the time they arrive at the hospital, they present as model citizens, calm, coherent, and peaceful. Since an emergency petition is limited to getting a psychiatric evaluation done and is not a guarantee of admission or securing treatment, you must take the initiative to speak to the attending psychiatrist or mental health worker in the emergency room. Without your input, the staff may not have enough cause to justify involuntarily hospitalizing your young person.

An even more troubling legal option is to initiate the process to have your young person incarcerated. If you, for instance, find illegal substances, you could initiate legal action by calling 911. For some, the deterioration that occurs in the wake of substance abuse is so severe that jail can be a lifesaving option. For the parent of a drug user engaging in life-threatening behaviors, jail at least ensures shelter, three meals a day, and an increased probability that she will live healthier and longer than if left on her own in the community.

Given the traumatic nature of watching a loved one being led off in handcuffs and leg irons, parents should discuss and share their feelings and thoughts regarding such a possibility. Are both of you capable of seeking police intervention should conditions degenerate to such a level that this becomes a necessary option? What would it take to raise the ante to such an extent that this form of intervention is necessary? If your prior experiences with the police have been negative (this is a definite concern for many minority parents and those from lower socioeconomic conditions), could you trust the police to do the right thing? Talk about these concerns and issues now so that, should the day arrive when incarceration becomes a viable option, all involved will understand each other's position and be prepared to act in a unified manner.

Sometimes your son's or daughter's substance-induced actions will result in an arrest. In such an event, what would you do when you get that call from the police? Would you post bail so your child will not have to stay in jail, or would you let your beloved remain incarcerated and thereby experience the logical consequence of violating the law? Would you hire a lawyer, or would you step back and allow your son or daughter to be underrepresented by an overworked public defender? If you post bail, you must ask yourself, *Why are we thwarting logical consequences?* If you hire a lawyer, you need to examine the amount of enabling you are doing. Most youth involved in criminal behaviors know that a "pay lawyer" means you don't do any jail time, or just a minimal amount, with probation the normal outcome. Is that the message you want to give your young person—that you will pay for a lawyer to keep him out of jail and thereby prevent him from experiencing the logical consequences of his actions? If this is your bottom-line motivation in hiring a lawyer, you need to reread the sections on enabling and codependency. If your bottom line is to utilize the lawyer to increase the probability that your son or daughter will receive court-ordered treatment, then hire that lawyer, for you will be enhancing the chance that a positive, treatment-centered outcome can be realized.

Should you choose not to hire a lawyer, expect the court to pressure you to hire a lawyer for your child. By law, everyone is entitled to legal representation, and since you are lawfully responsible for the underage substance abuser, you will probably be pressured to assume responsibility for hiring and paying for her lawyer. Before you commit to this, learn the extent of your actual liability if you don't hire a lawyer. You also need to decide how to handle this dilemma. Would you continue to refuse to hire a lawyer and be willing to suffer the possible legal consequences, or would you yield to pressure and thereby thwart a very powerful logical consequence? Before you decide, you might want to talk with your family lawyer and find out exactly what your actual legal responsibilities are. You also might want to consult with those in your support group. These experienced individuals will be able to assist you in developing tactics that allow logical consequences to be fully experienced while keeping you from running afoul of the legal system.

Many readers have experienced unpleasant, often biased or prejudiced treatment from various sections of the legal system. Others distrust the legal system on principle and have a real problem turning over a beloved son or daughter. How deep-seated is your distrust of the legal system—the police, corrections, or the courts? Take time now to talk about your concerns. Is your distrust so grave that you could never trust the legal system? Might you be able to cautiously involve the system, or would you be able to utilize the legal system without any qualms? Not sure? Then turn to your Al-Anon and Nar-Anon group and seek out the advice of others who have experience with the legal system. If you belong to a racial, ethnic, or religious minority group, seek out members from your race, nationality, or religion and get their feedback.

Utilizing the legal system opens your young person to many helpful resources that are accessible only if he is found "guilty," "delinquent," or "involved" in criminal activity. Many a troubled youth has been able to change by utilizing treatment options reserved for adjudicated youth. Unfortunately, in many areas the system is so rancid with prejudice, discrimination, and biases that parents cannot command the confidence and willingness to trust it. For those parents with strong and well-founded concerns about the legal system, utilizing this potentially valuable resource may not be an option. You should, however, still discuss what you would do if your son or daughter were arrested. Will past experiences thwart logical consequences and force you into an enabling position, or can you, in an act of last resort, reluctantly turn to the legal authorities? These are weighty issues that need to be openly and honestly discussed now.

While incarceration may appear to be a harsh option, remember that not only will your young person have shelter and food, but she will be removed from the dangers of the streets and have less of a possibility of overdosing or getting some "bad drugs." Danger, violence, and drugs do exist in adult jails and juvenile facilities, but overall, your young person is still safer within the setting of a correctional facility than on the streets. Remember, if you choose to or are forced to interact with the legal system, make sure that when your young person is found "delinquent" or "guilty," the judge specifically orders her into drug and/or mental health treatment. I have years of experience working in youth detention, so believe me when I say that there are resources available to help your kid, but without a court order mandating your son or daughter into treatment, your child will never experience these resources. Correctional facilities do honor all court orders, but few will take the initiative to place a young person into a specific treatment modality if it isn't ordered. So make sure that treatments such as drug treatment, psychological evaluation, and therapy are ordered, even if you must speak out in order to get the judge to place your young addict into these treatment programs.

Sometimes a combination of court-ordered treatment and institution-alization can do wonders to motivate a person, but parents must be prepared and willing to utilize it. Therefore, it is strongly urged that both parents speak openly with the family lawyer and seek out information from parent support groups and their wealth of experiences. While it is hoped that you will never have to exercise legal options, there is no time like the present, while things are relatively calm, to become adequately informed so you can judiciously utilize legal options should things deteriorate. This is also a good time to explore each parent's mind-set. Which options are both of you able to follow through on, and will you be able to reinforce, support, and sustain each other?

Step 8: Hospitalization

As you do your strategic planning, be sure to consider the option of hospitalization. This is probably one of the more agreeable of your options, since it implies that treatment will be initiated. To start this, you can take your son or daughter to the hospital by yourself, providing a life-threatening situation doesn't exist and your safety isn't compromised, of course. If your health and welfare or that of your son or daughter is in immediate danger, prompt intervention and assistance from others is needed. If you call for an ambulance, don't be surprised to find the police accompanying the EMS staff. Your son or daughter may be undergoing a life-threatening emergency, but your youngster has most likely created a situation that requires police attention or support.

If you must call for an ambulance, remember that many seemingly distraught addicts have an amazing ability to pull themselves together when sirens and flashing lights appear. If your addict is able to sufficiently compose herself, the police and/or the paramedics will likely downgrade the situation and refuse to take your addicted young person to the hospital. By law, emergency personnel cannot involuntarily remove a person whom they do not witness acting out, engaging in threatening behavior, or presenting in such a manner that he or she is seen as seriously ill or a threat, so be aware of the constraints emergency workers must operate under. Act calmly and don't argue with the police or EMS. You cannot change the system, the law, or their analysis of the situation by yourself, so show them any records you may have that would support you (another reason for having that properly documented ledger) and calmly explain how your son's or daughter's actions pose a real threat. Should the police or EMS still refuse to remove your troubled young person, and you believe conditions would be unsafe if your young addict is not removed, ask to have a supervisor come to the scene.

Should the police and EMS find cause to transport your young person to an emergency room, be sure to follow. Your input will help emergency room staff reach a valid, therapeutically sound treatment conclusion. You should be aware, as you drive to the emergency room, that while hospitals treat overdoses, intoxication, and life-threatening conditions such as suicide attempts and suicidal ideation, emergency rooms are primarily designed for physical ailments and life threatening medical conditions. An emergency room can connect a patient to a detoxification program, but it is not their primary function or job. Drug treatment on demand is an ideal, but the reality is that there are far more addicts and alcoholics seeking treatment than there are available beds, a condition that hampers emergency room personnel from ensuring a detoxification bed. Unless there is an immediate threat to harm self or others, such as homicidal ideation or an attempted suicide, the individual will probably be discharged from the emergency room as soon as she is stabilized, with phone numbers of possible drug programs that may have beds in the near future.

If a case can be made for dual diagnosis (mental illness coexisting with substance abuse), your young person will gain entrance into a psychiatric ward where detoxification can occur under medical supervision and treatment for the mental illness initiated. Length of stay in these units, unfortunately, is very brief, and the time frame for placement is governed by insurance carriers rather than based on what you might consider to be therapeutically sound.

Should the emergency room staff determine that it is primarily a substance abuse condition, your addicted son or daughter will be sent home. In short, hospital emergency rooms can access a bed for someone who is suffering from mental illness or presents as a threat to self and/or others, but it is unlikely they will provide a substance abuse treatment bed. Unless the hospital has a detoxification unit within its facility with an empty bed (a rare occurrence), your son or daughter will most likely be returned home once stabilized.

In addition to a severe shortage of available beds, in this era of managed care, insurance carriers are less willing to pay for substance abuse treatment. Being a threat to self or others is a condition that offers a legitimate reason for inpatient treatment and forces insurance companies to pay for hospitalization, albeit briefly. This at best is a short-term solution with minimal hope for long-term sobriety. Once your young person's mood is stabilized and safety can be ensured, the insurance providers will have your young person sent home, often without any follow-up treatment. If you are able to get a child into a hospital, take advantage of the brief time he is behind locked doors by diligently working on securing placement in a follow-up treatment program. Many treatment programs want new clients to have already undergone detoxification, a fact that makes locating substance abuse treatment beds a lot less challenging if your son or daughter is undergoing hospital detoxification.

Here is a tip for parents unfamiliar with hospital dynamics: On admission day, make contact with the unit's social worker. Get this person's name, phone number, and an understanding of what you hope she can do—namely, follow-up placement. On day two, begin to make a nuisance of yourself and remain in that mode until follow-up placement is obtained. This doesn't mean being rude or mean. Rather, it means being persistent and tireless in your efforts to get the unit social worker to secure that follow-up treatment slot. Think of the old adage: "The squeaky wheel gets the grease."

Step 9: Aftercare

Since residential treatment usually becomes the treatment modality of youth who persist in resisting early strategies, aftercare, the adherence to a treatment plan following discharge from a program, must be part of any good planning. Whether the young person returns home from jail, a residential drug treatment program, a government-run program, a court-ordered program, a hospital, or a structured community-based program, he will need a treatment plan that is relevant and practical. Without a strong aftercare plan, the benefits received from any treatment program will be swiftly and dangerously compromised.

To prevent this from happening, consideration should be given to making Twelve Step meetings, such as NA or AA, serve as the centerpiece of your son's or daughter's aftercare program. This is a commonly used strategy that for some is supplemented by weekly individual or group sessions with a therapist. By regularly attending NA and AA meetings, learning the principles of the Twelve Step program, acquiring a sponsor, and associating with the clean and sober people of NA and AA, your young person will be able to find the reinforcement he needs to maintain recovery in the community.

To a large extent, the effectiveness of any aftercare program is contingent upon Mom and Dad's pledge to adhere to all components of the aftercare treatment plan. For this to occur, parents should honestly determine the amount of time and energy they have available to commit to aftercare and then tailor the program accordingly. Since parents have oversight accountability, it is imperative that they assume only those commitments they can realistically accomplish in light of family schedules and time constraints. For instance, will a parent be able to make daily treks to an NA meeting? If not, then what is realistic? Four meetings a week? Five meetings a week? Or maybe you can discuss the idea of putting the responsibility for getting to meetings upon the recovering young person. What would be Mom and Dad's role then? Being a backup driver when all else fails? And what should happen if your young person fails to responsibly look for rides? How often do you expect to drive her to meetings before you consider your daughter to be irresponsible regarding aftercare treatment adherence? And what will be the logical consequences for being irresponsible?

Whatever you decide, remember, if you are not able to provide reliable oversight and remain consistent, you will severely cripple the positive effects of the previous treatment program, so take time to fully assess and examine your capabilities and what would be a viable plan. Then create a draft of a behavioral contract that reflects your decisions.

Additional aftercare suggestions can also be obtained from those in your Al-Anon or Nar-Anon group. Don't develop an aftercare strategy without the experienced input of these knowledgeable people. Take your time, talk with those who have "been there, done that," and listen carefully. The insight and practical suggestions they offer will prove invaluable. In addition to speaking with these experienced parents, you should ask staff at your child's current program about suggestions for follow-up treatment. These program staff are knowledgeable about various community follow-up programs in your area, and they often discharge patients with established aftercare plans—just make sure that you are involved in that planning.

Step 10: Removal from the Home

Finally, there is one last horrendous option—removing the addicted young person from your home. If your young person hasn't reached the legal age of maturity, don't try this! You are legally responsible for your young person and will be charged with neglect, abandonment, or abuse if you fail to provide food and shelter. You can, however, utilize some of the other options we have already discussed. Use these legitimate, legal methods to remove your son or daughter from the home. There are sufficient legal alternatives to keep you from resorting to illegal actions.

If your young person has reached the legal age, usually eighteen, you do not have to let him or her into your home. Your legal duty to provide food and shelter ended on the magical birthday that your state legislature determined a young person to be of legal age. Discharged from parental legal constraints because of age, you now are at liberty to exclude your young person from your home and thereby allow the consequences of a drug-centered life to be felt without the shock absorber of Mom and Dad's protective shelter.

Before you decide whether to remove your young adult from the home, take time to discuss the ramifications of such an action while conditions are still relatively calm and you can dialogue in a rational manner. Together, determine if each spouse is capable of carrying out such an option. It will do no good for Mom to put her son out of the house and then have Dad support him with a different residence, or counter his wife by allowing him back into the home. We saw what happened in our all-too-typical story about David when Rose and her ex-husband failed to support each other.

Take time now to determine how each of you will react to the real possibility that your son or daughter might acquire HIV or hepatitis C, become incarcerated, become a prostitute, overdose, or die from a violent act after being banned from the home. If any of these tragic events happened, could you live with yourself and your decision? Would you be able to accept that you did the best thing you could for your young person, even if removal from the home resulted in catastrophe? Or would guilt and grief victimize you, as in, *If I had only kept her home, she wouldn't be in trouble/diseased/jailed/dead now.*

It is crucial that both parents openly and honestly discuss how they would react should conditions deteriorate to such an extent that removal from the home is needed. Would you be able to function not knowing where your beloved is, what she is doing, or how she is? Could you live under the cloud of uncertainty and with the fear that expelling a son or daughter brings? If a negative outcome were to occur, would you engage in such paralyzing thinking as, *I never should have put her out. It's my fault.* Or would there be accusations such as, *I never should have listened to you. She'd be okay now if I hadn't listened to you.*

These are concerns that cannot be lightly dismissed, and parents should honestly explore them, since putting a son or daughter out of the home is a crapshoot at best. You never know how the dice of life will roll. Dismissal from the home can be the very consequence that an addicted young person needs in order to earnestly seek treatment (it is for many), or it could give her the freedom to descend even further into dangerous, drug-centered behaviors. It is a weighty decision that has to be made rationally, openly, honestly, and jointly.

When the law considered your young person to be your responsibility, you had the authority to place him in supervised alternative treatment settings. Then you had options, unlike now, when the only choices are banishment to the streets or engaging in useless, unhealthy, enabling behaviors by continuing to provide food and shelter.

Given the weighty consequences that removal from the home brings, parents must take all the time they need to share how they feel about this option. How will you cope? Can you support your spouse and expect support in return? Do both of you have the ability, willingness, endurance, and detachment necessary? Can both of you live with the emotional devastation of worsened drug dependency, imprisonment, permanent physical and/or mental disability, or death? Would you and your spouse be able to cope and support each other should your decision result in a negative, devastating outcome?

Talk it over. One day you may be forced to consider this, so take time now to make sure everyone involved will be supportive of this distressing but sometimes necessary anti-addiction weaponry. Communicate honestly and candidly with each other now, while there is time, and then pray that you never have to resort to such an action.

It should be noted and emphasized that for every removal from the home—and no removal from the home should take place without this—it must be clearly communicated that you love your son or daughter, and they are more than welcome to come home once there is a cessation of drug use or a willingness to enter treatment. By emphasizing this, everyone knows this banishment is not permanent. Regardless of everyone's excitability at the time of removal, this understanding must be emphasized and expressed. This must be seen as a temporary measure that will end whenever drug usage ceases or a sincere willingness to enter treatment is expressed. By emphasizing this, you not only demonstrate that your love still exists, something that must be communicated if this is to be effective, but you also enhance the probability that some degree of peace of mind will be found amid all the emotional turmoil and trauma. So deliver the message assertively and clearly: "We love you, and when you are ready to stop your drug use, you are more than welcome in our home and lives."

In Summary

Combating the powerful grasp of addiction requires a strategically sound, well-devised, cooperative plan of attack. It's akin to military leaders masterminding a war plan to ensure victory over the enemy. It requires intimate familiarity with all available resources and a well-organized plan of action that maximizes them in a timely and strategically sound manner. Parents of addicted youth who are about to engage in their personal war on drugs must design a cooperative, systematic, well-calculated strategy (the ten-step plan of action) that progressively and logically elevates the consequences of continued drug use until that highly personalized motivational point of misery is reached. To execute this plan, parents must be prepared to resist the natural inclination to protect their sons and daughters from misery, pain, and discomfort. They must be willing to attack the enemy of addiction through actions that appear contrary to the love and care that parents instinctively offer. They must be prepared for months and possibly years of actively intensifying a loved one's misery and suffering. They must admit that to fail in this effort significantly lessens the possibility of successful recovery.

Maybe you will be lucky and discover that parental interventions within the home are sufficient. Maybe, like many other parents, you will be fortunate enough to find a community-based program that motivates your young person into recovery. Maybe you will find that your son or daughter will be receptive to drug treatment through a combination of a short-term inpatient program followed by a strong community-based aftercare program consisting of therapy and regular Twelve Step meetings. If any of these relatively mild, early strategic options bring your young person into permanent recovery, consider yourself blessed.

Whatever your fate, begin preparing now by sitting down and starting the strategic planning, focusing on how you will make your son's or daughter's life increasingly miserable. Resolve now to make your ten-step plan of action. Attempt to work out any spousal or family difficulties so that you present a unified front. Determine how far you and your spouse are willing to go and what each other's level of commitment is—and while you are at it, don't forget to talk with other parents who have addicted sons and daughters so you can benefit from their expertise. Finally, hope (or pray if you're a spiritual person) that your son's or daughter's bottom may be easily reached.

�֍

CHAPTER 20

Treatment Programs Compared

Parents can quickly become stressed out as they attempt to locate the most beneficial treatment modality. A mountain of information must be investigated, sorted through, and narrowed down, a process that can make locating suitable treatment a perplexing undertaking. For financially stressed parents, this undertaking becomes more complex as insurance providers shrink program allocations while governmental funds focus upon interdiction efforts instead of treatment programs (although, fortunately, this is changing).

Parental angst further rises as parents try finding a program that corresponds to the progressive stage of their young person. *Where exactly is my addicted offspring on addiction's pathway? Does she need the community-based programs or should I consider residential programs that are appropriate for later-stage addicts who are drug dependent?* To further complicate the search, financial and insurance resource depletion become major issues as parents look at the price tags of various programs. Multiple questions arise. *Should I deplete the family's resources on an expensive inpatient program, or could I choose a less costly option such as community treatment? What are the criteria that tell me when to place my young addict into an expensive inpatient program, and when would it be appropriate to utilize less costly options?*

To demystify and clarify the process and to prevent treatment choices from being made out of frustration and exasperation, we will explore various treatment modalities. To assist the reader, I have chosen to classify the various treatment modalities into seven generalized categories. We will begin with the program modality to which your health care provider will most likely refer you. After this, we will examine two types of inpatient programs, followed by three treatment options that offer intriguing alternatives, before closing with an overview of governmental treatment programs.

Community Outpatient Programs

If you utilize your health care provider, this will be the first program your addicted young person will most likely be referred to. The goal of any community outpatient program is to maintain the addict within the community while initiating and/or sustaining sobriety. By utilizing community outpatient programs, sobriety is established and maintained within the same community where the abuse of brain-altering substances developed. For addicts early in addiction's progressive march, it makes sense to treat the addiction within a community setting. After all, what better a place to begin recovery than within the same environment where drug use started, and within which the young person will hopefully again live drug and alcohol free?

Community outpatient programs also have the added advantage of saving money, which makes them favored by insurance providers. Some are operated by private individuals or for-profit companies. Others are funded by the government through grants, mostly to nonprofit organizations. Community-based programs monitor the addict through urine testing while he attends group and/or individual sessions on a regular basis. Some have a family component in which parents and sometimes siblings are involved in the treatment process. Since addiction creates a dysfunctional family, you are strongly urged to locate a community-based treatment program with a strong family component—if you can find one. Out-of-pocket expenses for community-based programs are usually predetermined co-payments or determined by a sliding fee scale, and even if you have to pay full price, these community-based treatment programs are significantly less expensive than the costly inpatient programs.

Community-based programs also allow the young substance abuser to maintain his schooling and other favorable ties within the community, an important consideration. This treatment modality, however, will not be beneficial for addicts whose addiction has progressed to the later stages: preoccupation or powerlessness. For those who have advanced this far along addiction's pathway, the many powerful, drug-related stimuli within the community will likely render treatment ineffective, since individual counseling sessions once or twice a week cannot compete with those familiar, powerful drug triggers that are so ubiquitous within the community.

Should you choose a community-based program or be forced into it by your insurance carrier, be sure the personnel are experienced and skilled in addiction work. Individuals who have personally experienced the addiction or the anguish of seeing a loved one overcome by addiction's forces are often more effective than those who have not personally experienced it. This is not to discount those lacking a personal background, but generally, those with firsthand experience are more successful in convincingly relating to your addicted young person. At a minimum, the counselor, who is intimately familiar with drug addiction, will be able to cut through the games and cons your addict son or daughter will be playing. The experienced counselor will quickly spot a manipulation developing, effectively counter it, and, over time, prove to be an invaluable guide and model for your young addict to emulate.

In addition to having experientially savvy counselors, it is essential that the outpatient program have clearly established controls in place. Some programs test urine on a regular basis while others do it randomly, so it is imperative that you inquire about their urine testing policy. Since many drugs have a short detection period, random testing is preferable since the addict never knows when he will be subjected to a urine test and therefore cannot plan his drug use. You should also ascertain what the consequences would be if your kid comes up with "dirty" urine, refuses to give up any urine, or shuns other aspects of treatment. Are the consequences powerful enough to motivate your young person? Remember, your youthful addict will still have a lot of free time within the same community where he learned to use illicit substances and within which his drug-using and -dealing friends still freely roam. Unless the program has experienced staff, firm controls, and guidelines with clearly established consequences, a successful outpatient treatment outcome could be dubious.

A good drug treatment program should mandate parent involvement. Many parents are surprised when they are told that there is an expectation that they should be involved in treatment. Far too many parents see addiction as their son's or daughter's problem and think that their responsibility is completed once they have gotten their son or daughter into treatment. This mind-set is unfortunate since parental involvement is imperative. As the young person learns about addiction and the tools of recovery, parents should have a parallel experience. They need to learn what addiction means, understand what recovery entails, and be able to identify with their young person's treatment. If recovery is to be maintained, parental understanding of the addiction and the tools of recovery is indispensable. Any holistic treatment modality will insist that parents attend regular parent counseling sessions so that they march in unison with their recovering addict.

If you are unable to locate a program with a strong parent component, and this very well may happen, turn to Al-Anon and Nar-Anon. The individuals in these groups will be able to direct you to family-oriented programs. They will also educate you, support you, and help prevent you from relapsing into enabling and codependent behaviors, actions that must be avoided if you are to support a drug-free life for your young person. Combining a community-based treatment program that mandates parental involvement with Al-Anon or Nar-Anon is the ideal. But whatever you do, please do not let the lack of a parent component leave you ill prepared and thereby place your young person's sobriety in jeopardy. Join a Twelve Step self-help support group!

Short-Term Residential Programs

These programs generally provide no more than a month of residential treatment and are costly. You will need deep pockets or access to a good insurance plan. Some parents have cleaned out their child's college fund for such programs, rationalizing that she will never get to college anyway unless the addiction is addressed. Others have taken out a second mortgage or otherwise gone into debt. Regardless of the cost, some young addicts, particularly those who have progressed to the third (preoccupation) or fourth (powerlessness) stages of addiction, *must* start their recovery journey within a residential facility. When addiction has progressed to these stages, detoxification and treatment in a facility isolated from the community is imperative.

Upon admission to an inpatient facility, a treatment plan for your child will be developed that confronts conditioned, drug-centered thinking and behavior. Depending on her preferred drugs, your young person might initially endure a few horrendous days in which she suffers aches, pains, nausea, and other discomforts of withdrawal. As the physical withdrawal decreases, generally in about seventy-two hours (this varies according to drug of choice, extent of use, and detoxification medicine administered), she begins to experience life again without drugs flowing through her body. She feels better, she looks better, and her thinking improves. It is at this point that the young addict begins to exhibit the first signs of progress as she verbalizes how great it feels to be drug free and resolves never to use drugs again. For parents who have endured the wasteland of hopelessness, this comes as an exhilarating experience, a dream suddenly revitalized—but this is short-lived as ambivalence, which is normal for those in early recovery, takes hold. A typical addict's stay in a short-term inpatient program is like an emotional roller coaster powered by ambivalence. Parents who haven't cast off their codependent mode will find themselves sharing their young person's emotionally charged ups and downs. For these parents, the drug rehab experience is as emotionally wild and volatile as it is for their addicted son or daughter.

When you consider how long it has taken her to acquire her addiction, up to a month of treatment isn't long enough to reverse months or years of negative thinking and behaviors. A short-term residential program, however, does expose the addict to the tools she needs to remain clean and sober. When she returns home, armed with her tools of recovery, there is an exhilaration that comes with being drug free and having a new desire to remain clean and sober. Armed with knowledge about the addiction and the tools needed to sustain recovery, she returns to her home and community—but her recovery has yet to be tested in the environment where the addiction originated and grew. She has proven she can stay clean and sober within the protective confines of the treatment program, but can she do it in the community? How well she survives reintegration into the community will be contingent on many factors, such as how sincerely motivated she is and, most important, whether her parents are sufficiently prepared and educated to properly support her.

In the drug rehab business there are no guarantees. If the truth were told, short-term rehabs would have to admit that they have a very low long-term success rate. Parents must, therefore, realize that their "new" drug-free young person may return home clean and sober, but she is still a babe in the world of recovery, barely able to stand up and, from a statistical point of view, likely to relapse eventually. She will need support from her parents, as well as from the recovery community (NA and AA). And even then it may not be enough. Cautious hope is appropriate. Become recovery savvy so that when your beloved returns home, you will be able to intelligently enforce aftercare plans and provide the appropriate support needed to sustain recovery.

Long-Term Residential Programs

Our next treatment modality, long-term residential programs, provides care and intensive treatment that generally spans from six to twenty-four months. This extended stay serves as an excellent option for addicts who have been unsuccessful in remaining clean and sober following multiple treatment episodes in community-based and short-term inpatient programs. Due to the length of stay, these programs have more than enough time to clean your young person's body of unhealthy chemicals while cleaning his mind of unhealthy, drug-centered thinking. Conditioned thought processes and behavior patterns, which developed during drug abuse, are challenged and altered.

Initially, there is a period of detoxification and adjustment during which family interaction is severely limited. The focus during this early period is on the addict, who is forced to confront himself without external pressures, such as family. After this initial phase of treatment, the addict is expected to become increasingly responsible and accountable as he progresses through each of several established phases. Well-designed long-term residential programs have a series of phases, and with the completion of each increasingly responsible phase, there is a resultant improvement in self-esteem and self-respect.

Interaction with the family begins when the recovering addict has completed predetermined requirements. Early family visitations are within the facility and are time limited. Home visits begin only after certain expectations are met by the young person, and then these begin with a day visit, often supervised by an upper-phase peer client, who serves as a support and companion. As your recovering young person advances in the program, unsupervised weekend visits are granted. Reintegration into the larger community is also gradual. With initial home visits successfully accomplished, the recovering addict begins limited job experiences or community schooling. His evenings are filled with support from staff and peer counselors as he daily shares his feelings, temptations, and successes. Through this support, the recovering addict is strengthened, encouraged, and eventually realizes his final program accomplishment—graduation and a return full-time to his home and community, well equipped for sustained recovery.

The process of gradually phasing back into the community allows the young person to become comfortable with his ability to maintain a clean and sober life outside of the security of the treatment facility. This comfort level is reinforced by self-esteem enhancement through the accomplishment of difficult, challenging phases. Since many young addicts have little awareness about what it feels like to finish anything, these successes become major, self-affirming events that enhance the recovering addict's self-concept. By progressing through the challenging phases established by the program, upon graduation the young person reenters the community with considerably more self-respect, self-esteem, and self-confidence.

Part of your preparations should be visiting various residential treatment programs in your area. When you visit these programs, look for the same things you looked for in other programs, such as a staff that is intimately acquainted with recovery. You should also make sure that the residential program is not cluttered with distractions. A facility with nice amenities presents well to parents about to drop a large sum of money, but these amenities can be distracting. The more spartan the program, the fewer distractions, which allows for more time working on self.

Long-term recovery programs are expensive, and you may have to be financially creative to secure a bed, although some insurance carriers still share a portion of the costs. Some are for profit, while others are church based and subsidized by religious organizations. For parents with limited finances, try to locate programs that are grant funded or run by nonprofit organizations. Many of these programs operate on a shoestring budget that is supplemented by highly dedicated individuals. Some expect parents to contribute time and energy in lieu of writing a sizable check. Find out what your obligations will be and how much of your time and finances will be expected.

A comparison of the success rates between short- and long-term treatment programs is also recommended. A rule of thumb is to view short-term residential programs as having a relatively good completion rate, but a less satisfactory long-term sobriety rate. Long-term residential programs, in comparison, have a low graduation (program completion) rate, but a higher long-term recovery rate for those who graduate. In other words, if you enroll your young person in a short-term program, he will likely complete the program, but is less likely to remain clean and sober once he is back in the community. If you enroll your son in a long-term program, he is less likely to complete the program, but his chances of remaining clean and sober are significantly higher should he graduate.

You now have an overview of the main drug treatment program options. There are, however, other interesting and creative approaches, and you should be aware of these concepts. We will now explore three of these programs.

Self-Esteem Development Programs

Programs in this category vary in composition and structure, but they share the common belief that troubled youth will be less inclined to engage in acting-out behaviors if self-confidence and self-esteem are enhanced. Many of these programs are survival based, taking troubled youth into wilderness settings where they have to outlast the elements by using their ingenuity and creativity. By weathering the challenges nature throws their way, these survivors return home feeling accomplished (often for the first time in their young lives) and with a heightened sense of self-esteem.

A less costly form of self-esteem development is Adventure Therapy, in which youth are challenged to overcome physical obstacles and work as a group to conquer various challenges. These programs can be found within your community and are usually just for the weekend. The vast majority of young people who complete a well-executed survival or Adventure Therapy program return home feeling accomplished and fulfilled with significantly heightened self-esteem and self-respect. Both modalities give troubled youth a sense of achievement, the novel realization that they can accomplish difficult things, an appreciation of the importance of working as a group, and a boost in self-respect and self-esteem.

Designed to primarily address self-esteem and self-confidence, these programs do not specifically address the young person's addiction problem. Since the addiction is primary, these programs will not in and of themselves effectively address the substance abuse. Treatment specific to addiction must be the addict's primary treatment focus and cannot be replaced by self-esteem programs. Self-esteem programs are excellent additions to substance abuse programs, but parents cannot expect them to succeed in addressing their young person's addiction alone. They can, however, serve as an excellent complement and enhance the chances for recovery to be sustained.

Self-Help Groups

Regular attendance at Twelve Step meetings such as NA and AA, reliance upon a sponsor, living a Twelve Step–centered life, seeking support from the self-help community of recovering addicts and alcoholics, and changing "people, places, and things"—these are some of the basic tenets of this treatment modality. For those who are highly motivated, self-help groups can bring the individual into recovery and sustain it. The power and strength that these supportive groups provide will work wonders for any addict who is motivated. Many addicts have been able to utilize self-help groups to stop substance abuse without entering any formal treatment program.

Twelve Step programs serve as an effective follow-up for the addict who has completed a residential treatment program and/or as a supplement to ongoing treatment programs within the community. If a young addict graduates from a residential treatment program with a firm desire to remain drug free, there is no better follow-up program than local self-help groups. Regular participation in NA and AA groups provides recovering addicts and alcoholics with the support that is so desperately needed to remain sober and clean. With the strength, encouragement, and acceptance received from the Twelve Step community, the prognosis is significantly enhanced.

Parents must also be involved in parallel self-help groups. Much has been said about the need to be involved in Al-Anon and Nar-Anon, and that will not be repeated. If, however, you haven't committed to becoming involved in self-help groups, do it now. You cannot fight the enemy of addiction alone, nor can your young person.

Grassroots Programs

These programs vary widely in structure and mostly operate quietly within your community with a broad array of philosophies and modalities. Some of these programs are highly structured, while others are loosely organized, but all keep the focus on promoting drug-free independent living within the community. Many of these programs are sponsored by religious and nonprofit organizations, but recovering addicts and alcoholics also operate many of these programs. Most exist on limited budgets, and although few become significant moneymaking ventures, they do excellent work under less than desirable conditions. Most grassroots programs begin when an organization or an individual takes over a house in either a poor neighborhood or a community that is undergoing transition (stable, middle-class neighborhoods typically offer too much resistance to locate such a program in their community). The doors are opened, and those wishing a safe, drug-free environment while they work on their recovery are welcomed.

Since most grassroots programs lack significant external resources, they survive by having residents contribute a portion of their income to the house, whether that income is from entitlements, family, or wages. The house manager, who is in recovery himself and manages the house for room and board, rotates housekeeping assignments, and provides needed support and operational coordination. Houses have varying rules and standards, but attendance at Twelve Step meetings and maintaining sobriety are standard expectations. Some programs have a requirement that a new member be isolated from friends and family for a period of time that can range from a couple of weeks to a couple of months. Each house becomes a small, supportive community with the seasoned members encouraging each other while working with the newcomers.

Since these programs generally offer few amenities, life in some houses can be downright austere. While the trappings most of us would consider necessities might be minimal, communal care and support for those motivated to remain clean and sober outweigh any physical shortcomings in the house. Support is an integral hallmark of daily living and sustains those seeking to maintain a clean and sober life. For those who are mature enough to capitalize on the benefits of these supportive programs, the prospect of long-term recovery is good.

For many legitimate reasons, these programs do not normally service those under eighteen years of age. A person must have a good level of commitment and a high level of maturity if she is to effectively utilize these programs, a factor that parents and their young person should not treat lightly. If she has sufficient maturity and motivation, your young adult might find the supportive, drug-free environment that a grassroots program provides is just what she needs to maintain a clean and sober life.

Many of these programs function as halfway houses or step-down facilities. For addicts emerging from a residential treatment program and in need of a supportive, drug-free environment while they assimilate back into the community, these programs are central in helping the addict and alcoholic gradually and safely reintegrate back into the community. Depending on your geographic area, these houses may be referred to as "recovery houses," "sober houses," "transitional houses," or "treatment houses." They provide reasonably priced housing. The average price in the area where I live is $80 to $100 a week. For this price, the addict is offered food (at least two meals a day), shelter, and most important, a supportive environment that promotes assimilation into the community. Since these programs don't advertise, you can only learn of their locations by inquiring within your parent support group or by talking with those who work in the recovery community.

Government-Supported Programs

Government-sponsored recovery programs address a wide variety of needs. They treat dually diagnosed patients through both inpatient and outpatient programs. Inpatient programs treat those needing intensive, secure treatment in order to detoxify, initiate or restart medications, and treat ideation to harm self or others, as well as serious mental illnesses. Outpatient modalities, such as community mental health centers, treat dually diagnosed clients who are already living at home as well as those being transitioned from inpatient programs.

Some government agencies specifically treat juveniles who have been declared "delinquent" (guilty) by the court. Other juvenile programs address the needs of youth who are considered "at risk" or "in need of supervision." Access to these programs is through the legal system, and parents should consider how they would feel about the court taking over control of their youngster. One way to have some say in what you would like to have happen to your young person is to get the judge to write specific treatment orders.

A combination of community and institutionally based government programs are found in nearly every state. Some states are actively working to minimize the number of expensive institutions they operate by shutting down residential facilities and creating a network of community-based programs. More and more states are favoring this cost-saving idea. The availability of residential programs in your community depends upon your state's approach toward institutionalization. Because of the wide variations from state to state, it is advisable for you to turn to your local support group and speak with those parents who have placed their young people in government programs. Learn from them what "the real deal" is concerning various programs—and don't forget to ask these experienced parents about various other ideas, strategies, and approaches that can help access programs.

In Summary

The success of your war on drugs will be contingent on how well you understand the various treatment modalities and how discerningly you develop a strategically sound, appropriate plan of action to access these programs. Take time to learn from those in your support group. Have them share their experiences about various programs, then contact recommended programs and ask the program gatekeepers about their entrance requirements and the population they serve, and set up an appointment to explore the facility. Do this now so that a strategically sound plan of action can be developed and ready for implementation should it become necessary.

CHAPTER 21

Pragmatically Living with an Addict

The next weapon to counter addiction within the family—behavioral contracts—promotes an atmosphere within the home that is significantly less tense and conflicted. It is based on the recognition that if a family is to reasonably coexist with a substance abuser living in the home, the day-to-day existence must be governed by clearly understood, relevant expectations. This is accomplished by developing and maintaining behavioral contracts that direct the addict's daily activities through clear guidelines.

To be effective, behavioral contracts must have a set structure that I will refer to as the ABCs of a good contract: Achievable, Believable, Concrete, and Specific. These principles and standards are reinforced and made viable through mutually agreed-upon sanctions and rewards as well as time limitations, all of which we will discuss. But let us first consider the ABCs of a good contract.

The first standard of a good behavioral contract, *achievable*, means that both parties agree that a goal is attainable—that the behavior change and schedule under discussion are possible. To agree to a goal that the individual cannot commit to, or that would be unrealistic due to constraints of time or money or other concerns, will not be effective. Parents need to make sure that they and their child are working toward a realistic goal.

Paul wants to start his first job when he turns sixteen in late November. His grades on the last report card were all Cs except for one B. As concerned parents, Mom and Dad want Paul to develop work skills but, given his grades, which they consider vastly underrepresentative of his capabilities, they fear working would only harm him academically. They explain their concern that the hours he will be working (about twenty hours a week) could be an obstacle to achieving the grades they know he can acquire. Paul admits that he has been lackadaisical in his attitude toward school, but he also considers himself smart enough to achieve good grades while holding down a job. "Like you tell me all the time, I just need to apply myself. I know I can do this." By this statement, Paul is meeting the "achievable" criterion for a good behavioral contract.

Our second standard, *believable,* means that the individual believes he can accomplish that which is being considered. If Mom and Dad believe that Paul can do A-level work in school, but Paul is convinced that he is only a B student, then a grade of B should be the contracted goal, no matter what Mom and Dad personally believe to be attainable. Without a belief that the goal can be met, Paul will feel he is agreeing to something impossible and thus will not strive to meet the goal.

Paul firmly expressed his belief that he can work twenty hours a week and still improve his grades. He admits that his current grades reflect a lack of maturity and responsibility and not his academic abilities. He is adamant that not only could he work twenty hours a week, but that he could show his maturity and responsibility by raising his grades with no Cs on the next report card. Paul is resolute in his *belief* that he can do this, and since what matters is what Paul *believes* he is able to do, the second criterion is met.

Not wishing to lose a possible motivator for Paul to get better grades, his parents agree that he can work as long as no C grades are brought home. The grade expectation has been agreed upon, an expectation that Paul *believes* is viable and possible. Since Paul *believes* he can work and still maintain his agreed-upon grade level, the second standard is met.

The next standard, *concrete,* requires that the goal can be touched. You cannot contract with your young person to "be good" since "good" is a concept that cannot be touched. In the situation with Paul, the goal is touchable, his report card, a very visible and touchable document

Specific, the final standard, requires that the contract be so precise and clear-cut that there is no room for ambiguity or loopholes through which the young person can maneuver. Questions such as *Who? What? When? Where?* and *How?* must be answered. There can be no vagueness, especially with a person who has a history of manipulating people and situations to get and use drugs. If a contract lacks specificity, then your young person will creatively find ways to circumvent its intent. In our ongoing example with Paul, the contractual agreement is very specific. It details the *who* (Paul), *what* (earn grades of B or above), *when* (on the next report card), *where* (the academic work is done in school and at home), and the *how* (by holding Paul to his commitment to be mature and responsible).

The ABCs are the structure of a good contract. They provide the framework, the guidelines within which the final components of a good contract, *mutually agreeable rewards and sanctions for an agreement that is time limited*, are inserted. In order to give meaning and life to a contract, rewards and sanctions that are meaningful, relevant, and agreed upon by all concerned parties must be included. Since Paul wants to work while going to school, a strong motivator to keep his grades up, the contracted agreement must reflect that he will continue working as long as his grades meet the agreed-upon goals.

The contract must also be time limited, something that is critical for youth who operate in the "now." This contract is very specific in its duration— the next report card. The issuing of the report card will terminate the contract and therefore will not leave Paul feeling overwhelmed by an ambiguous or extended time frame.

The final step is to write and sign the contract. "On Paul's next report card his schoolwork and homework will demonstrate his ability to be mature and responsible in managing his time by earning grades that will meet or exceed Bs in order for him to continue working." When Paul and his parents affix their signatures, they endorse an agreement that meets the ABCs of a valid behavioral contract.

Behavioral contracts can be used in any number of situations, but they are particularly effective when living with addiction in the home. For those living with an addict, a properly constructed behavioral contract brings a level of sanity into the family by providing agreed-upon expectations. It is also a very effective tool in assisting your efforts to create effective logical consequences. For parents, behavioral contracts become a no-lose situation. By setting up predetermined consequences, the young substance abuser is fully aware of what will happen if he chooses to use drugs, an awareness that, for some developing addicts, can serve as a motivation to cease or at least modify drug use. If the drug use persists, there are established consequences that can be enacted without a lot of controversy and chaos.

James's mother finds a packet of cigarette papers in her son's jacket when she is doing the laundry. She confers with her husband. They are not sure if he is using drugs or the extent of his drug use, if any. They are, however, concerned over what the drug paraphernalia represents. They decide to sit down with James and share their apprehension about the cigarette papers, his new phantom "friends," and the statement one of Mom's friends made that some of his new associates are known to use drugs. They also share their concern about James's increasing secrecy and his lack of openness with them.

After a heated discussion in which James vehemently denies that neither he nor any of his friends are using drugs, Dad informs his son, "We cannot in good conscience allow you to continue hanging out in these circles. You've changed, you've changed friends, and you've become more remote and closed off. And now Mom finds papers used to smoke marijuana in your jacket. These are all signs of involvement in drugs. We want to work with you to figure out a way to address our concerns so that you don't end up addicted to drugs. We cannot allow you to continue the way you are going."

Angry at his parents' accusations, James forcefully states, "I'm not using drugs, but I guess your mind is made up. What do you want from me? To piss in a cup every day?"

Realizing that the talk with James is deteriorating into a confrontational interchange, Dad chooses to become assertive, "I FEEL scared ABOUT your new friends, the pack of cigarette papers Mom found, and the secrecy you have developed BECAUSE these are proven signs of involvement in drugs."

James turns stoically silent while Dad continues, "I FEEL scared ABOUT what is going on with you BECAUSE drugs can ruin your life."

"So what do you want from me? I ain't using drugs."

"I'd FEEL more comfortable and less scared ABOUT possible drug use if we could develop a way of monitoring you BECAUSE I love you too much to see you get caught up in drugs."

Thanks to Dad's assertive communication and the impact the feeling format is having, James turns from being argumentative and defensive to mumbling, "So what do you want?"

A less hostile interchange follows, thanks to Mom and Dad's continued assertiveness. They discuss his various friends, and it was agreed that the names of friends James wishes to hang out with must be presented and approved by Mom and Dad prior to any activity. Mom and Dad also insist that his new friends be introduced to them prior to James's being given permission to associate with them. His parents also share their uneasiness about places he has been frequenting recently. After considerable interaction marked by continued assertiveness by Mom and Dad, which kept James unable to mount a full counter, an agreement was reached:

> James will not possess drug paraphernalia or use drugs. He will not visit the Main Street Mall and the convenience store on the corner of Fourth and Main Streets. He will inform his parents of the names of those he will associate with when he goes out. Individuals whom Mom and Dad don't know are to meet with them for approval. James will attend school as scheduled, and for all other activities, he must provide an itinerary before leaving the house, and if he must deviate from it, he will get prior approval from one of his parents. This agreement will end in forty-five days. Should, however, James violate any of the above, the agreement will be extended another forty-five days from the day of the violation and he will be immediately taken to the community drug treatment program on Central Boulevard for evaluation.

James doesn't like the contract, but he believes he can do it since it is time limited, and he is convinced he can adjust his behaviors for this short period of time. He also believes he is slick enough to maneuver around the contract, and besides, he wants to silence his parents so he can be free to come and go as he wants. Although his motivation is anything but ideal and laudable, James believes that he can do what he must to satisfy his Mom and Dad. Thus the contract is *achievable* and *believable.* It is also *concrete,* since drugs and drug paraphernalia are touchable and observable, as are the people and locations he must avoid. The contract is also very specific. It lists *who* James cannot see, *what* he cannot do and has agreed to do, *when* it expires, *where* he cannot go, and *how* the agreed-upon consequences will be executed whenever a violation occurs (by going to the drug program on Central Boulevard). Time specific, it also provides appropriate rewards (the restrictions of the contract end after forty-five successful days) and sanctions (contract extension and involvement with the Central Boulevard community drug treatment program).

Everything appears to be going well for five weeks until Mom receives a call from James's high school saying he is absent. James has violated the terms of his agreement by not being where he was supposed to be—in school. When James comes home, he is immediately taken to the Central Boulevard community drug treatment program, where he tests positive for marijuana and opioids, which James admits he obtained by taking some of his mother's prescription OxyContin. In accordance with the agreed-upon contract, James is enrolled in the community drug treatment program on Central Boulevard. There is no need for discussion, arguing, or typical parent reactions such as lecturing, shouting, or unilateral punishment. James has violated the agreement and expected consequences are being enforced.

A good behavioral contract condenses multiple issues into a single agreement. In James's situation, drug paraphernalia, possible drug use, secrecy, unacceptable and unknown peers, his presence in known drug hangouts, and holding James accountable for his whereabouts were all combined under one contract. By not treating these issues separately, which most parents would have done, they are addressed in a unified, comprehensive, relevant manner. Had the contract not been developed, Mom and Dad would most likely have addressed the truancy as a separate issue and would have missed the opportunity to place him in drug treatment.

Behavioral contracts are also advantageous for those who have a son or daughter in recovery. Whether a recovering addict is returning from a residential program or involved in a community based treatment program, a well-constructed behavioral contract is essential in promoting sobriety at home. Do not neglect this powerful weapon in your war on drugs arsenal.

In Summary

Whether living at home or preparing to return home, youth who are drug-free operate best under properly constructed behavioral contracts. Youth and parents new to recovery need clearly delineated, written behavioral guidelines and expectations in order to sustain their new, fragile recovery. With clearly understood expectations and consequences, parents have no need to engage in useless, emotionally charged, arbitrary behaviors that characterized the past. Now all they have to do is to uphold the contracted consequences.

Behavioral contracts must be the underpinning of the day-to-day existence of a family with a young person involved in drugs. For the young person actively using drugs, behavioral contracts impose mutually agreed-upon consequences and provide much-needed structure for the addict and the entire family. Guidelines reduce the level of insanity within the family, but more important, the contract removes the onus of having to make decisions in the heat of the moment or under stress. Parents only have to read the contract, thereby reducing potential insanity. Do not minimize the importance of creating and following a behavioral contract.

CHAPTER 22

Avoiding Common Mistakes:
More about Bill and Susan

Let's continue with the story of Bill and Susan. Because of Sean's addiction, Susan and Bill developed a Saturday morning tradition of coffee and conversation at a local bagel shop before heading to their eleven o'clock Al-Anon meeting. On one particularly gray Saturday morning, while Bill was savoring his cup of coffee and sesame bagel, Susan announced, "I'm not having a lot of success making consequences work. I know consequences can change Sean, but now he seems to be immune to them."

Bill placed his coffee cup down, with concern in his eyes. Susan continued, "I enrolled Sean in the county's outpatient drug program and he stayed clean—for a while. Then I put him in a residential program and he stayed clean—for a while. Then I put him in another residential program and he stayed clean—for a while."

Looking down at the table, she said, "This relapse, recovery, relapse thing is getting to be too much."

With apprehension, Bill said, "Please, don't tell me Sean has relapsed again."

"We are back into another relapse mode. He knows it will cost him—yet he continues using." Tears filled her eyes. Bill reached out and clasped her limp hand. Based on his daughter's multiple relapses, he knew that every time a parent starts another horrendous relapse cycle, the pain never gets any easier.

Choking back her sorrow, Susan confessed, "I'm tired of it all, Bill. I'm fed up. I'm worn out."

"You're sure he relapsed?" Bill asked, hoping against hope.

Striving to retain control of her emotions, Susan explained, "I began to see some of those behaviors he shows when he is using, but I was hoping it was something else. Last Tuesday he got expelled for fighting. I knew I had a problem since the fight made no sense. According to Sean, it was one of those 'he looked at me wrong' deals. I've had him keep up with his schoolwork, and he has managed to stay civil around the house. I kept hoping it was nothing more than a fluke, but he was back using drugs.

"He had come so far—eighty-seven days of sobriety—or so I thought. I was counting. I was so hopeful that I started to believe he had finally worn himself out. I knew I was worn out."

Susan gripped her coffee mug tighter. "Anyway, when the fight happened, I kept hoping it was nothing more than one of those crazy adolescent things, but last night Sean shattered any denial I was having."

"What happened?"

"He slipped out of the house to go to some forbidden party and came home this morning high as a kite, full of himself, and with a nasty attitude to boot. He threatened to smack the mess out of me."

With a voice choking with sorrow she continued, "I'm at the point that I can't take it anymore. I enforce and raise consequences and he does all right for a while, but then he relapses. I impose consequences and once again he gets clean and sober. Even becomes polite and civil for a while, but it never lasts."

Susan reached for a napkin to dab her eyes. "I'm too tired and worn out to ride this roller coaster one more time."

While Susan wiped the dampness from her cheeks, Bill shared, "When my daughter was using drugs, it seemed like I was waging a losing battle. There were a few rare glimpses of hope, but they were always shattered by yet another drug-induced mess. It got so bad I eventually wrote her off as a lost cause.

"Things got so bad that I would tense up when I reached home. There were times when I would pull into the driveway and just sit in the car, trying to muster the courage to walk through that door and deal with whatever waited for me inside."

"And I thought that was just me," Susan said. "Each time I drive down our street, I get knots in my stomach. Sometimes I sit in the driveway dreaming about leaving, about driving away forever. But then reality takes over. I've got a second son to care for, so I stay in my misery.

"How did you handle it?" Susan asked.

"When things got really bad, I went to the only place I had left to go to: my higher power, God in my case. Over time, I turned everything over to him. The crazier things got, the more I turned to God."

"I used to be like that. Well, my faith is gone. I pray and nothing happens. I even use the higher powers God supposedly sends me, like my friends in Al-Anon. I do everything you all tell me to do, but when it is all said and done, Sean keeps relapsing. God has abandoned us."

"When Barbara was deep into drugs, it seemed I had lost my faith. I kept asking God over and over, *Why me? Why my family?* I was mad at God. I blamed him. *After all*, I thought, *If he is supposed to be so all-powerful, how come he can't take care of my family?*"

"You've said your faith sustained you. I've heard you say that time and time again," Susan said, confronting.

"There was a period when nothing I did worked. Things just got worse, and the worse things got, the madder I got at God. If there was a God, he certainly wasn't watching over my life."

Susan's eyes locked on Bill, "What is it? Are you with God or not? You can't have it both ways. Please don't lie by saying you hated God. You're one of those 'turn it over to God' people. That's all I've been hearing from you for some time now."

"When my daughter was deep into drugs, nothing I tried worked. I'd get frustrated and angry with God. I'd question his very existence and why he allowed this to happen. But in the end I did turn things over to him. It was all I had left to do."

"An act of last resort," Susan exclaimed sarcastically. "You became one of those 'turn it over' people as a last resort. That's not faith. That's desperation."

"Remember those horrible three months when Barbara had run away? Nothing that I tried worked. I put up posters around town. I called all her friends' parents. Didn't get a single lead as to where she was. Even the cops couldn't find her."

Bill tried to ignore those horrible memories. "In my frustration, I blamed God. He could have brought her home and stopped her drug use, but he didn't. And since he didn't, I found myself wondering if he even existed. After all, why would this supposedly loving God let my family go through the living hell I was enduring?"

Bill responded to the scowl settling over Susan's face, "Yes, I questioned his very existence. Yes, I felt abandoned. Yes, I felt alone. Yes, I was angry at God, and if he did exist, which I seriously questioned at that time, I was holding him responsible because, as far as I was concerned, he had failed."

Bill paused, attempting to quiet a rush of disturbing recollections. "Eventually I admitted that I couldn't do it by myself, that I was powerless, and that I could no longer control things. With nothing left within me to draw upon, I had no other choice but to surrender my will and turn things over to my higher power, God. There was nothing else I could do."

Sarcastically, Susan asked, "And how, pray tell, does someone who is angry at God and halfway doesn't believe in him come to turn it over to him?"

"Each morning I faithfully plopped on my knees and I prayed that God, wherever he was, whoever he was, if he even was, would watch over my kid. Each night I got on my knees again and offered a prayer of thanksgiving to that same elusive God, thanking him that I hadn't gotten a phone call telling me my daughter had succumbed to death, disease, jail, or violence. Crazy, isn't it? Staying mad at God, questioning his existence, and all the while asking him to take care of my daughter."

"This whole drug thing is craziness."

"That it is. It leaves you feeling helpless and powerless. It did, however, lead me to understand and live that Twelve Step slogan, 'Let go and let God.' I had no choice. When all was said and done, he was the only power that could bring my daughter back. Obviously, I couldn't do it."

"So when you turned in prayer to God, it was an act of frustration and desperation. Your turning to God was the act of a pained and hopeless man." Susan could be so biting at times.

"If that is what it took, so be it. I admit that I was just going through the motions when I prayed, but I had no other recourse left—and besides, I wasn't crazy enough to turn my back completely on God. I had the same doubts that you appear to be having, but I wasn't ready to completely give up on him."

Susan volunteered, "I used to be in church every Sunday, and religion was always comforting. I used to be a strong believer. When I first heard, 'Let go and let God,' it was consoling, but now it's so empty."

"Turning to a higher power was hard for me," Bill responded. "I had never been anything but a nominal churchgoer, so the God thing wasn't as big an issue as being mad because I couldn't take charge of things. It was really a control thing. I'm used to being in control, and I have a major problem surrendering control, but addiction took care of that. It was a long and torturous process for me to finally admit I was powerless. I couldn't control my daughter; I couldn't make her stop using drugs. And when I finally admitted to this, I knew I needed to turn my pathetic self to something or someone who has the power to deal with my daughter."

Thoughts of his transformed daughter, who would be graduating from community college, soothed Bill's spirit. "I painfully learned that I was truly powerless. I could raise consequences, consistently interact at a feeling level, remain assertive when Barbara was nasty and aggressive, but when all was said and done, I was still powerless over my daughter's addiction. When I came to truly accept my powerlessness, I suddenly found myself liberated enough to turn her over to my higher power."

"I know I don't have the power to stop his drug use. If I did, Sean wouldn't keep relapsing over and over. That is not the issue."

"Yes it is," Bill countered. "Admitting to powerlessness is the issue. You're upset because all your efforts to control Sean's addiction haven't worked. You may be tired, worn out, disgusted, mad at God, but you still want to control things. You still want God to respond to you on your terms. You haven't fully admitted to your powerlessness."

Bill massaged his coffee cup while he waited for Susan to respond. After several uncomfortable, awkward moments, Bill predicted, "In time, your exhaustion and disgust will lead you to accept your powerlessness. That's what happened to me. When I finally admitted to my powerlessness, I accepted the fact that drugs had taken control of my daughter and I no longer could control her. I had to honestly admit that I was truly power-less, which freed me to turn to a higher power, where my true power laid.

"Turning to God as an act of desperation, as a last resort, isn't faith-based," Susan replied.

"You would be surprised what a last resort can do for you. I have a strong faith now, but that is because I was brought to my knees, finally admitting to my powerlessness. I couldn't do it alone. I needed help from someone more powerful than me. My daughter's addiction was too big."

"All those things that people have been telling me to do," said Susan, "like letting consequences happen, seem like they are basically useless efforts. Now these same people are saying I need to turn it over to my higher power. How can I believe this will work when everything else they've been telling me hasn't worked?"

Bill said, "I believe we should always strive to do whatever is in our power, even if it doesn't feel like enough. Your higher power expects you to do those things that have been proven to work. The way I figure it, my higher power, God, wants this to be a team effort—his divine protection and intervention, combined with our best efforts to follow proven approaches in dealing with addicted kids." Susan stared over Bill's shoulder at the wall behind him as he continued. "That's why it is so important to remain steadfast and continue to do what you have to do."

Resignation was in her voice. "I hear you, but I'm not sure that I have anything left. Everything seems so hopeless."

"I know the hopelessness and emptiness that having an addicted kid brings. How do they put it, 'Been there, done that'?"

"But your wife was with you," Susan quickly countered. "You had help. I have no one. Just in case you forgot, I happen to be a single parent."

"Sometimes I think it would have been easier if I had gone it alone. Drug-using kids are great dividers. They know how to play one parent against the other. My daughter was a great divider. She would come to my wife after being denied something by me and end up getting her way. At other times she would come to me after being denied something by her mom. She kept us divided and fighting. The support we should have offered each other, well, it simply wasn't there. We were like two strangers, each with our own way of operating, highly critical of each other. Not a very supportive way to live."

With his voice low and confidential, Bill continued, "You are intimately aware of our marital problems, and those problems were there before drugs entered our lives, but when my daughter became addicted, it intensified our divisions. I really think that if my daughter hadn't become addicted, we might still be limping along in our marriage, but after she introduced the craziness of drugs, things just plunged downward."

"I'm not sure I have the strength to do this alone," Susan volunteered.

"At least you don't have to deal with marital problems at the same time. Being single may be better than what I had to deal with—an addicted kid and a troubled marriage. Besides, you're not alone. You've got a lot of support from Al-Anon."

"When I'm home, I feel like I'm alone."

"Your phone works. You can talk with your friends in Al-Anon. You also have your higher power, who is waiting to take over when you turn it over. You definitely are not alone."

"Is that your response to everything? You sound like some kind of hustling preacher. Give me your money and God will take care of your needs, or in your case, turn Sean over to him and everything will be okay."

"I'm a far cry from some hustling preacher, but I do know that you can't do this alone. None of us can combat drugs singlehandedly."

Bill paused, weighing whether he should say what he wanted to. He threw caution to the wind, "Because you are a mom, you are accustomed to being in control, but since drugs have invaded your family, you have lost that control."

"Now you're trying to say I'm a control freak!" Susan was very combative today. Bill censured himself for not being cautious.

"I admit I was one too. Being a parent is being in control—it is a part of parenting. You've been controlling Sean since he was born, and it's hard to change seventeen years."

Susan turned silent. It was only after a sip of his coffee that Bill chose to end the uneasy silence. "I have a job where I say 'jump' and they say 'how high?' I'm in charge, and all day long I am running things, and I'm okay when I'm in charge. To surrender control over Barbara was unnatural, and it took a while before I realized I had no choice but to turn her over—totally and completely. Surrendering control meant admitting my powerlessness over my kid, and that wasn't easy. As a matter of fact, it was a long, hard process before I fully turned things over."

"So you're saying that all I need to do is to turn Sean over to a higher power?"

"The fact that Barbara is currently clean and sober, I attribute that to a good treatment program and surrendering control to her higher power and mine. I bumbled through my attempts to maintain consequences, to interact assertively and on a feelings level—not to mention messing up the united front thing my wife and I were supposed to have. As far as I'm concerned, prayer brought us through. We were too busy fighting each other, and besides, Barbara's addiction was more powerful than either of us could handle. A higher power was needed."

"I'm too mad at God to turn to him now."

"I hear you. That's completely understandable."

"That's big of you to say."

"It was big of him to tolerate my halfhearted prayer and then answer my prayers, despite how I felt about him."

"So prayer is the magic bullet, the answer to all of my son's craziness?"

"Admitting that you are powerless over Sean is the magic bullet," Bill clarified. "As long as you uselessly try to control the outcome of things, you will remain stuck where you are."

"So your answer to Sean's latest relapse is to turn him over?"

"You're not doing very well on your own. It can't hurt."

Looking at her watch, Susan said, "It's time to go to a higher power I can see. We need to be going to our meeting."

Sliding his chair away from the table, grateful to leave the bagel shop and their intense interchange, Bill said, "See, you are still doing what you need to be doing. You are still acknowledging your need to access a higher power."

Gathering her purse, Susan said, "Al-Anon isn't God."

"Ah, that is true, but it does serve as a fine higher power."

Susan allowed, "That's one good thing I've gotten out of all this. Al-Anon has given me a lot of friends I'd never have met otherwise. I need them now."

"They were my mainstay. They kept me together during those horrible days."

Developing an Awareness of Some Common Mistakes

The verbal exchange in the bagel shop between Bill and Susan exemplified a few of the commonplace mistakes that parents of addicted youth tend to make. In the interest of helping you avoid these mistakes, let's explore them, along with other frequently committed parental errors.

Turning from the God of One's Understanding

After riding the emotional roller coaster of addiction for far too long, Susan had become emotionally drained, repeated relapses having crushed her morale. With hope hard to maintain, her despair and discouragement became so deep that, despite a faith that was once strong, Susan could no longer honestly turn to her God. The forces of addiction had beaten her down, robbed her of her spirituality, and left her discouraged and struggling. Without the assurance that comes from faith, Susan was having difficulty enduring another relapse. Her son's addiction led her into a true desert experience.

Her Al-Anon supports, including Bill, kept advising her to turn it over, to "Let go and let God." Failing to acknowledge her powerlessness, her personal and spiritual lives became more and more tormented. Bill, however, was confident that in time she would come to realize that the only option left to her would be to turn to her only true power source, the God of her understanding—but first, there had to be an admission of her powerlessness.

It wasn't until the forces of addiction had beaten him through repeated failures that Bill finally came to accept his own powerlessness and, in turn, discovered the power of spirituality. He believed Susan's faith would be restored, but first her desert experience would have to run its course. Her epiphany would come, but only after she experienced enough pain and hopelessness to compel her to admit she was truly powerless. For now, at least, Bill consoled himself with Susan's determination to remain actively involved with her other higher powers, Al-Anon and the friends she met through that group. As long as she utilized this supportive network, Bill was convinced she would endure until her epiphany arrived.

Below is a story that is often passed around in Twelve Step groups. Authorship is in question, but its message is fixed.

Footsteps

One night a man had a dream. He dreamed he was walking along the beach with God. Across the sky flashed scenes from his life. For each scene he noticed two sets of footprints in the sand: one belonging to him, and the other to God. When the last scene of his life flashed before him, he looked back at the footprints in the sand. He noticed that many times along the path of his life, there was only one set of footprints. He also noticed that it happened at the very lowest and saddest times in his life. This really bothered him and he questioned God about it. "God, you said that once I decided to follow you, you would walk with me all the way. But I have noticed that during the most troublesome times in my life, there is only one set of footprints. I don't understand why, when I needed you the most, you would leave me."

God replied, "My precious child, I love you and I would never leave you. During your times of trial and suffering, when you see only one set of footprints, it was then that I carried you."

Failure to Accept Powerlessness and to Surrender Control

Susan may have been able to apply logical consequences and carry out other counter-addiction weaponry, but she wasn't yet competent in admitting her powerlessness over the results. She was having difficulty accepting the fact that enrolling her son in treatment programs (a logical consequence for drug use) couldn't guarantee Sean would stay clean and sober. She knew logical consequences can force someone into treatment, but was unable to accept the reality that no consequence could guarantee a sincere, ongoing commitment to recovery. Until Susan accepted this reality by admitting she is truly powerless, until she learned the art of letting go by surrendering her desire to control and detaching herself from the results of logical consequences, until she honestly admitted that she can neither guide nor control the outcomes of her efforts, she would continue feeling hopeless and helpless.

The first of the Twelve Steps, "We admitted we were powerless over alcohol [or our addiction]—that our lives had become unmanageable,"[1] reminds all parents of addicted youth that they must fully admit they are powerless over brain-altering substances. Drugs are in control, not the values, morals, and standards imprinted on their sons and daughters. Those out-of-control urges are now in charge.

To admit to powerlessness is to admit that the weaponry taught in this section cannot guarantee an instantaneous, successful outcome. Like any commander, parents must realize that no weaponry can guarantee immediate victory since war is a prolonged and drawn-out process of wearing down, weakening, and crippling the enemy until he surrenders. The strength, power, and hold that addiction has is so influential that, for many parents, victory will occur only after long, extended warfare. To accept this truth is to embrace one's powerlessness over addiction.

Loss of Determination

Susan lacked the determination that parents must have to be victorious in their personal war on drugs. Unable to control things, she became exhausted, became frustrated, and felt defeated. Despite her best efforts, Sean continued relapsing, evoking in Susan feelings of hopelessness, helplessness, and discouragement, the by-products of being unable to control Sean. These were all weakening her determination, but this could be changed if Susan adheres to the following suggestions:

Cease Personalizing the Outcomes

The tactics, strategies, and weaponry deployed to fight addiction offer no guarantee of immediate success. Because of this, many parents (including Susan) tend to personalize the failure of deployed weaponry and blame themselves, God, and anyone else they can for failed outcomes. Susan must cease this behavior or she will find herself immersed in private pity parties and thereby cripple her resolve to continue executing her war arsenal in a determined manner. Parents must accept their powerlessness over the outcomes but never stop being powerful in deploying weaponry.

Take Charge of What You Can Truly Take Charge Of

Susan has to take charge by continuing to reach out to others, especially her Al-Anon friends. She also needs to stop her pity parties and cease letting her codependency govern her emotions and her life. She has to take charge by reinstituting personally satisfying activities. When life becomes enjoyable, determination increases to the point that it can support a positive outcome in her personal war on drugs.

Remember to Remain Silent

Failure to utilize the highly effective weapon of silence is another common error. We've already spoken about this strategically important weapon, but it cannot be repeated too often. Parents must control their inclination to talk too much and at inappropriate times, which deflects attention from the event onto the speaker. Remember, when parents fail to utilize silence, they provide the addict an "out" by allowing the young person to focus on parental words and actions instead of the real issue—the abuse of brain-altering substances.

The next time your son or daughter engages in negative behaviors, instead of resorting to the frequently used phrase "I told you . . . ," which is a prelude to an extended, useless monologue that damages the potentially valuable learning that the incident offers, turn to silence. Take time to choose your words carefully. Be silent or say as little as possible so that the natural and logical consequences of the addict's actions can speak powerfully and persuasively for you. Consequences are far more eloquent and powerful than any "gems" of wisdom you have the urge to offer.

Use the Feeling Format

Much has been discussed in this book about communicating on a feeling level. Screaming, shouting, arbitrary punishment, and lecturing are so deeply entrenched that many parents are hesitant to try alternatives, while others find the use of the feeling format to be so awkward and uncomfortable that they stop using this most capable weapon. If you aren't comfortable using it, practice. Practice until you feel secure enough to express yourself in the suggested manner of "I FEEL _____ ABOUT _____ BECAUSE _____ ." It works. Even though it may feel awkward at first, with sufficient practice you will become comfortable enough to triumphantly communicate with your young person as well as others in your life.

Be Consistent

The tendency to ease off consequences and behavioral expectations too hastily by prematurely compromising and granting concessions was mentioned earlier, and it is very common. Young addicts know that when parents impose and maintain various weapons to combat addiction, their resolve must be compromised. To this end, young addicts will go out of their way to relax parental resoluteness by demonstrating rapid improvement, ingratiating themselves, and conforming to parental expectations. As the son or daughter demonstrates these tokens of compliance, parents too hastily appraise their efforts as successful. Hope resurfaces. Grateful that their efforts are working, parents quickly become vulnerable to compromise and slacking their adherence to that which has been working.

While it is exciting to see an addicted son's or daughter's behavior improve, be on guard against early concessions. Early positive change in behavior must not be perceived as a permanent change. We are all capable of making impressive temporary changes, and youthful addicts can quickly transition into desired behaviors. As the parent of an addicted young person, don't be deceived by early results.

Consistency also implies that you stop engaging in such meddling behaviors as reminding your young person, "Don't forget your NA meeting tonight," or "When was the last time you talked with your sponsor?" This is enabling. It is also an example of codependency. Your young person is fully aware of what must be done. She is fully cognizant of what has been agreed to and is sufficiently aware of the consequences if she fails to meet her commitment. So why are you interfering? Instead, determine to keep quiet and cease your enabling. Remember, this is your young person's recovery program, not yours.

※

CHAPTER 23

Shutting Down the Underground

Addicted youth run away from home or treatment programs from time to time. Some runaways flee in order to engage in prohibited activities, while others flee program or parental restrictions. Whenever a son or daughter vanishes, parents understandably become anxious, upset, and angry. They feel they need to do something, but they are unsure about what to do, so all too often they get in the car and roam around the area, hoping they will be lucky enough to spot the child. Unsuccessful in their initial search, they return home and enlist relatives and friends in order to organize a wider search. One parent usually remains at home to coordinate the search and have someone at home just in case the absent child reappears. At day's end, everyone reassembles empty-handed, frustrated, and more anxious and fearful than they were at the start of the day.

There is a more productive way of getting your missing young person back home. While there are no guarantees that this process will always work, it is certainly more effective than wandering aimlessly around the community.

What you must do is effectively shut down the underground that exists in every community. Since most runaways do not go far from their community, shutting down the underground—yes there is an underground, even in your community—will quickly compromise the freedom of movement for your AWOL son or daughter. Below are eight suggestions that can shut down that underground and increase the chance of your runaway's return.

Step 1: Information Gathering

Initially, begin by gathering as much information about your young person's friends as you can. Since many of her friends have become phantoms, this can be a difficult undertaking—but it is possible. Begin by gathering recent cellular phone bills and examine those numbers, highlighting those that were very brief (remember what was mentioned earlier about the connection between drug deals and brief phone conversations). Separate those phone numbers from the numbers you are familiar with. You should also go through your son's or daughter's possessions, looking specifically for phone numbers. That number on a piece of paper on the desk may be the key number that will lead you to your youngster. Take your time and be very careful as you again go through clothing, book bags, textbooks, notebooks. Thoroughly examine every pocket and items of clothing lying on the floor, thrown on the bed, or hanging in the closet. Find those numbers, but be careful you don't get cut or stabbed by a sharp object.

Step 2: Call 911

While you are looking for phone numbers, call the police. Tell them your son or daughter has run away and you need to file a police report. If you are told that the individual must be missing for twenty-four hours, inform the officer that since there has been an increase in abducted kids, the twenty-four-hour waiting period is null and void for kids. Insist on having an officer come to your residence. If they refuse, go to the police station and file the report there. If you run into resistance, practice your newly learned assertiveness. Do not get distracted from your dual mission of (1) getting that important missing person report number, and (2) developing an alliance with the police. You never know when they will be needed, so keep them on your side.

Step 3: Make Those Phone Calls

Call every one of those numbers you found. Say to the individual who answers the phone, "This is Mary's mother. Who is this?"

Write down the name of the youthful voice.

"I am looking for Mary. Have you seen her?" You will probably get a "no" response.

"Are your parents around?" you continue.

An uncooperative response will most likely occur. "I don't know."

"Could you give me a number so that I can talk with them? This is an emergency and I need to talk to your parents." Be persistent.

It is imperative to talk with the parents, so remain steadfast. Once you are able to contact the parent or get one on the phone, begin with, "Hi there. I am Mary's mother and she has run away. Since I know she had been talking with your daughter, I was wondering if you could keep an eye out for her. If you see her, please call me at (give your phone number) or call the police. I will give you the police missing person report number so that you can give it to the police if you see her. Thank you very much for your time."

As you are talking, write down the parent's name as well as any other phone numbers you manage to acquire, the time and date the call was made, and the parent's response. Repeat this process for each phone contact that you make. When you finish the calls, put the notes that you have just created in a safe place. You will need them later, so don't lose them.

Be forewarned, this is a very humbling and distasteful process, but persist until all numbers have been called. Remember, with each phone call, you are potentially shutting down a part of the underground. It will be very difficult for your child to remain a runaway if you keep closing off her options. So put your discomfort and embarrassment aside and keep making those phone calls.

Step 4: Gather with Your Supports

After you have finished this emotionally exhausting third step, do yourself a favor by getting together with your supports. You need emotional support, so either call or visit those who constitute your supports. Attending an Al-Anon or Nar-Anon meeting, where you can share your feelings about what has happened, can be a great emotional release. You might also find suggestions regarding what to do when your runaway does return home. Get their ideas now so that you will have material to complete the next step.

Step 5: Planning for the Return

It is now time to plan what to do when the child returns. With your spouse, draft a behavioral contract (refer to chapter 21). It is imperative that when the runaway returns home, there is a drafted plan of action ready—so begin the process now. Your preference might be treatment at home with NA or AA meetings and counseling, underpinned by a behavioral contract. If this is the preferred option, be sure to have a backup plan just in case she arrives home belligerent, out of control, and unmanageable.

Sit down together and review the various weapons we have discussed in this section. Which ones might be relevant at this time? For instance, would both of you be willing to take her to court and ask the court to declare her out of control? If you believe that drug treatment is mandated, then discuss how far you believe she has progressed on addiction's pathway and what treatment modality would be most appropriate—community based, short-term residential, or long-term residential. If no arrangements for admission have been made, who will do this? If arrangements with a treatment program have been initiated, who will accompany you to the treatment program? How quickly can your help respond, and how rapidly will the treatment program take her? If you choose to utilize the court system, have you taken the time to learn what that entails, and have you updated your ledger of past behaviors and your responsive actions?

Step 6: Follow-Up Phone Calls

It is now time for uncomfortable follow-up work. Pull out that list of the people you called in step three and make those calls again. "Hi, this is Mary's mom calling to follow up on the call I made to you regarding my daughter on Sunday at noon. Have you seen her or heard anything about her whereabouts?"

The response will normally be no, to which you respond, "Please don't forget to keep a look out for her. Once again, I thank you, and if you don't mind, I want to give you my phone number and the missing person report number again."

As you speak with the parent, be sure to state the day and time you first spoke. This tells the parent you are keeping records. When you give your phone number and the missing person police report number a second time, the parent will most likely take your call more seriously. Since the parent doesn't want to get involved, if nothing else she will be more vigilant than she was prior to the second call. Your young person's friend will most likely be warned, "Mary's mom called again. Mary has run away. If you know anything about her whereabouts, please tell me."

The word is spreading. Mary's mom is on a mission to find her. Mary is getting too hot to associate with. The underground shuts down further.

Step 7: Distributing Flyers

Prepare a missing person flyer, making sure you have a contact phone number (you might want to buy one of those inexpensive prepaid cell phones so you don't have to put out your personal phone number). Go to the local mall security office and give the head of security a few flyers. For mall security, give them the number of the missing person report. Having that number handy will make it easier should they actually find your young person. Then go to the convenience stores and other places your runaway hangs out. Ask the storeowner for permission to post a flyer and ask him to keep an eye out for your son or daughter. If possible, spend a few minutes chatting so that a bond is developed that may result in a call being made.

Step 8: Wait by Taking Care of Yourself

If you haven't already, it is now time to turn things over to your higher power and start taking care of yourself. Let go by getting some exercise, going to a movie, bowling, or spending an evening out with your spouse. Be sure to get to an Al-Anon or Nar-Anon meeting. Access your supports and seek out their fellowship. If you conscientiously take care of yourself, you will be better prepared mentally and emotionally to utilize the weaponry you have determined to be most appropriate when your missing son or daughter finally arrives home.

CHAPTER 24

Drugs and Suicide—They Are Intimately Related

There is a strong connection between addiction to brain-altering substances and suicide. It is not a chance relationship for, as we have already seen, anyone who engages in the use of brain-altering substances experiences decreased judgment and increased impulsivity, a condition that can be fatal for any young person who is by nature already impulsive and lacks coping skills. In addition, youthful substance abusers generally have poor self-esteem and are often depressed. As the addiction progresses, hopelessness and helplessness become more and more dominant, markers of an increasingly severe depression. For young addicts who are unable to see a way out of their misery, suicide becomes an attractive solution.

In the following report, the Centers for Disease Control and Prevention states that suicide is the third leading cause of death for our youth. For parents with family members who completed or attempted suicide or who have a child with a mental health disorder and/or a substance abuse problem, the following is a must-read.

Suicide (i.e., taking one's own life) is a serious public health problem that affects even young people. For youth between the ages of 10 and 24, suicide is the third leading cause of death. It results in approximately 4,500 lives lost each year. The top three methods used in suicides of young people include firearms (46%), suffocation (39%), and poisoning (8%).

Deaths from youth suicide are only part of the problem. More young people survive suicide attempts than actually die. A nationwide survey of youth in grades 9–12 in public and private schools in the United States (U.S.) found that 15% of students reported seriously considering suicide, 11% reported creating a plan, and 7% reported trying to take their own life in the 12 months preceding the survey. Each year, approximately 149,000 youth between the ages of 10 and 24 receive medical care for self-inflicted injuries at Emergency Departments across the U.S.

Suicide affects all youth, but some groups are at higher risk than others. Boys are more likely than girls to die from suicide. Of the reported suicides in the 10 to 24 age group, 83% of the deaths were males and 17% were females. Girls, however, are more likely to report attempting suicide than boys. Cultural variations in suicide rates also exist, with Native American/Alaskan Native and Hispanic youth having the highest rates of suicide-related fatalities. A nationwide survey of youth in grades 9–12 in public and private schools in the U.S. found Hispanic youth were more likely to report attempting suicide than their black and white, non-Hispanic peers.

Several factors can put a young person at risk for suicide. However, having these risk factors does not always mean that suicide will occur.

Risk factors:

➡ History of previous suicide attempts

➡ Family history of suicide

➡ History of depression or other mental illness

➡ Alcohol or drug abuse

➡ Stressful life event or loss

➡ Easy access to lethal methods

➡ Exposure to the suicidal behavior of others

➡ Incarceration[1]

The use of brain-altering substances is a significant risk factor for suicide, and if the young person also suffers with depression, you should be very concerned. Depressed youth don't think like their normal peers, and this keeps them from planning, dreaming, and looking forward to a fulfilled life. The young person can't see past today's darkness. Mired in the hopelessness and helplessness of depression and addiction to brain-altering substances, he believes there is no way out. Thoughts of ending his life become more and more of a tempting escape as he turns further inward, becomes more isolated, and becomes preoccupied with not wanting to continue living.

Schizophrenia is another mental health disorder that can lead to suicide. Although this mental illness is primarily associated with adults, its onset usually takes place during the late teen years and early twenties, so it deserves to be mentioned. The individual who suffers from schizophrenia sees visions or is plagued by voices that are typically disturbing, are threatening, and may be urging him to engage in self-destructive behaviors. With schizophrenia, there is a loss of contact with reality, thinking is distorted, and behaviors become bizarre. When you add brain-altering substances, these symptoms are magnified, reality is further distorted, and conditions can become so overwhelming that suicide becomes a major concern—

which is enhanced by verbal hallucinations commanding the person to end his life.

If your young person is abusing drugs and simultaneously suffers from a mental health disorder, the risks in her life are significantly elevated. Parental awareness is critical, and professional treatment is essential. Talk with your young person. Be direct, open, and honest. Find out about any suicidal ideation (thoughts about suicide) she currently has or may have had in the past. Determine if she has ever acted on any suicidal thoughts. Try to get your young person to be as specific as you can, and remember, this is not a time for you or your young person to engage in avoidance. The ideation must be addressed and dealt with—but for that to occur, it must be exposed.

Don't make the potentially fatal mistake of pretending that your young person doesn't harbor suicidal thoughts or conclude that raising the subject of suicide will only insert the idea into her mind. Such a mind-set is dangerous, is erroneous, and can be fatal. If your young person is without suicidal ideation, talking about it will not make her suicidal, but if you fail to give her permission to talk about any harmful thoughts she may have, you allow them to fester and develop. Without the opportunity to be expressed, suicidal thoughts will only grow until they potentially lead to fatal consequences.

While you are talking, do not become circumspect with your young person. Keep your interactions honest and open. Be candid, remain calm, and provide support through emotional identification, sympathy, and upholding the validity of her statements. Be nonjudgmental in all you say and hear—even if you don't agree. The feelings and thoughts expressed are valid since they are your young person's, and they make sense to her, so respect her feelings.

Take all the time necessary to accurately ascertain any suicidal plan that may exist and carefully determine whether your son or daughter has the ability and means to carry that plan out. Your young person needs your loving, tender, concerned support, so be patient. Here are some of the things you should ask about as you talk with a troubled young person.

Does the Person Have a Plan to Take His or Her Life?

The more specific the plan to take one's life, the higher the risk of acting on a suicidal ideation. Examples of an individual with a specific plan would include such statements as: "Take Dad's gun and shoot myself when you guys leave for work," "Overdose on Mom's pills," "Hang myself using the shower rod and a sheet."

The more precise a plan, the more your young person's life is in danger. Should you get a response similar to the above, act immediately. If there is no specific plan, but your young person has acquired a melancholy instigated by emotional events, such as the loss of a boyfriend, consider the risk to be moderate. The chance that she will *immediately* attempt to end her life is less, but action is still required. Keep the lines of communication open, closely watch for any further suicidal clues, and seek out professional help.

Does the Person Have Access to the Instrument to Kill Him- or Herself?

Any suicidal ideation requires an instrument in order to execute the act. If the ideation involves a gun, rope, or poison, immediate action is needed. Guns, as already noted in the CDC quote, are the most fatal of all the instruments used to complete suicide. They are often preferred by males more than females. Rope or any other item that can be used to hang oneself must also be treated as highly lethal. Hanging (suffocation) is the second most common way to complete suicide for youth, with poison listed as a distant third. The presence of other items, such as knives, should raise concern since they are lethal instruments as well, with many people cutting their wrists in an attempt to end their life. Often, individuals overdose with pills or illegal drugs, with many winding up in emergency rooms to have their stomachs pumped out while being forced to consume nasty-tasting charcoal. If there is access to the instrument to end one's life, remove it at once. Should walking into traffic or jumping off a bridge or out of a window be the plan, watch that person closely until professional help arrives. These actions can be fatal, but they also have the potential to leave the individual permanently crippled.

How Available Is the Means?

When you discover the planned instrument, take appropriate action. Remove that item at once and secure it. If, for instance, your child plans to shoot himself with your gun, immediately remove the gun. Since he has probably figured out a way to bypass your security procedures, get that gun out of the house. If your child plans to overdose on your pills, secure those pills under your direct control at all times. If jumping out of a window or walking in front of cars is the plan, watch his comings and goings. To be safe, remove all possible means of suicide from the home while you get help by calling 911. A person who is suicidal will easily switch to a new method if it is available and he or she is determined.

Are Suicidal Intentions Stated?

Pay close attention to what your young person is saying. Suicidal ideation is generally announced prior to the actual event. Don't ignore statements such as: "No one will miss me," "Nothing matters," "It's no use," "Everyone will be better off without me around," "You will not have to worry about me much longer," or "I'll be going away soon."

These and similar statements are clear warnings that suicide is being contemplated. You can't afford to minimize them. If your son or daughter expresses such sentiments, view them as honest feelings that need to be released. They must never be minimized, ignored, or superficially dealt with, nor should they be confronted abrasively. They are expressions of your young person's reality, and even if that reality is contrary to yours, it doesn't matter, for it is your young person's reality and should be respected and acknowledged. To respect that reality, you have no option but to engage in assertive communication, using the feeling format to its fullest advantage. If you have not yet bothered to begin utilizing it, this is the time to start.

Has the Person Been Giving Away Valuable Things?

While this is not always a warning sign, it is something to consider. When some people have made the plan to end their lives they begin tying up loose ends, which may include giving away belongings. However, young people often borrow clothes and other items from each other. They also change tastes and styles often. Or they might sell items to earn extra money, which could be a warning sign if you suspect drugs and alcohol are involved. If you notice a stereo is missing or favorite clothing has disappeared, find out what happened to these possessions. Make a note of it. If other warning signs are present, then it might be a concern.

Has the Person Suddenly Become Busy Cleaning Up?

Teens preparing for suicide will often busy themselves by cleaning their room and otherwise preparing to end their life by leaving things in order. As they are doing this, their mood is upbeat and bright, misleading parents about the real reason they are suddenly energized. This *sudden* change in mood and presentation is due to the fact that the depressed young person has finally found a "solution" to her problems—suicide. She no longer feels overwhelmed, hopeless, or helpless, and she is experiencing the elation that all of us feel when something weighing heavily on us is removed.

Does the Person Express Feelings of Hopelessness and Helplessness?

Suicide can seem like a way out of a seemingly impossible situation. Those who consider suicide generally feel hopeless and helpless since life seems so burdensome, miserable, and complicated. There seems to be no resolution, no solution. Should your young person seem sad or down, talk with him. If, during your conversation, it becomes evident that feelings of hopelessness and helplessness dominate, take time to process these feelings and the events that instigated them. Showing a caring and empathetic attitude can help decrease the feelings of hopelessness and helplessness, but this is usually not sufficient to safely defuse the situation, so it is strongly advised that professional help be accessed. Hopelessness and helplessness often arise from feelings of rejection following a breakup with a boyfriend or girlfriend, conflicts with friends, feeling overwhelmed by school, family discord, or from living with someone (self included) with an alcohol or drug problem.

Sometimes an individual will experience hopelessness and helplessness without any perceptible reasons. If you find yourself concerned about your son's or daughter's troubled mental state, but are frustrated because you cannot determine a rationale, don't further bewilder yourself. Instead, share your concerns with a trained professional and get immediate help before it is too late.

Is the Person Depressed?

Depression is a chemical imbalance in the brain. It has been found that people suffering from depression have altered levels of certain brain chemicals. People who make violent suicide attempts have been found to have a reduced level of serotonin, a "feel-good" chemical in the brain. Chemical imbalances create thought problems, and this can be tragic for the substance abuser who is already suffering from unclear and distorted thinking. Taking medications that are prescribed by a psychiatrist can improve this condition, as long as there is no concurrent consumption of illicit drugs. A favorable outcome with the use of medication depends on the depressed young person remaining in treatment with a psychiatrist and therapist, taking her medication as prescribed, and remaining free of illicit, brain-altering substances.

Depression and suicide are interrelated. The majority of people who are depressed do not complete suicide, but individuals who attempt suicide are usually depressed. It, therefore, is important that as a parent you remain acutely alert to any signs of depression in your young person, especially if drugs are involved. The best way to determine if depression exists is to look for a pattern that lasts for at least two weeks and consists of the following:

- Change in sleeping patterns as manifested by not sleeping well at night, having trouble getting to sleep, sleeping more than normal, or napping more frequently than normal.
- Change in appetite and weight. Depressed people do not eat the way they once did. Some will overeat while others hardly eat at all.
- Speaking and moving with unusual slowness.
- Withdrawing from friends and family (isolating).
- Loss of interest in things that once gave pleasure and enjoyment.
- Loss of energy and an increase in fatigue.

- Decreased ability to think or concentrate. This can be manifested through slow thinking and indecisiveness.
- Feelings of worthlessness, self-reproach, and guilt.

When depression is coupled with other suicidal clues or substance abuse, the probability that your young person is contemplating suicide rises significantly, and immediate action should be taken.

Has There Been a Recent Suicide within the Peer Group or Larger Community?

Experienced youth workers will tell you that once someone completes suicide, other youth will often imitate. One can debate and discuss the various explanations for this copycat phenomenon, but the fact remains that once a young person within the school or community setting completes suicide, a sudden increase in suicide attempts by the surviving peers follows. This copycat trend should propel parents to take time to process any suicides within the community with their young person. Be proactive. Conduct an open and honest discussion regarding the recent suicide, sharing feelings about the event, and learning what your young person thinks about the suicide. Failure to conduct this conversation could result in your son or daughter becoming the community's next casualty.

Has the Person Experienced a Recent Loss?

Susceptibility to suicide rises to dangerous levels whenever a loss or humiliation (which is a loss) occurs. Doing poorly on a crucial test, breaking up with a boyfriend or girlfriend, parental separation or divorce—these are only a few examples of highly charged loss moments during which a discouraged adolescent is susceptible to suicide. The death of someone your young person is close to, such as a brother, sister, parent, grandparent, significant relative, or a close friend, can significantly raise the probability of suicide being considered. Remember also that losing someone due to moving away, going to another school, or a romantic breakup can be as devastating as the actual death of someone close. As a parent, you must process with the young person any significant loss that may have occurred.

This dynamic makes sense when one recalls what was said earlier about teens possessing poor coping skills and their lack of experience in handling problems. Just as retreating into brain-altering substances is an easy way to avoid dealing with problems for which one doesn't have sufficient coping skills, so is turning to suicide another way for the inexperienced adolescent to deal with life's burdens. Your experiences may have allowed you to develop coping skills as an adult, but don't expect your young person to possess the same skills. They are novices in coping with the tribulations of life and can be easily overwhelmed. They need your expertise and help. Give it to them.

Have There Been Prior Suicide Attempts?

Prior suicide attempts, either by a family member or by the young person, give rise to the probability that there will be future suicide attempts. This is because prior attempts make the contemplation of suicide less prohibitive by significantly reducing the taboo against it. The principles and value systems that prohibit suicide have been eroded, and this makes it much easier to sanction or approve ending one's life. Regardless of who in the family attempted suicide, prior suicide attempts should be considered as an indicator that there could be future ones. Has there been a prior suicide attempt within your family? If so, keep the lines of communication open, talk about it and its significance with your young person, and remain highly vigilant as you monitor the moods and disposition of your offspring.

Is the Person Engaged in Drug or Alcohol Use?

For youth who are actively engaged in alcohol or drug use, the risk that suicide will occur is significantly raised. Alcohol is a depressant that only worsens a preexisting depression, while brain-altering drugs distort thinking, which can lead to and promote suicidal ideation. Combining drugs or alcohol with a mental illness such as depression or schizophrenia creates a condition that is ripe for suicidal thoughts.

Practical Suggestions to Save a Life

Get Help
Encourage the suicidal person to allow you to accompany her to the emergency room. If this is impossible, or you deem it to be unwise (if you fear she may jump out of the car or otherwise jeopardize herself or you en route to the hospital), call 911 and have the police/EMS accompany both of you to the hospital.

Never Challenge or Dare a Suicidal Person
It is totally erroneous to think that telling someone who is considering suicide to "go ahead and do it" will shake him into rational thinking. This tactic doesn't work and may actually push the suicidal person into acting upon the suicidal thoughts. Instead, offer the despondent person what he really needs: acknowledgement of his feelings, reassurance that help is available, and your assurance that the things that are troubling him can be overcome. Get help while encouraging, supporting, and providing hope— just never challenge or dare him to go ahead and engage in a suicidal act.

Openly Discuss Suicide
In a nonjudgmental and open way, talk about suicide. Don't shy away from talking about it. Silence is not golden where suicide is concerned, so give that suicidal person the opportunity to openly and honestly share with you his thoughts and feelings.

Be Supportive
Let your young person know that you care. Stay close to your emerging adult and let her know that you are there for her. Assure her that those suicidal feelings are temporary, that depression is treatable, that it doesn't have to plague her forever, and that whatever is upsetting her can be addressed. Pledge to her that, together, both of you can deal with today's problems. Supportively encourage her to get help and keep the lines of communication open.

Don't Judge
Openly listen to your loved one's concerns and feelings. At this point, lectures on whether suicide is right or wrong, your personal beliefs about

it, or how hurt you would be are not going to be helpful. Now is a time to focus on how your loved one feels.

Periodically Check Responses to the Questions Listed Above

Ask your child where her mood falls along a range of one to ten, with one being very despondent and ten representing an extremely good mood. Ask your young person to give you a word that describes her mood. If she seems very despondent, ask questions about suicidal ideation and if she has access to the means to go through with it. If a high risk is found, get help.

If, on the other hand, she is reporting an elevated mood, continue actively interacting with your young person. Don't stop just because things are improving, since improved mood and energy can be precursors of impending suicide. Many suicidal individuals are initially so depressed that they don't have the energy to hurt themselves, but once the energy levels begin to elevate, they are entering a dangerous zone since now they have the energy to carry out the suicidal plan. Remaining involved and active in your son's or daughter's life is an essential safeguarding tactic.

Get Professional Help Immediately and Make Sure Appointments Are Kept

Get your young person into counseling with a therapist or mental health professional, along with a psychiatrist who can prescribe medications to stabilize his mood if necessary. Do not try to deal with a suicidal person alone. Contact either your community mental health center or your health insurance carrier. Most health insurance providers have a mental health call number posted on the back of the insurance card.

Be Patient

The underlying reasons for the hurt and pain that led to drug use and suicidal thoughts can be many and can run deep. It will take time for your young person to reveal her personal pain, openly share her feelings, and find resolution to her problems. Until that occurs, support her by letting her know that you are there for her, and remain attentive to any signs of suicidal ideation.

Make the Environment Safe

Remove any and all means for suicide, such as ropes, medications, drugs, household cleaning products, knives, scissors, razors, and so forth. Remove all guns and rifles from your home. With firearms as the leading suicide method, how can you rationalize maintaining weapons in a home of a person with a suicidal profile?

In Summary

You began this section by learning how to effectively communicate and, through your words, disarm your addicted son or daughter. This was followed by learning how to be assertive in your interactions instead of resorting to passive or aggressive behaviors. The importance of allowing natural and logical consequences to flow unimpeded was stressed. We took time out to emphasize the importance of maintaining an up-to-date, detailed ledger, and you developed a ten-point strategy to combat addiction. You are now armed with your plan of action. You also learned how to successfully govern daily interactions within the family through behavioral contracts. We also explored some of the more common mistakes parents make, such as not utilizing the powerful weapon of silence. Finally, you were introduced to two of the dangerous behaviors that the young addict resorts to when the misery that consequences bring becomes unbearable— running away and suicide. You know how to counter both.

May the God of your understanding be with you as you begin to employ these weapons to combat addiction, and may you persevere through the upcoming final section as we get an update on Susan, attend an Al-Anon meeting, and see how the suggestions offered in this book impacted other parents of addicts.

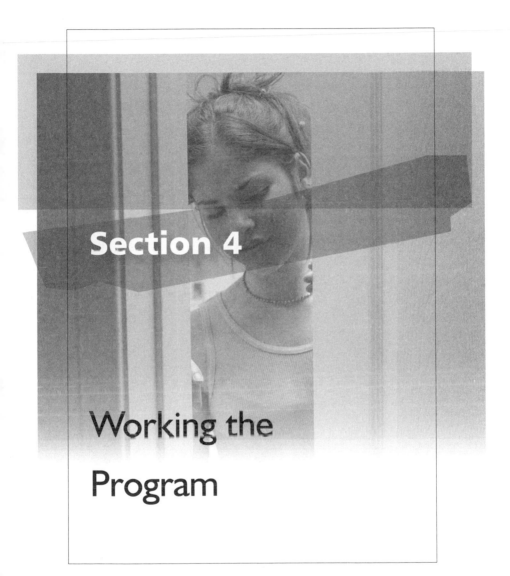

Section 4

Working the Program

CHAPTER 25

The Meeting: The Conclusion of Bill and Susan's Story

Bill and Susan's story concludes with Susan telling her story at an Al-Anon meeting. Susan had asked her Al-Anon group if she could speak and share her story with the newcomers. As she explained to Bill, "I know we don't have speakers often, but I have a story to tell. And I feel some of the new people in Al-Anon need to hear it. If you can, I'd like for you to be there."

Bill promised he would be there, but multiple setbacks were conspiring against him. Wedged in traffic, Bill looked at the clock on his dashboard. He was five minutes away from the meeting, which started in ten minutes. But with traffic stopped, he had no idea how long it would be before he started moving again. The dashboard clock read 7:05 when traffic finally began to creep forward. He would be able to make most of the meeting!

Bill slid into an empty seat in the rear of the room just in time to hear Susan's first words: "It was three years ago that I first came to this room. My neighbor introduced me to Al-Anon, but after two meetings I stopped coming. It wasn't until my son's program demanded that I attend at least one Al-Anon meeting a week that I began to show up. When he came home from residential treatment, he had to attend NA or AA meetings, which meant I had to drive him here each Friday, so I figured, why not kill the hour attending an Al-Anon meeting in the same place? It was that thinking that got me into this room, but I never realized what was in store for me."

She was somewhat tense, an unusual state for the new and serene Susan, but Bill attributed her uneasiness to the nervousness of public speaking. She continued: "At that time, coming here made no sense to me. Alcohol and drugs were my kid's problem, not mine. He was the one who needed to be in meetings getting help, not me. I really believed that addiction was his problem.

"Like others with loved ones addicted to drugs and alcohol, I had filled my life with my kid's craziness. I didn't know this until this group showed me that I needed to reclaim my life and free myself from my entanglement with my son. When I first came here, I wasn't aware how deeply I had allowed my life to be intertwined with his. I definitely didn't think I needed help."

Susan's eyes spotted Bill adjusting his coat on the back of the chair. Bill acknowledged her glance with a nod as she continued. "Not a lofty reason for being in this room, but it got me here. And once I sat in this room for a few weeks, I discovered the power in this room: the power of Al-Anon and the power of the Twelve Steps. But I could still rationalize leaving, so I thought when he was doing well, I would drop out."

Looking around the room, she proudly announced, "Now I faithfully show up each Friday. I wouldn't miss it for anything. I am involved in this group and deeply appreciate and depend on the power of the people in this room. Without this program, my kids and I would not be the people we have become."

Susan paused briefly before proudly resuming. "The whole family is involved with Twelve Step groups. My addicted son is doing well—for today—and right now he is here in the AA meeting down the hall. His brother is in a room further down the hallway in his Alateen group and is flourishing there, getting the support and help he needs. As for me, well, I'm finally my own person, happy with myself, and at peace—something that I haven't experienced since my husband died thirteen years ago.

"When he died, I stopped taking care of me. For years, my life was centered only on my two boys. I did it all—and I did it well—but I became so wrapped up in my kids I forgot to take care of myself. I faithfully monitored homework and served as chauffeur for practices, musical performances, ball games, and so forth. I just never chauffeured myself to anything I wanted to do. So when my kid started using drugs, I did what I do best. I sacrificed myself. It was all that I knew."

Susan paused to sip from a bottle of water. "If you have a loved one controlled by drugs or alcohol, you will learn, if you haven't already, that you can't control them or their addiction. I didn't realize this until I came to these meetings. Coming here regularly changed my thinking. I stopped trying to save my son and began saving myself by taking care of me.

"That's when my family changed. Thanks to the self-help groups here, we are all getting better now. My addicted son attends AA and NA, since he is addicted to both alcohol and multiple drugs. Thanks to Alateen, my other son understands what living with an addicted brother means. He was a good kid until the craziness of addiction attacked my family, and then he started to act out—but thanks to his Alateen group, he is back to his old self and is growing into an upbeat, independent, together young man.

"Because this hospital holds AA, Al-Anon, and Alateen meetings at the same time each Friday, coming here has become a family tradition. We meet and then we eat together. Together we are all living the Twelve Steps—thanks to the support, help, and friendship that these groups offered us. Without their assistance, I am convinced we would still be in the crazy, chaotic mess we were in."

Susan thrust her right hand into the air, a key chain dangling from her fingers. "My son gave me this last Friday after our meetings. It was the greatest present he could ever give me. It's made of nothing more than cheap plastic with a plain ring attached. You could buy something like this at any discount store—but I carry it with pride and love. You see, the key chain has an inscription. It says, 'Clean and sober for six months.' My kid has been clean and sober for 180 days! A miracle!"

With tears of happiness streaming down her cheeks, Susan attempted to continue, but joy choked her. The meeting secretary handed Susan a box of tissues and placed his arm on her shoulder saying, "That's all right. Take your time. You have a lot to be grateful for." A crescendo of supportive applause flooded the room.

While Susan tried to control herself, Bill looked around the room. He recognized so many people with whom he had shared a multitude of trials and moments of indescribable joy. In the front row he spotted Tom, whose wife was an alcoholic. Despite all he was going through, Tom took a day off from his job to help Bill transport his daughter to a treatment program. Bill's wife, Gloria, drove the hour it took to get to his daughter's rehab program while he and Tom struggled in the backseat trying to control Barbara as she cursed, thrashed about, and resisted every effort to be contained. It was one of the longest hours Bill had ever experienced, and he would always be grateful for Tom's support.

Gwen was sitting next to Tom. Bill wondered if she had ever gotten the surgery to cover up the scars she sustained when her son dumped scalding hot water on her arm because she wouldn't let him go out and satisfy his drug cravings.

Bill spotted Mark, whose son overdosed on the same bad batch of drugs that Barbara almost died from. An image of two sets of parents anxiously pacing the emergency waiting room flashed before him. Like soldiers holed up in a foxhole all night long, Mark and Bill bonded as they anxiously awaited word from the doctors who were trying to save both their kids' lives. Would death escape them tonight? Would one die and one live? That night of shared terror had left them comrades for life.

At the end of the row, Bill spotted Bernice, a mother of two young children living with an alcoholic husband. When her husband arrived home intoxicated, he would beat her and terrorize their children. After months of sneaking out of the home while her husband was working in order to attend Al-Anon, she became sufficiently empowered to finally make the bold move of having her husband arrested for assault and having him legally banned from the home.

Bill recalled the meeting several months after their separation, when Bernice revealed to the Al-Anon group that she was considering bringing her husband back home since she was unable to financially survive alone. The support and feedback she received that evening was nothing short of phenomenal. She remained separated. She continued to struggle financially, but her Al-Anon supports upheld her. Someone in the group found her a better-paying job, while donations of clothing and food would periodically arrive at her doorstep. She appeared to be at peace. He would talk with her after the meeting.

Behind Bernice sat Connie, who some three years ago revealed to the group that she was raised in an alcoholic family and married an alcoholic—not once but twice. Through Al-Anon, she found the support that she needed to begin the process of recovering from the aftereffects of the disease of alcoholism. When Bill saw her two months ago, she was attending both Adult Children of Alcoholics and Al-Anon meetings. She was becoming more confident in herself, had gotten a divorce, and was much more personable. He decided that he would approach her after the meeting as well.

Susan was wiping the tears from her cheeks when Bill spotted Harry, with whom he had developed a close relationship. Harry had a daughter who was completely out of control and kept running away. It seemed that she knew all the drug havens and was a master in using the underground. Bill wondered how Harry's daughter was doing. The last time they had talked, a month ago, Harry indicated with pride that his daughter was living in an apartment in the city, had gotten her GED, and was preparing to attend community college. Bill hoped that she had maintained her direction.

Yolanda and Bill made eye contact. Bill remembered the time Yolanda invited him to attend her daughter's first anniversary of sobriety. As with so many Twelve Step anniversary meetings, emotions ran so deep and intense that the meeting was an emotional roller coaster. Bill recalled the image of Yolanda's daughter standing before her NA home group, her one-year key chain tightly clasped in her hand as if she were gripping a precious jewel. "Mom, could you come up here?" she had said.

As Yolanda had worked her way to the front of the room, her daughter confessed: "I am one of those hardheaded addicts. You all know the kind. Probably are one yourself—if you're honest. Don't listen to anything anyone tells you and think you got all the answers. Well, I put my mom through a living hell with my hardheaded self, but she hung in there. No matter how bitchy I got, she never gave up on me. Eventually she stopped her enabling, which robbed me of my Chief Enabler. When she did that, I really hated her. She wouldn't fix things anymore. We would fight—but despite our struggles, she never stopped believing in me, even when I stopped believing in myself. She kept her faith in me, but she never again bailed me out or fixed things. And that was what I needed, or else I'd still be out there doing my thing and counting on Mom to take care of my messes."

When Yolanda arrived at the front of the room, mother and daughter hugged. "Mom," her daughter had said, "I want to say in front of all these people, thank you for being there. You never gave up on me, no matter what I did. You were there, but not in your old enabling ways. I hated the rooms of Al-Anon because they taught you to let me feel consequences and stop rescuing. I know it hurt you to see me go through what I did: jail, institutions and hospitals, living on the streets. I'm just so grateful that you became a strong mom and stopped enabling, because if you hadn't, I'm sure I'd still be out there. I thank you. You are truly my higher power, and I love you so much."

She handed the one-year key chain to Yolanda, "Mom, this is for you. You earned it. Thanks." Mother and daughter embraced as the room burst into a round of heartfelt applause. Eyes dampened, especially those who had witnessed the difficulties that Yolanda and her daughter had endured.

With her joy now under control, Susan continued, "This key chain is the greatest gift my kid ever gave me. There is nothing better than having a clean and sober son."

Several people nodded in agreement, knowing intimately the delight having a loved one living in recovery can bring. "For those of you new to this group, stay with us. What the people in that rehab program told me is true. If you stay in Al-Anon, if you learn the Twelve Steps and live them, if you use the care and support in this room, your loved one is likely to work his program. His chances of getting truly drug and alcohol free are so much greater!

"My kid told me as much just last weekend. We were talking, something we do on a regular basis now, and we began discussing the difference between this present period of clean time and his past efforts at sobriety. He said that since I'm working my program by staying in Al-Anon, by working the Twelve Steps, by taking care of me, and by not letting anything ruin my serenity, he knew he had to work his program. In the past when he got drug free, I would leave Al-Anon and stop taking care of myself. He told me that once I left Al-Anon, he knew it would only be a matter of time before he could outmaneuver and use me again. He said that since I'm staying in Al-Anon now and taking care of me, he knows life would be hell if he doesn't stay clean and sober."

Susan briefly paused before continuing, "When I stopped attending Al-Anon meetings, the insanity quickly returned. Again I'd be beaten down emotionally, yet I was too embarrassed and uncomfortable to return to this group. I eventually found the courage to reappear in this room—it was my only option—and when I did, no one criticized me or told me that I should have stayed. Instead, you welcomed me, reached out, and helped me. I burned phone lines with many of you, and somehow we not only got through my family's various crises, but I grew to love and take care of myself.

"This is the one place where I feel safe and free to talk openly without anyone judging me. You don't make me feel guilty or like I have to explain myself. You understand me, and that means a lot, especially when you challenge my tendency to revert to old behaviors."

Susan paused, looked around the room, and then declared, "You not only took me back, but you continued to support me. I will never forget the time that my kid relapsed and did his usual runaway thing, and I did my usual thing—stopped taking care of me. Some of you came by my home and reminded me that I was relapsing into my old behavior of putting my son over myself. You weren't critical. You just gently reminded me what I was doing to myself. You got me back on track.

"You also helped me by teaching me how to close the underground. And it worked. On my kid's last runaway, I successfully closed the underground all by myself, and he was forced back home in record time. He returned high on drugs and nasty, but he was home. And what did I do? I called some of you, and you quickly appeared at my door to support me. While he was gone, you helped me decide what I should do when he came back home—and I listened this time. We had a plan of action, and I wasn't sure I could summon the strength to execute it, but once again you were there for me. With your help, I managed to get my kid into court and then court-ordered him into residential mental health treatment.

"I had no idea how to do this, but you taught me. Some of you even went to court with me! I doubted my ability to remain strong, and I did break down in the courtroom when my kid was taken out in handcuffs—just like I knew I would—but you were there to sustain me, to wipe my tears, to support me. You literally held me up."

Triumphantly raising the key ring a second time, Susan said, "My son may have earned this, but if it hadn't been for those of you in this room, this chain and all it represents would never have been. Because of the many supportive people in this room, I have this key ring. But I have more. I have the power and personal strength that came when this group got me to focus on my needs and self. And when I started taking care of myself, well, that's when my kid really got better."

Susan paused to look around the room, taking quick inventory of those present. "I see some new faces. Those of you who are newcomers don't know my story except for what I have just told you—and you don't need to know any more of my story, because if you have an addicted loved one, you already know the pain and agony that is my story. Your story may appear to be different from mine since the names and particulars are different, but they are really the same. You see, we all have the same problem—the wretched pain that comes with having an addicted loved one and the subsequent loss of ourselves into the loved one's craziness. Just as I did, you are probably trying to cope with the insanity of substance abuse by focusing on the addicted person instead of taking care of yourself. Like I did, you are so entangled in the addicted person's behavior that you have lost yourself—and have become miserable.

"I was on a lack of self-care mode for a long time. Thirteen years ago on this very date, a drunk driver killed my husband on his way home from work, leaving me with two young kids. For over a decade, I existed in a gray cloud of self-pity and sorrow that I covered up with my determination to compensate for the loss of their father. I tried to be everything to them. It wasn't until I got into these rooms that I discovered that I had no life of my own. My life was my kids. I didn't date. I didn't go out. If I was out of the house, I was either hauling a kid somewhere or working. I was happy when the kids were doing well, and since they were, I declared me and my world to be okay. Despite my loneliness, I convinced myself that I was okay."

Susan paused briefly. "I remember one memorable night when I sat in this room and someone mentioned the three Cs—cause, cure, and control. He said he got better when he realized that he didn't cause his daughter's addiction, he couldn't cure it, and he definitely couldn't control it. That was an earth-shattering statement for me, a life-changing statement that left me thunderstruck. I had stressed myself out to such an extent that I was having stomach problems, couldn't sleep, couldn't laugh or smile—yet what I was stressing myself over was something that I didn't cause, couldn't cure, and definitely couldn't control.

"I'll never forget that meeting. I went home repeating the three Cs to myself. I had repeatedly proven their validity. The more I tried to fix things, the more unsuccessful I was.

"I decided that night that I would cure myself by taking care of myself. I had caused my misery by not taking care of myself, by becoming so absorbed in my kid's addictive behaviors that I made myself sick. I also realized—it was one of those lightbulb moments—that if I took care of myself I'd get better."

Susan paused before emphasizing, "That person was so right! I didn't cause my kid's addiction, but I did cause my misery. I couldn't cure my kid's addiction, but I could cure myself. I couldn't control my kid, but I could definitely control my life, my emotions—myself."

Susan scanned the room. "To those of you new to Al-Anon, I can't encourage you strongly enough to hang in here with us. Don't half-step like I did for far too long. Take advantage of us. Learn to live the Twelve Steps. Stay here, and one day your story may parallel mine. One day you may proudly show the world your symbol of liberation. Mine happens to be a key chain.

"The Twelve Steps tell us a power greater than ourselves can restore us to sanity, and a large part of that power resides in these rooms—here lie so many of my higher powers! I also rediscovered my ultimate higher power—God. The power that I doubted, got mad at, didn't want to talk with. But he remained there for me. I know some of you can relate to that tumultuous spiritual walk we parents go through as we question God.

"It's amazing how we want to isolate from society when we discover addiction in our families. I was so afraid of ridicule and criticism that I didn't want to show my face. I thought I was alone—like my kid is the only kid ever to get hooked on drugs and alcohol—so I retreated inward and spent my days in private pity parties."

Susan spotted Bill's knowing smile. "My next-door neighbor is in the back of the room. I see by the expression on his face that he remembers those good old days. A long-time member of Al-Anon, he tried to get me out of my isolation. Used to come over to check on me and tried to get me out of myself. But he couldn't do it alone. I was too good a pity party thrower for that. It took this whole group to make stop feeling sorry for myself.

"At first I thought this was a gathering of folks who got together to talk about their problems. I thought that I had found an even bigger pity party, but I quickly came to realize that this wasn't the case. Rather, it was a gathering of positive people who were taking charge of their lives—and enjoying themselves in the process. They weren't complaining to be complaining. As a matter of fact, what I initially mistook for complaints and tales of woe were really positive discussions about ways to effectively deal with substance-induced craziness. This group began to make sense, especially when they talked about the Twelve Steps."

Susan looked around the room. "I am rambling, but I must stress to the newcomers that the folks in this room patiently guided me and stood by me, and now, thanks to them, my life is about me and not what my kids do. Oh, I'm happy that my kid is sober, but I know I'd be okay even if he wasn't. That is an honest statement. You see, I've come to admit that not only am I powerless over drugs and alcohol, but I am powerless over my kids and what they choose to do. I've come to realize that they are free-thinking people who make choices independent of me. I can't control them. Nor can I control things that happen in other parts of my life, like my husband's death. What I can control is myself. I, and only I, am responsible for my moods and how I feel. So I make sure that I take care of me. I exercise regularly. I talk to Al-Anon friends daily. I'm back in school to sharpen my skills and advance my career—all things that I am enjoying and are beneficial for me.

"I may be rejoicing in my son's accomplishment—and I am—but more importantly, I'm rejoicing in the new me. I now have a life—a social life. After over a decade living in isolation, I'm now dating a great man. Life is good, and I'm only sorry that it took so long for me to reclaim my life. But I turned things over to the God of my understanding, admitted to my powerlessness, and relied upon my higher powers, including the people in this room. And it worked! Never in my wildest dreams did I think I'd be able to say anything close to this when I decided to kill an hour on Friday nights by hanging out in this room.

"Don't get me wrong. I know there will be problems in the future, and relapse can happen. But I'm ready. I have the Twelve Steps, my higher powers to whom I can turn, and since I've turned my life over to the God of my understanding, I'm able to trust him instead of myself. What more can a lady ask for?"

Susan looked around the room. "I've talked long enough. Thank you for your attention, and as we say in the Twelve Step world, keep coming back. It works, if you work it."

The room burst into an appreciative round of applause while Susan drank from her bottle of water. The meeting secretary waited for the applause to subside before announcing, "At this time, I ask that anyone who wishes to make a comment regarding what was said tonight or has a burning issue that needs to be shared, please speak up. The floor is open."

Susan's talk was powerful and moving. Bill hoped the comments would be as dynamic and insightful. Gwen spoke first. "My name is Gwen," she began.

In unison the group responded, "Hi, Gwen."

"I've been battling with my son's addiction for seven years now. He's been in and out of recovery, in and out of treatment, in and out of trouble. When this craziness first started, I was like Susan, feeling good when he was doing well, feeling lousy when he was doing awful. The Twelve Steps and this group, through which I received so much support and love, kept me going. As happened with Susan, this group showed me that I am able to once again have a life of my own.

"My kid is over age now, and I have absolutely no idea where he is. It has been that way for about six months since he quit rehab. I'm not going to say that I don't worry and fear for his welfare. I do. But I don't let it rule my life like I used to. Instead, I'm reclaiming my life. We are powerless over our addicted loved ones, but we don't have to be powerless over our own lives. Just like Susan, this group has become my higher power, and together with the God of my understanding, I am able to keep my priorities in order and my mind intact."

Looking at Susan, Gwen said, "You were on time for me tonight. I needed to hear what was said. I needed that focus, the reinforcement that you gave me. I thank you."

"And I thank you for sharing," Susan responded.

Mark, Bill's comrade from that terrifying night in the emergency room began, "I'm Mark, a proud member of Al-Anon."

"Hi, Mark," the room responded.

"I've watched Susan grow in this program. I was in my second year in Al-Anon when Susan first showed up, angry and isolating herself."

Susan nodded knowingly as Mark continued, "I didn't think she would stay, and for a while it seemed like I was on target with my prediction. She came when her kid was drinking and drugging, but we never saw her when things were going along okay. But after a few relapses, Susan became a part of this group and a big part of my program."

Turning to Susan, he said, "I'll always be grateful to you when you joined my wife and me that night in the hospital. My kid had once again overdosed and was rushed to the ER. You stayed with us that night and supported us. This was the second time that this had happened, and you were there. I'm not sure how I would have handled things if you hadn't been there."

Mark's glance covered the room. "You have to picture this. There I am once again in the emergency room waiting to see if my kid will survive another overdose, and here comes Susan talking the Twelve Steps. My kid's life is hanging in the balance, and she has us working the Twelve Steps. By the time she got there, I had pretty much concluded who sold my kid the bad drugs, and I was plotting to do some serious bodily harm. I'm plotting revenge, and here comes Susan, giving me focus through the Twelve Steps.

"It's no wonder that her son is now clean and sober. Her program is so strong but, as she mentioned, it wasn't always that way. There was a time when she was a miserable person and her kid was just as miserable. Thanks for a great talk, Susan, but even more, thanks for being there and being the inspiration you have been."

Harry spoke next, "My daughter is an alcoholic and drug addict."

"Hi," the group responded.

"This is why I continue to come to these groups. It seems that every time I come to a meeting, I hear exactly what I need to hear. My daughter, who is now an adult, vanished right after Christmas. In the three weeks since her disappearance, I've learned that she abandoned her apartment, lost her job, and no one seems to know where she is. I lost perspective. I allowed myself to return to my old ways. I notified missing persons, but I forgot to notify myself that I was powerless and to turn to my higher powers.

Bill's heart went out to Harry. He resolved to talk with him tonight. "Then, this afternoon I received a call at work. She had managed to travel over a thousand miles before being arrested in a city she had never been to before. My first impulse was to catch a plane, but then I said to myself, *Slow down. Take time to use your supports.* So I'm here, hoping that I can get some positive ideas and feedback so that I do the right thing this time.

"Tonight, Susan, it seemed like you were talking directly to me. I need to get back into my program. It's so easy to fall back into old ways. I've been stuck in my old ways for three weeks now. Susan, your talk gave me a lot of insight and perspective. I thank you and I think I know what I need to do, but I sure could use some feedback."

Bill's mind drifted into a self-reflective mode. He was lucky. His daughter was still doing well—at least for today—but he knew he needed to be back in the rooms. His program had been weakened by neglect. It is so easy to drift into complacency, and that is the worst thing a parent of an addict or alcoholic can do—even one whose kid is doing well and living on her own. Bill asked himself, *Would I be able to enforce consequences if she relapsed?* He seriously doubted it. His program had become too weakened through neglect. He had retreated into his own world of travel for a week or two at a time with no effort to remain connected to the program. Travel, Bill had to admit, was an excuse. They have Al-Anon meetings throughout the country. When his daughter was out there using drugs and drinking, he had faithfully attended Twelve Step support groups, no matter what city he found himself in.

Bill admonished himself. Twelfth Stepping means reaching out to others, strengthening one's program while helping them. He couldn't think of a single person he had reached out to lately. *Let's face it,* he thought, *I haven't done any Twelve Step work in a while. There has been no outreach. I've become too self-centered, too complacent. I need to get back into these meetings.*

Bill decided to share his resolve with the group and ask them to hold him to his resolve.

NOTES

Introduction

1. "NIDA Infofacts: High School and Youth Trends," National Institute on Drug Abuse, http://www.drugabuse.gov/Infofacts/HSYouthtrends.html.

2. "Results from the 2009 National Survey on Drug Use and Health: Volume I, Summary of National Findings," U.S. Department of Health and Human Services, Substance Abuse and Mental Health Services Administration, Office of Applied Studies, http://www.oas.samhsa.gov/NSDUH/2k9NSDUH /2k9ResultsP.pdf.

3. Ibid.

Chapter 1

1. "Healthy Youth! Health Topics: Alcohol & Drug Use," Centers for Disease Control and Prevention, accessed May 13, 2011, http://www.cdc.gov /healthyyouth/alcoholdrug/index.htm.

2. *The Surgeon General's Call to Action to Prevent and Reduce Underage Drinking* (U.S. Department of Health and Human Services, Office of the Surgeon General, 2007), quoted in "Healthy Youth! Health Topics: Alcohol & Drug Use," Centers for Disease Control and Prevention, accessed May 13, 2011, http://www.cdc.gov/healthyyouth/alcoholdrug/index.htm.

3. Centers for Disease Control and Prevention, "Alcohol-Attributable Deaths and Years of Potential Life Lost—United States, 2001," *Morbidity & Mortality Weekly Report* 53, no. 37 (2004): 866–870, quoted in "Healthy Youth! Health Topics: Alcohol & Drug Use," Centers for Disease Control and Prevention, accessed May 13, 2011, http://www.cdc.gov/healthyyouth/alcoholdrug /index.htm.

4. "Fatality Analysis Reporting System (FARS) Web-based Encyclopedia," U.S. Department of Transportation, National Highway Traffic Safety Administration, http://www-fars.nhtsa.dot.gov/Main/index.aspx, quoted in "Healthy Youth! Health Topics: Alcohol & Drug Use," Centers for Disease Control and Prevention, accessed May 13, 2011, http://www.cdc.gov /healthyyouth/alcoholdrug/index.htm.

5. *The Relationship between Mental Health and Substance Abuse among Adolescents* (Rockville, MD: Substance Abuse and Mental Health Services

Administration, 1999), http://www.oas.samhsa.gov/NHSDA/A-9/comorb3c
.htm#TopOfPage, quoted in "Healthy Youth! Health Topics: Alcohol &
Drug Use," Centers for Disease Control and Prevention, accessed May 13,
2011, http://www.cdc.gov/healthyyouth/alcoholdrug/index.htm.

6. T. S. Naimi, R. D. Brewer, A. Mokdad, C. Denny, M. K. Serdula, and J. S.
Marks, "Binge Drinking among US Adults," *JAMA* 289 (2003): 70–75,
quoted in "Healthy Youth! Health Topics: Alcohol & Drug Use," Centers
for Disease Control and Prevention, accessed May 13, 2011, http://www.cdc
.gov/healthyyouth/alcoholdrug/index.htm.

7. Centers for Disease Control and Prevention, "Youth Risk Behavior
Surveillance—United States, 2009," *Morbidity & Mortality Weekly Report*
59, SS-5 (2010): 1–142, quoted in "Healthy Youth! Health Topics: Alcohol
& Drug Use," Centers for Disease Control and Prevention, accessed May 13,
2011, http://www.cdc.gov/healthyyouth/alcoholdrug/index.htm.

Chapter 2

1. "Facts About Alcohol Poisoning," National Institute on Alcohol Abuse and
Alcoholism, accessed May 17, 2011, http://www.collegedrinkingprevention
.gov/OtherAlcoholInformation/FactsAboutAlcoholPoisoning.aspx.

2. Ibid.

3. Ibid.

Chapter 6

1. *HIV/AIDS Surveillance Report,* 2004, vol. 16 (Atlanta, GA: U.S. Department
of Health and Human Services, Centers for Disease Control and Prevention,
2005), 1–46, quoted in "HIV/AIDS among Youth," Centers for Disease
Control and Prevention, accessed February 10, 2010, http://www.cdc.gov
/hiv/resources/factsheets/youth.htm (original page no longer available).

2. "HIV/AIDS among Youth," Centers for Disease Control and Prevention,
accessed February 10, 2010, http://www.cdc.gov/hiv/resources/factsheets
/youth.htm (original page no longer available).

3. Substance Abuse and Mental Health Services Administration, *2004
National Survey on Drug Use & Health,* http://oas.samhsa.gov/nhsda.htm,
quoted in "HIV/AIDS among Youth," Centers for Disease Control and
Prevention, accessed February 10, 2010, http://www.cdc.gov/hiv/resources
/factsheets/youth.htm (original page no longer available).

4. B. C. Leigh and R. Stall, "Substance Use and Risky Sexual Behavior for
Exposure to HIV. Issues in Methodology, Interpretation, and Prevention,"

American Psychologist 48 (1993): 1035–1045, quoted in "HIV/AIDS among Youth," Centers for Disease Control and Prevention, accessed February 10, 2010, http://www.cdc.gov/hiv/resources/factsheets/youth.htm (original page no longer available).

5. "Hepatitis C Information for Health Professionals," Centers for Disease Control and Prevention, http://www.cdc.gov/hepatitis/HCV/index.htm.

Chapter 7

1. Lloyd D. Johnston, Patrick M. O'Malley, Jerald G. Bachman, and John E. Schulenberg, *Monitoring the Future National Results on Adolescent Drug Use: Overview of Key Findings, 2011* (Ann Arbor: Institute for Social Research, the University of Michigan, 2012); Lloyd D. Johnston, Patrick M. O'Malley, Jerald G. Bachman, and John E. Schulenberg, "Marijuana Use Continues to Rise among U.S. Teens, While Alcohol Use Hits Historic Lows," press release, December 14, 2011, http://www.monitoringthefuture.org/.

2. Ibid.

3. "Prescription Drug Abuse," National Institute on Drug Abuse, accessed May 8, 2011, http://www.nida.nih.gov/tib/prescription.html.

4. "NIDA InfoFacts: Inhalants," National Institute on Drug Abuse, accessed May 8, 2011, http://www.nida.nih.gov/Infofacts/Inhalants.html.

5. Ibid.

6. "'Dusting' Is the New Killer High for Teens," *Today,* accessed May 8, 2011, http://today.msnbc.msn.com/id/8714725/ns/today/t/dusting-new-killer-high-teens/#.TsaRV_E5CL8.

7. "In Search of the Big Bang: What Is Crack Cocaine?" accessed May 8, 2011, http://www.cocaine.org/.

8. "Cocaine," National Institute on Drug Abuse, accessed May 8, 2011, http://www.nida.nih.gov/DrugPages/Cocaine.html.

9. "NIDA InfoFacts: Cocaine," National Institute on Drug Abuse, accessed May 8, 2011, http://www.nida.nih.gov/Infofacts/cocaine.html.

10. "NIDA InfoFacts: Methamphetamine," National Institute on Drug Abuse, accessed May 8, 2011, http://www.nida.nih.gov/Infofacts/methamphetamine.html.

11. N. D. Volkow, L. Chang, G. J. Wang, et al., "Association of Dopamine Transporter Reduction with Psychomotor Impairment in Methamphetamine Abusers," *American Journal of Psychiatry* 158, no. 3 (2001): 377–382, quoted

in "NIDA InfoFacts: Methamphetamine," National Institute on Drug Abuse, accessed May 8, 2011, http://www.nida.nih.gov/Infofacts/methamphetamine .html.

12. E. D. London, S. L. Simon, S. M. Berman, et al., "Mood Disturbances and Regional Cerebral Metabolic Abnormalities in Recently Abstinent Methamphetamine Abusers," *Archives of General Psychiatry* 61, no. 1 (2004): 73–84, quoted in "NIDA InfoFacts: Methamphetamine," National Institute on Drug Abuse, accessed May 8, 2011, http://www.nida.nih.gov /Infofacts/methamphetamine.html; P. M. Thompson, K. M. Hayashi, S. L. Simon, et al., "Structural Abnormalities in the Brains of Human Subjects Who Use Methamphetamine," *Journal of Neuroscience* 24, no. 26 (2004): 6028–6036, quoted in "NIDA InfoFacts: Methamphetamine," National Institute on Drug Abuse, accessed May 8, 2011, http://www.nida .nih.gov/Infofacts/methamphetamine.html.

13. G. J. Wang, N. D. Volkow, L. Chang, et al., "Partial Recovery of Brain Metabolism in Methamphetamine Abusers after Protracted Abstinence," *American Journal of Psychiatry* 161, no. 2 (2004): 242–248, quoted in "NIDA InfoFacts: Methamphetamine," National Institute on Drug Abuse, accessed May 8, 2011, http://www.nida.nih.gov/Infofacts/methamphetamine.html.

14. Richard Rudgley, *The Encyclopedia of Psychoactive Substances* (New York: Thomas Dunne, 1999), 92.

15. "Club Drugs Facts & Figures," Office of National Drug Control Policy, accessed May 8, 2011, http://www.whitehousedrugpolicy.gov/drugfact /club/club_drug_ff.html (page no longer available).

16. Ibid.

17. Ibid.

18. "Hallucinogens Facts & Figures," Office of National Drug Control Policy, accessed May 8, 2011, http://www.whitehousedrugpolicy.gov/drugfact /hallucinogens/hallucinogens_ff.html (page no longer available).

19. Ibid.

20. Ibid.

21. "NIDA InfoFacts: Hallucinogens—LSD, Peyote, Psilocybin, and PCP," National Institute on Drug Abuse, accessed May 8, 2011, http://www.nida .nih.gov/Infofacts/hallucinogens.html.

Chapter 9

1. "Mental Illnesses: Dual Diagnosis and Integrated Treatment of Mental Illness and Substance Abuse Disorder," National Alliance on Mental Illness, accessed May 30, 2011, http://www.nami.org/Template.cfm?Section =By_Illness&Template=/TaggedPage/TaggedPageDisplay.cfm&TPLID =54&ContentID=23049.

2. Ibid.

3. *Alcoholics Anonymous,* 4th ed. (New York: Alcoholics Anonymous World Services, 2001) 59–60.

Chapter 12

1. Melody Beattie, *Codependent No More: How to Stop Controlling Others and Start Caring for Yourself* (Center City, MN: Hazelden, 1987, 1992), 36.

Chapter 19

1. "Dual Diagnosis in Adolescence," National Alliance on Mental Illness, accessed April 29, 2011, http://www.nami.org/Content/ContentGroups /Helpline1/Dual_Diagnosis_in_Adolescence.htm.

2. Ibid.

3. Ibid.

4. *Diagnostic and Statistical Manual of Mental Disorders,* 4th ed., Text Revision (Washington, DC: American Psychiatric Association, 2000), 197.

5. Ibid, 199.

Chapter 22

1. "The 12 Steps," 12Step.org: Resources and Information about the 12 Step Program, http://www.12step.org/the-12-steps.html; *Alcoholics Anonymous,* 4th ed. (New York: Alcoholics Anonymous World Services, 2001), 59.

Chapter 24

1. "Suicide Prevention," Centers for Disease Control and Prevention, accessed August 31, 2010, http://www.cdc.gov/violenceprevention/pub/youth_suicide .html.

George E. Leary Jr., M.A., provides mental health services to addicts and those living with HIV/AIDS. He established and operated two recovery houses in Baltimore, Maryland, and served for nine years on a mobile crisis intervention team.